Contents

How to Use This Book

ABOUT THE MAPS

This book is divided into chapters based on regions that are within close reach of the city; an overview map of these regions precedes the table of contents. Each chapter begins with a region map that shows the locations and numbers of the trails listed in that chapter.

Each trail profile is also accompanied by a detailed trail map that shows the hike route.

Map Symbols

-------	Featured Trail	🛣 80	Interstate Freeway	○	City/Town
-------	Other Trail	101	U.S. Highway	✈	Airfield/Airport
═══════	Expressway	21	State Highway	⚲	Golf Course
═══════	Primary Road	66	County Highway	⟋	Waterfall
═══════	Secondary Road	🅣	Trailhead	🢒	Swamp
········	Unpaved Road	★	Point of Interest	▲	Mountain
············	Ferry	🅟	Parking Area	⚐	Park
—·—·—	National Border	⛺	Campground	)(	Pass
—··—	State Border	■	Other Location	✦	Unique Natural Feature

ABOUT THE TRAIL PROFILES

Each profile includes a narrative description of the trail's setting and terrain. This description also typically includes mile-by-mile hiking directions, as well as information about the trail's highlights and unique attributes.

The trails marked by the **BEST** ◖ symbol are highlighted in the author's Best Hikes list.

Options

If alternative routes are available, this section is used to provide information on side trips or note how to shorten or lengthen the hike.

Directions

This section provides detailed driving directions to the trailhead from the city center or from the intersection of major highways. When public transportation is available, instructions will be noted here.

Information and Contact

This section provides information on fees, facilities, and access restrictions for the trail. It also includes the name of the land management agency or organization that oversees the trail, as well as an address, phone number, and website if available.

ABOUT THE ICONS

The icons in this book are designed to provide at-a-glance information on special features for each trail.

- The trail climbs to a high overlook with wide views.
- The trail offers an opportunity for wildlife watching.
- The trail offers an opportunity for bird-watching.
- The trail features wildflower displays in spring.

- The trail visits a beach.
- The trail travels to a waterfall.
- The trail visits a historic site.
- Dogs are allowed.
- The trail is appropriate for children.
- The trail is wheelchair accessible.
- The trailhead can be accessed via public transportation.

ABOUT THE DIFFICULTY RATING

Each profile includes a difficulty rating; the ratings are defined below. Remember that the level of difficulty for any trail can change considerably due to weather or trail conditions. Always phone ahead to check current trail and weather conditions.

Easy: Easy hikes are 5 miles or less round-trip and have less than 700 feet of elevation gain (nearly level). Thay are generally suitable for families with small children and hikers seeking a mellow stroll.

Easy/Moderate: Easy/Moderate hikes are 4-8 miles round-trip and have 500-1,200 feet of elevation gain. They are generally suitable for families with active children above the age of six and hikers who are reasonably fit.

Moderate: Moderate hikes are 5-9 miles round-trip and have 1,000-2,000 feet of elevation gain. They are generally suitable for adults and children who are fit.

Strenuous: Strenuous hikes are 5-10 miles round-trip and have 1,800-2,800 feet of elevation gain. They are suitable very fit hikers who are seeking a workout.

Butt-kicker: Butt-kicker hikes are 7-14 miles round-trip and have 3,000 feet of elevation gain. These hikes are suitable only for advanced hikers who are very physically fit.

INTRODUCTION

Author's Note

The Portland area has amazing trails. I know: I have been hiking them for years. I hike them with my family, with my friends and neighbors, with school groups, and with conservation organizations. As a matter of fact, I hike the trails around Portland whenever I can. Winter or summer, rain or shine—it doesn't really matter to me. I find that wherever I hike there is so much natural beauty to enjoy that little else matters.

There are so many hikes within two hours of Portland that it was a struggle to narrow them down to a reasonable number. I thought hard about my annual favorites, my frequently visited sites, and the hikes that have excited my various hiking partners over the years. I talked with my children, friends in conservation groups, and the many helpful folks at management agencies. *Moon Take a Hike Portland* represents my own unique perspective on Portland hiking, which means it includes some trails that are hugely popular, some that get few visits, and some that may be a little off the map. I often get asked what my favorite hike is. My answer is always the same: It's the hike I'm on at that particular moment. I find equal amounts of joy in a stroll around the Eastbank Esplanade as in a day-long leg-burner up to Tanner Butte.

I hope you'll use this book to get out and explore some of the Portland-area trails I so love. In doing so, you'll be creating your own list of favorites and hopefully will begin to take along your family and friends. Get out and take a hike! You'll be glad you did.

Barbara I. Bond

Best Hikes

❰ Best for Bird-Watching

❰ Best Butt-Kickers

❰ Best Hikes with Children

❰ Best for Peak Baggers

【 Best for Waterfalls
Trail of Ten Falls, Portland and the Willamette Valley, p. 52.
Multnomah-Wahkeena Falls Loop, The Columbia River Gorge, p. 77.
Eagle Creek, The Columbia River Gorge, p. 99.
Ramona Falls, Mount Hood, p. 140.
Falls Creek Falls, Southwest Washington, p. 227.

【 Best for Wildflowers
Catherine Creek, The Columbia River Gorge, p. 117.
Vista Ridge-Cairn Basin, Mount Hood, p. 146.
Timberline Trail-Paradise Park Loop, Mount Hood, p. 161.
Butte Camp-Loowit Trail, Southwest Washington, p. 242.
Stagman Ridge, Southwest Washington, p. 251.

【 Best Views
Powell Butte Nature Loop, Portland and the Willamette Valley, p. 46.
Cape Horn, The Columbia River Gorge, p. 71.
Tom McCall Point, The Columbia River Gorge, p. 120.
Horseshoe Ridge-Zigzag Mountain, Mount Hood, p. 137.
Gnarl Ridge, Mount Hood, p. 156.

Hiking Tips

HIKING ESSENTIALS

There are some important things you should carry whenever you are out hiking. These are commonly called the 10 Essentials. It's easy enough to put together your own 10 essentials in a small stuff sack or zippered plastic bag. When heading out, just throw it in your daypack along with your other gear. While a small daypack will suffice for many hikes, for trips lasting all day, use a small backpack to carry what you need.

Clothing

In the Pacific Northwest, outdoor folks often say, "There is no such thing as bad weather—only bad clothing choices." The point is, the weather in and around Portland is notorious for its changeability, so be ready for it. When you are out hiking, you must be prepared for all conditions. Wearing synthetic or wool clothing is preferable to cotton, which loses its insulating ability when wet and dries slowly. Good outerwear of waterproof/breathable material is available in lightweight styles for hiking. Nearly year-round, you will need to carry a wind/rain jacket, light hat and gloves, and a light, insulating layer such as a fleece vest. Even in August, the snow levels can drop quickly to below 6,000 feet, surprising hikers with a dusting of pretty white stuff and cooling temperatures.

When hiking in the mountains, wind and/or rain pants are also an essential. Add in a hat with a brim for sun protection and good eye protection for those hikes near timberline where the sun is harsh.

Sturdy shoes or hiking boots will help keep you safe and comfortable while on Portland-area hikes. It's often wet, muddy, or even icy on the trails, and shoes with non-slip hiking soles will keep you on your feet. Wear shoes that are comfortable

THE 10 ESSENTIALS

The 10 Essentials have been around since the 1930s when The Mountaineers climbing club pioneered the concept. Whether or not you carry the basic 10 Essentials on your hike can make the difference between an exciting outdoor adventure and an epic disaster. Store these items together in a zippered plastic bag so that you have them every time you hit the trail. The only things you'll need to change are your extra clothing choices, extra food and water, and the map. Remember to check your headlamp/flashlight batteries at the beginning of each hiking season.

- Compass
- Extra clothing
- Firestarter
- First-aid kit
- Food and water
- Headlamp or flashlight
- Knife
- Map
- Matches
- Sunglasses and sunscreen

and use wool-blend or synthetic socks to keep your feet warm and dry, and to help prevent blisters. Add thin liners under your socks, which also can prevent blisters. If you are a winter hiker, add gaiters to your list of equipment. Gaiters will keep rocks, mud, and water out of your boots. Additionally, light traction devices can help when trails are icy.

Food and Water

Hiking uses a lot of energy, so a little planning will enhance your enjoyment while on the trail. Carry adequate food for the distance you are hiking, taking into consideration the elevation gain and length of time you estimate you'll be out. Snacks come in all shapes and sizes—there is nothing like a good old peanut-butter-and-jelly sandwich when out on the trail. Carry a little extra food, you never know when you may want to extend your outing.

Staying well hydrated while hiking is important. Even when you are just heading out for a "short" hike, take along some water. There are many systems for carrying drinking water on the trail—pick one you like and use it! A backpack hydration reservoir with a hose and nozzle can make drinking easy. If carrying water bottles, try and keep them in an easy-to-reach location. For extreme heat or long days on the trail, you may want to supplement your supply with an endurance or electrolyte formula, but water is still the best choice for most circumstances. Your local sporting goods or running store will have a good supply of these supplements. The amount of water you carry will depend on many factors. It's best to overestimate the amount you will need, or carry water treatment supplies in case you run out. Never drink untreated water from natural sources; lightweight water filters as well as several chemical treatment methods are available at camping stores.

Gear

You can spend a lot of time trying to figure out what "gear" to take hiking. The good news is that you really don't need more than a daypack in which to fit your 10 essentials, including clothing, food, and water. The bad news is there are *lots* of products that can add to your outdoor enjoyment. Lightweight hiking poles have gotten more popular in the last decade or so. These sectional poles can be a great help on rocky, wet ground or when descending steep trails for extended periods of time. Carrying a headlamp, which allows you to keep your hands free, instead of a flashlight can be more versatile if you find yourself heading back to the trailhead in the dark. When hiking with your children, make sure they have a daypack that fits them properly and have older children put together their own bag of 10 essentials. Kids love having their own gear and it will help make them enthusiastic hikers.

Fitness

Hiking is an aerobic activity, particularly around Portland where you often find that the trails gain some elevation. Walking in your neighborhood, riding your bike, or taking part in other aerobic activities will help prepare you for the trails. If you plan on doing longer hikes with significant elevation gain, and are inexperienced or could use some conditioning, do a little pre-trip training. Get out for regular walks with friends or join a community group for an organized walk. You'll want to be fit enough to see the sights and have fun while you're out.

Navigation

It's usually simple stuff to stay on route when hiking well-established trails like the ones in this guidebook. Sometimes, though, conditions necessitate a little extra skill.

MAPS AND COMPASSES

Always carry a map of the area where you are hiking. Topgraphical maps are useful, although many state or local parks have trail maps that are almost as good. Always carry a compass and be sure to know how to use it.

Sometimes the most difficult part of the hike is getting to the trailhead. Make sure you have the road maps you need for your specific destination. For navigating on secondary roads, use the USDA Forest Service map for the area or a state atlas. Delorme and Benchmark both make very good road atlases and these are widely available.

GPS SYSTEMS

If you have a Global Positioning Satellite receiver (GPS) and understand how to use it, bring it along. It can be a great tool for navigation, particularly if you want to do any off-trail exploring or if you find the trail washed out. Today's GPS devices have many features that can be useful on long hikes in new territory; you can track your mileage, elevation gain, and time on the trail, and even create a breadcrumb trail to follow. (Remember to check the map datum and set your GPS to the same datum for waypoint accuracy.)

BLAZES

Blazes are color markings along a trail that can help you stay on route. They can be painted on trees or might be a wood or plastic symbol and are typically about six feet high. Many forests still have carved blazes on trees—these are marks that look like an upside-down exclamation point. Blazes can be useful when trails are obscured by snow or have been washed out by flooding.

To keep from getting lost (above tree line or in sparse vegetation), mark your route with **trail ducks,** small piles of rock that act as directional signs for the return trip.

Rock Cairns

Another common navigation aid is a rock cairn, also called a trail duck; it consists of a small pile of stones indicating a turn in the trail. (It's best not to disturb existing rock cairns along a path.) Sometimes hikers affix plastic tape to mark a route in the snow; this is called flagging. Note that flagging is a temporary navigation tool; if you use flagging to mark a trail, remove the tape when hiking back to the trailhead.

Getting Lost

Even with these navigational tools, sometimes it can be possible to wander off the trail. When you hike a lot, you are bound to get lost or disoriented once in a while. If you do get lost, try not to panic—this is when your map and compass come into play. If you are in a safe location, stop. Take a look around at the area's physical features and use your compass to find yourself on the map. If you have a GPS—and a good signal—take a reading and use that information to find yourself on the map.

First Aid

First-aid Kit

A basic first-aid kit is, well, basic. In a marked stuff sack or plastic bag, carry some bandages of various sizes, a roll of gauze or gauze pads, antibiotic cream, and tape. Carry some extra moleskin and small scissors for padding blisters. You may also want to carry a 24-hour supply of any personal medication you need. Add a bandana or elastic bandage and some pain relievers to round out your kit.

Emergencies

Accidents do happen in the outdoors, so it is useful to make sure someone in your party has had first aid training and carries a kit. If faced with an accident, first calmly assess the situation, then decide on an action plan. Remember the ABCs of first-aid basics: check the Airway, stop any Bleeding, and check for Circulation (heartbeat, pulse). If there is an accident due to a natural phenomenon, such as a rockslide, get yourself and everyone else out of danger if you can. Call for help if you are faced with a life-threatening situation and determine whether you have to send a party member to the trailhead to get help. If there are any injuries, keep the injured hiker warm, dry, and hydrated (unless their injury contraindicates food and/or water).

ON THE TRAIL
Trail Etiquette
Practicing some trail etiquette basics will contribute to your enjoyment of the outdoors:
- Treat other trail users with respect.
- Hike single file on narrow trails and yield to faster hikers.
- When hiking downhill, yield to the uphill hikers.
- Obey trail closures, restrictions, and other posted signs.
- Practice low-impact hiking (see the *Leave No Trace* sidebar).
- Stay on the trail; please don't create shortcuts or cut switchbacks.
- Yield to horses and riders on shared trails.

HIKING WITH CHILDREN
Introducing children to the outdoors at a young age is a gift they will never forget. Some basic considerations can make it a lot more fun for everyone:
- Make sure your children stay on the trail.
- Teach them not to kick rocks off the trail or throw sticks or other objects.
- Kids can be slow on the trail, so yield to faster hikers early and often.
- Teach children about low-impact hiking by encouraging them not to pick flowers, feed wildlife, or litter.

HIKING WITH DOGS
The Portland area is home to a lot of dog owners, and many take their pets hiking. When you do hike with your dog, follow these simple guidelines from the Sierra Club. They'll keep your pet safe and make sure everyone has an enjoyable outing:
- Respect the rules—not all areas allow dogs.
- A 6-foot leash is recommended for all dogs, at all times. Even when your dog is leashed, make sure he's under voice control. Small children and others may become afraid if your dog rushes toward them suddenly.
- Make sure your dog is fit enough for the hike you are doing.
- Keep your dog hydrated.

- Watch out for trails that are rough on paws; your dog may need booties.
- Check your dog for ticks, foxtails, or burrs after every hike.
- Pack it out. Take your dog's droppings with you rather than leaving them on or around the trail.
- Did you know that your dog can carry up to one-third of his weight? You can train your dog to wear a dog backpack.
- Finally, check with local outdoor groups such as The Mazamas for dog-friendly hikes. If you do join an organized hike, check ahead of time to ensure dogs are welcome.

CONSERVATION AND PRESERVATION

Conservation is the responsibility of all outdoor enthusiasts. Although hiking takes place on trails, these are still sensitive environments that require protection. Hikers can become advocates for the preservation of our public lands. Learn more about the places you visit and practice low-impact techniques. Get involved in local preservation efforts, express your views at public meetings or by writing letters, and volunteer with conservation organizations.

LEAVE NO TRACE

Leave No Trace (LNT) is a nonprofit educational organization that has worked with land management agencies to promote the responsible use and stewardship of our public lands. Educating yourself, your children and friends, and your hiking party members about outdoor stewardship can be the best way to protect our natural lands.

The LNT principles are:
1. Plan ahead and prepare.
2. Travel and camp on durable surfaces.
3. Dispose of waste properly.
4. Leave what you find.
5. Minimize campfire impacts.
6. Respect wildlife.
7. Be considerate of other visitors.

See the Leave No Trace website (www.lnt.org) for more information on how you can get involved.

Wildlife

Hikers share the land with a wide array of wildlife. Be aware of the wildlife in the places you visit. Many Portland-area hikes take place in natural areas that black bears, cougars, deer, elk, and a variety of small mammals call home. For example, the Eastern Gorge and Southwest Washington are home to rattlesnakes. If you come across a snake, it is likely trying to get away from you as fast as it can. If you surprise a snake and it rattles, back away or go far around the area.

If an area has had recent reports of cougar sightings, avoid traveling alone. Animal attacks in the Portland area are rare, but if you do encounter a cougar, do not run away. Make yourself appear large by using your hiking poles or daypack to increase your physical size and avoid direct eye contact with the animal.

Nuisance Plants

Poison oak thrives in many popular hiking locations. In the Columbia River Gorge, it is a dominant shrub along low-elevation trails from Portland eastward to the edge of our hiking region—both in Washington and Oregon. Know how to identify poison oak by remembering the old adage: Leaves of three, let them be!

Poison oak looks slightly different in the Eastern Gorge but it's particularly thick along many favorite trails. Wear long pants if you are susceptible; even gloves and long sleeves may be necessary in some places. If you are exposed, wash afterwards using a specialty soap such as Tecnu Extreme. Fels-Naptha is also effective.

A few other plants have irritating needles and thorns. Stinging nettle thrives along many trails and Himalayan blackberry has nasty thorns that can rip your pants. Devil's club will catch any clothing you brush against it, and it may even pierce the cloth, irritating your skin. Learning what these plants look like and avoiding them is usually the best strategy.

Avoiding Poison Oak: Remember the old Boy Scout saying: "Leaves of three, let them be."

Insects

If you spend any time outdoors, you will have to learn to deal with a few irksome insects. When hiking in the spring you are likely to encounter ticks—they are abundant in Northwest forests and also thrive in the Eastern Gorge. Wearing long sleeves and slippery pants of light-colored fabric can make it easier to see and get rid of ticks. When back at the trailhead after hiking in a tick-infested area, take a moment to check yourself and other hiking partners for these little critters. It can save you the excitement of finding them on your clothing on the way home! In the mountains, particularly in alpine basins, mosquitoes flourish. Biting flies or wasps may also be present in some areas. Carry and use insect repellant to prevent painful bites. If anyone in your party has a sensitivity to bites or stings, make sure they have any neccesary medication and that you know where it is.

WEATHER

Weather in the Pacific Northwest has a lot of variability due to the effects of the Pacific Ocean and the Cascade Range. Always check the weather report for your specific destination regardless what the conditions are in town. The Coast Range gets a lot of rain and snow in winter, and generally has summer fog as you head west. The Cascade Range, particularly at higher elevations, often has rapid temperature variations even in summer. Snow may fall below the 6,000-foot level in July, so always be prepared when venturing into the mountains. The Columbia River Gorge gets drier as you head east. This means very cold temperatures in winter, less rain, and more heat in spring and summer. Gorge trails are often icy during mid-winter, so plan ahead and be prepared. Even trails in Forest Park can become icy on unusually cold days. You may also need to make provisions for driving on potentially icy roads as you head to or from the trailhead.

By learning what to expect in Portland-area hiking regions, you will never have to stay home because of "bad weather." Weather reports are updated often and are widely available on the radio, television, or Internet. Preparation, appropriate clothing and gear, and common sense will allow you to be out on the trails year-round.

Fall

Fall hiking allows you to experience the rich colors of falling leaves in the Columbia River Gorge. The trails become mushy with orange, brown, and yellow leaves and the forest fills with light. The trail experience changes as previously obscured views open up. Trails get quieter in fall as temperatures begin to drop and the light changes. Along Eagle Creek, the salmon thrash their way upstream to their spawning grounds, providing young hikers with the ultimate Northwest experience. The harsh mid-summer light gives way to a soft glow. Fall is often the last chance to visit the alpine hikes of the Cascades, unless you visit on snowshoes! Luckily there are ample trails with good access year-round.

Winter

Winter hiking usually means exploring trails that are often overlooked in the summertime. Winter may mean taking that trip to visit the Klickitat Trail in the Eastern Gorge, or taking a stroll along the quiet trails of Tryon Creek State Natural Area. The Marquam Nature Park is another winter staple for easy-access hiking. And, when the temperature dips, there can be snow on the upper reaches of Council Crest. This park is beautiful when glistening with a light dusting of snowflakes or frost.

Spring

Spring signifies renewal, and along the trails this means one thing: wildflowers. There is almost no way to describe the unbelievable assortment of wildflowers along Portland-area trails. I've been lucky to hike with quite a few flower experts—a fun and educational experience.

Wildflowers along the trails in the far Eastern Gorge begin to bloom as early as late February or early March and are plentiful by April. Washington's Catherine Creek and Dog Mountain have well-deserved reputations for their striking blooms. In Portland, Forest Park and Tryon Creek see early displays of pretty white trillium in late February. I visit the trails of Forest Park often in winter and spring, and always feel a little rush of excitement when I spy the first trillium blooms along the muddy trails. Alpine wildflowers don't bloom until winter snows begin to melt. Depending upon elevation, this can mean June in the Western Cascades or Coast Range. On the alpine trails of Mounts Adams, Hood, or St. Helens, big wildflower displays usually are on hold until mid-July or later.

Summer

Summer means that the trails of the Cascades and Coast Range are thawing out and ready for a visit. Early summer hikes in the Western Cascades blooming Pacific rhododendron amidst the crisp mornings that don't fade until July. Summer often means visiting alpine basins ringed with flower-filled meadows and timberline trees. And, for me, summer means getting onto some nearby summits for those classic views of surrounding peaks and valleys.

HIKING GEAR CHECKLIST

This basic list will get you started. It's not necessary to take all this stuff on your hike, you can personalize or modify your gear for specific preferences or weather conditions. For more information on clothing, gear, and equipment see The Mazamas' website at www.mazamas.org.

What to Carry
- Backpack
- Camera
- Emergency blanket
- Foot-care kit (moleskin, antiseptic liquid bandage, duct tape)
- Insect repellent
- Instant hand warmers (nice for unexpected temperature drops)
- Insulated sit pad (some packs include one)
- 10 Essentials
- Toilet paper and sealable plastic bags
- Trekking poles

What to Wear
- Fleece jacket
- Fleece or wool cap
- Fleece pants
- Gaiters (nice for winter hikes or hikes with many water crossings)
- Gloves (two pair for long or winter hikes)
- Hat with brim
- Lightweight balaclava (very versatile)
- Lightweight pants or shorts
- Long underwear
- Short-sleeved or lightweight long-sleeved shirt
- Sock liners, if desired
- Sturdy boots for longer hikes; lightweight trail shoes for quick trips
- Waterproof/breathable hooded jacket and pants
- Wool or wool-blend socks

Optional Gear
- Bandana
- Binoculars
- Cell phone or personal locator device
- Lens cleaner or anti-fog solution for glasses or goggles
- Two-way radios

PORTLAND AND THE WILLAMETTE VALLEY

© BARBARA I. BOND

BEST HIKES

❰ Bird-Watching
Warrior Point, **page 37**
Baskett Butte and Morgan Lake Loop, **page 49**
Woodpecker and Mill Hill Loop Trails, **page 60**

❰ Hikes with Children
Wildwood Trail-Leif Erikson Loop, **page 28**
Mount Tabor, **page 43**

❰ Waterfalls
Trail of Ten Falls, **page 52**

❰ Views
Powell Butte Nature Loop, **page 46**

Portland and its surroundings are home to some

of the most spectacular scenery in the West. Metro Portland and the Willamette Valley contain miles of trails in close proximity to major highways, so it takes little effort to get out and onto a trail. Portland and the Columbia River form the northern border of the well-known Willamette Valley. This interior Oregon landscape gets less rain than the neighboring Coast Range yet still has ample rainfall to maintain the woodlands, open grasslands, and forests that provide recreation for residents. It's a good thing too – most of Oregon's population lives in this relatively small geographic area. The opportunities for hiking are many in the lowland valley. The Tualatin Mountains contain Portland's well-known Forest Park, running nearly parallel to the Willamette River. Around Salem and Corvallis are the important preserves of the Willamette Valley National Wildlife Refuge Complex. Finally, the canyons and waterfalls of Silver Falls State Park invite visitors to explore the eastern border of Willamette Valley near Silverton. Whichever way you go, you are likely to find a trail to enjoy.

There is a great deal of variety amongst the trails of Portland and the Willamette Valley. Much of that is due to the origins of the valley's topography. The flat areas around Baskett Slough provide croplands and wetlands for migratory birds. On the eastern side of the valley are the foothills and dense forest of Oregon's largest state park. Silver Falls State

Park may feel familiar to hikers who frequent the Gorge – the dominant formations in the park are made of Columbia River basalts.

Within the city of Portland are a surprising number of destinations with natural settings that provide a wide range of opportunities for recreation in the fresh air. It's always a popular choice to hike the steep and winding trails of Mount Tabor. There and at Powell Butte we are reminded of the area's volcanic past. There aren't too many other places in the United States where hikers can explore cinder cones within city limits. On Portland's West Side you can hike the flat, wide paths along Tom McCall Waterfront Park and be back downtown in minutes. Further south lies Tryon Creek State Park – big trees, rich wildflower displays, and a barrier-free trail are the highlights of this urban wonderland.

Some of the hikers who regularly flock to the Coast Range or the Columbia River Gorge forget that they have wonderful hiking opportunities right in town. Many of Portland's natural areas are where hikers of all ages get their start. Along the walkway of the Eastbank Esplanade, you are likely to see small children toddling as well as a hardy group of senior citizens out for their daily constitutional. Sauvie Island attracts families, birders, and mushroom hunters – visit the island and check out the trails that they enjoy. With so many choices, it's easy to stay active and keep exploring – you'll be glad you did.

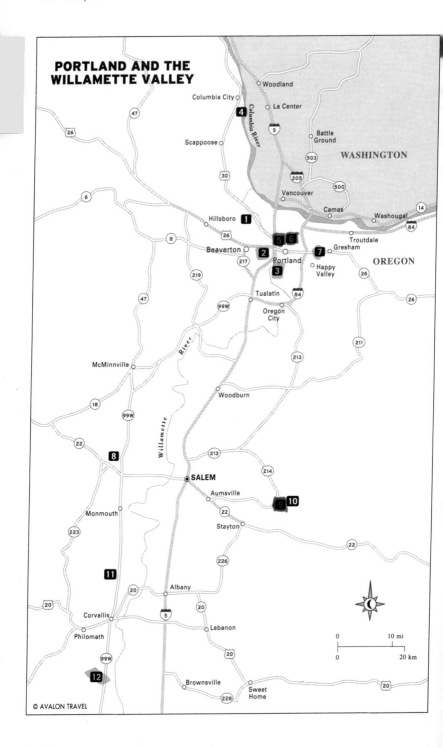

TRAIL NAME	LEVEL	DISTANCE	TIME	ELEVATION	FEATURES	PAGE
1 Wildwood Trail–Leif Erikson Loop	Easy	6.1 mi rt	3 hr	350 ft		28
2 Marquam Trail 4-19-15	Easy/Moderate	3.4 mi rt	2 hr	740 ft		31
3 Tryon Creek Loop 10-11-14	Easy	3.6 mi rt	2 hr	400 ft		34
4 Warrior Point	Easy	7.0 mi rt	3.5 hr	Negligible		37
5 Eastbank Esplanade Loop 10-12-13	Easy	3.0 mi rt	2 hr	Negligible		40
6 Mount Tabor 10-4-14	Easy	1-3 mi rt	2-3 hr	250 ft		43
7 Powell Butte Nature Loop 2-21-15	Easy	4.4 mi rt	2-2.5 hr	620 ft		46
8 Baskett Butte and Morgan Lake Loop	Easy	5.5 mi rt	3 hr	210 ft		49
9 Trail of Ten Falls 5-31-14	Moderate	8.7 mi rt	4.5 hr	900 ft		52
10 Buck Mountain Trail	Moderate	8.1 mi rt	4 hr	930 ft		55
11 Section 36–Powder House Loop	Easy/Moderate	4.0 mi rt	2 hr	900 ft		57
12 Woodpecker and Mill Hill Loop Trails 5-2-15	Easy	1.1-3.3 mi rt	3 hr	150 ft		60

1 WILDWOOD TRAIL-LEIF ERIKSON LOOP

Forest Park, North

BEST [

Level: Easy

Total Distance: 6.1 miles round-trip

Hiking Time: 3 hours

Elevation Change: 350 feet

Summary: Visit Portland's biggest city park and explore one of the nation's largest urban forests.

Forest Park has lured Portlanders into the wilds of the Tualatin Mountains since its official dedication in the 1940s. Touted as the largest urban forest in the nation, Forest Park has over 70 miles of trails and a host of recreation opportunities. The Wildwood Trail is iconic to many, winding its way nearly 31 miles on a serpentine path. The trail runs the length of the park from far north Newberry Road to its start near the Vietnam Memorial in Washington Park. This loop hike from Germantown Road will expose hikers to a wilder section of the park. Here

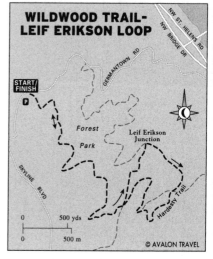

the dense forest of Douglas-fir, western hemlock, alder, and bigleaf maple creates a complex landscape in which wildlife thrives. Watch for coyote and blacktailed deer while listening for the loud hammering of the pileated woodpecker.

From the parking lot, hike uphill a short distance on the wide trail. You'll quickly pass the junction on the left for the Cannon Trail, then a blue diamond trail marker for "24.5 miles" high on a tree. Watch for these blue diamonds—they are unique to the Wildwood Trail, conveniently placed every 0.25 mile, and can be a useful navigation tool if you get lost or disoriented. You'll pass some larger Douglas-fir trees about 0.75 mile in as the forest becomes more dense. Shade-loving western hemlock fill in under the Douglas fir canopy and you might notice old red cedars, too. It's surprisingly quiet out here, so close to the city yet a lifetime away in the forest. As the trail rolls along the hilly terrain the elevation remains mostly level but with some very short changes. This is challenging in winter when the thick, slippery mud can make footing dicey at best. The trail winds around, in

Wildwood Trail, Forest Park's longest trail

and out of a couple of drainages on its way to the junction with Springville Road. As you make your way along this stretch, look out towards the Willamette River occasionally—when the trees thin you can catch some river views.

At mile 2.1 is the junction with Springville Road; turn left and head downhill on the wide gravel track. There is a trail map at this junction and signs marking the Wildwood Trail on both sides of the road. The short descent to Leif Erikson Drive doesn't take long. At Leif, turn right to head towards the Hardesty Trail junction. Leif Erikson Drive has a colorful past—for a time in the 1940s it was a scenic drive for dozens of vehicles carrying picnic-laden Portlanders. The city closed the road to vehicles in 1980 thus allowing it to become the recreational magnet it is today. On any given day you'll see bikers, strollers, dog-walkers, runners, and walkers. As you walk southeast, note the old concrete mileposts. The 0.3 mile on Leif quickly passes. Watch for the old foundation on the right; it's been completely obliterated by ivy—a stark reminder of the invasive quality of this tenacious species. At milepost 9.0 turn right uphill and onto the Hardesty Trail.

The Hardesty Trail climbs quickly 0.27 mile to get back to the Wildwood Trail. Along the way will be some huge, impressive stumps from the logging era. As you approach a boardwalk, check out the stump on the right side of the trail—it's enormous, with springboard cuts about halfway up the stump. When you reach the Wildwood Trail, turn right at the sign to return to the Germantown trailhead. From here it's about 3 miles to the parking area. Take a look at the variety of ferns and mosses along this section of the forest. The trees are covered with thick moss—hanging moss like witch's hair or methusaleh's beard—and it seems like every still surface is coated green. Huge sword ferns line the trail.

Options

Forest Park has many access points, making it simple to plan long or short hikes. A fun way to explore the park is through a shuttle hike along the Wildwood Trail. For solitude and a real feeling of wilderness, take the far north section south from Newberry Road. This amazing 5.75-mile (one-way) or 11.5-mile (out-and-back) trip zigzags through some of the least-visited miles of the park. Listen for the loud tapping of a pileated woodpecker up here, watch for black-tailed deer, and enjoy a profusion of wildflowers in spring that include a carpet of trillium. Numerous bridges span streams and creeks, making this a truly unique city hiking experience. Pull out along NW Newberry Road about 0.5 mile below Skyline Boulevard. There is a sign for the Wildwood Trail on the south side of the road.

Directions

From I-405 S, take exit 3 and drive 5.8 miles to NW Bridge Avenue. Turn left at the stoplight, then turn sharply right on NW Germantown Road. Drive uphill on Germantown Road, passing the parking area for Leif Erikson Drive on the left, to a pull-out parking area on the left in about 1.5 miles. (There is room for about eight cars.) A trailhead information sign and map are at the end of the lot, to the right of the trail. There are no services at the trailhead.

Information and Contact

Leashed dogs are allowed on Forest Park trails. There is no off-leash area in the park. For a good topographic park map and a bike map, contact Portland Parks and Recreation (www.portlandonline.com/parks). For current trail conditions and maps, contact the Forest Park Conservancy (1507 NW 23rd Ave., Portland, OR, 97210, 503/223-5449, www.forestparkconservancy.org). This non-profit group does the lion's share of trail work, offers guided hikes, and is the unofficial visitor information center for the park.

2 MARQUAM TRAIL

4-18-15

Council Crest Park

Level: Easy/Moderate

Total Distance: 3.4 miles round-trip

Hiking Time: 2 hours

Elevation Change: 740 feet

Summary: Enjoy panoramic views from 1,040-foot Council Crest Park, one of Portland's highest city parks.

There is nothing like standing on top of a hill and viewing neighboring volcanoes—something most Northwesterners appreciate. For Portlanders, the views from Council Crest are nothing new. On a clear day you can see several bridges and Cascade peaks including Mounts St. Helens and Hood. The trail travels through dense trees and a narrow canyon between the Marquam Shelter and Council Crest. Accessible year-round and easy to get to, this short but vigorous hike will become one of your favorite in-town getaways. While it may seem backwards to start at the top of Council Crest Park and hike downhill first, the bonus is that if you pack a picnic, Frisbee, or favorite book you can hang out at the park after your hike.

The Marquam Trail begins on the east side of the Council Crest Drive circle. (The trailhead sign is adjacent to the dog off-leash area.) The trail descends for about 0.2 mile through trees to the first of three street crossings. Cross SW Greenway and continue 0.3 mile down the second short section before crossing Fairmount Boulevard. (This road circles Council Crest, which was originally named Fairmount before a group renamed the peak in 1898.) From here it's a quick 1.2 miles down to the Marquam Park Shelter.

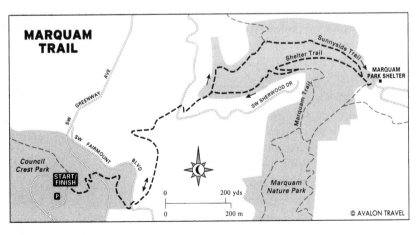

dense forest and ferns along the Marquam Trail

Descend some steps to enter the true city/nature interface of this hike. The steep-sided ravine has houses precariously perched in spots and some backyards push right up against the trail for a short distance. It's just a reminder of one way of being in the city and enjoying nature simultaneously. Wildflowers bloom alongside the trail here; watch for yellow violets in spring. As you wind your way downhill there will be some large mossy nurse stumps with ferns and flowers blooming in the rotting wood.

At 1.0 mile you will cross Sherwood Drive. There is only 0.7 mile to the shelter and 300 feet more of descent. Bear left at the trail junction with Sunnyside Trail. (You may even see some sun here.) This will take you on the first section of a clockwise loop through the Marquam Nature Park; you will pass a trail junction with the Broadway Trail on the left about halfway down. The forest here is thick with Douglas-fir and western red cedar and the understory includes the Oregon grape, salal, sword ferns, and a variety of fungi. After crossing a seasonally wet area on a turnpike—where there may be some horsetails and skunk cabbage blooming—turn left at the trail junction to reach the shelter. A series of interpretive signs and a garbage can mark your destination.

To return to Council Crest, retrace your steps until reaching the junction with the Sunnyside Trail. Keep left to complete your loop on the Shelter Trail, joining the Marquam Trail after 0.6 mile. Follow the Marquam Trail uphill 1.1 miles back to the views and your picnic.

Options

Extend your hike by taking the Marquam Trail to the Wildwood Trail in Washington Park. The continuation of the Marquam Trail is just prior to the trailhead at Council Crest. Turn northward to reach the Wildwood Trail in 1.8 miles. Once you reach the Wildwood Trail, you are limited only by your imagination and perhaps the size of your daypack. Retrace your steps to Council Crest when you are finished exploring.

Directions

From downtown Portland drive south on SW Broadway until it turns into SW Patton Road. Turn left onto SW Greenway Avenue and follow it for 0.5 mile, bearing right onto SW Council Crest Drive. (You are circling uphill to reach the park entrance.) Parking is along the circle. Reach the trailhead by walking to the dog off-leash area near the top of the circle on the east side.

The no. 51 TriMet bus has stops on SW Greenway Avenue at the north and south ends of the park.

Information and Contact

There are no fees. Dogs are allowed on leash on the trails and off-leash in the designated area. The park is open 5 A.M.–midnight and closes to vehicles at 9 P.M. Picnic tables, drinking fountains, benches, a paved path, public art, and a wedding site are available (call 503/823-2525 to reserve the wedding site). For more information, contact Portland Parks and Recreation (503/823-2223, www.portlandonline.com/parks). A trail map is available from Friends of Marquam Nature Park (email fmp@comcast.net).

3 TRYON CREEK LOOP   10-11-14
Tryon Creek State Park

🐎 🦯 🌿 🦌 👫 ♿ 🚌

Level: Easy

Total Distance: 3.6 miles round-trip

Hiking Time: 2 hours

Elevation Change: 400 feet

Summary: Enjoy a series of interconnecting short trails in Tryon Creek State Natural Area.

Hiking in Tryon Creek takes you across a suspension bridge, through a small canyon, and along ridges surrounded by wildflowers and towering trees. Well-known for displays of spring blooms including abundant trillium, pretty pink salmonberry, and delicate snowflakes, a walk through here brings you close to nature. There is a lot of wildlife here including the infamous barred owl, now competing with the endangered spotted owl for the same habitat. At any rate, high up in a cedar tree you may spot these nocturnal creatures. This lopsided figure-eight loop has a lot of turns, but don't let that confuse you. The trails are well signed and the loops allow a quick return to the Nature Center if you so desire.

Begin at the Nature Center where you can pick up a trail map. Follow the sign to the Maple Trail by walking on a wide, short path through the forest lined with spring blooms of trillium and bleeding hearts. The forest floor is covered with huge sword ferns, Oregon grape, and lots of flowers. Tangles of vine maples grow happily here amongst the alder, Douglas-fir, and bigleaf maples. It's just a few moments before you reach the Middle Creek Trail and go left to the High Bridge. There is a bench adjacent to the wooden footbridge across Tryon Creek. After crossing, continue north on the Middle Creek Trail. On the way to

trails in Tryon Creek State Park

the Terry Riley Bridge—an old, narrow suspension bridge—you'll pass some big cedars and some huge nurse stumps. Check out the growth from the stumps—mosses, licorice ferns, and sometimes a small tree. Tiny mushrooms often grow in the rotting bark.

After 0.4 mile you cross the bridge to begin the Lewis and Clark Trail to the right. This 0.4-mile section of trail leads to a super-short connector east to the North Horse Loop which you can use to head back to the High Bridge. It's a pleasant 0.6 mile back to the bridge. Cross it once again and turn left this time onto the Middle Creek Trail alongside pretty Tryon Creek. You're likely to see some ducks in the slow-moving water. The Cedar Trail is just ahead on the right.

Begin uphill on the Cedar Trail, going up some steps and past a lot of big western red cedar. The trail's namesake cedar trees are in evidence all around; some trees are enormous, including one lying on the ground that has become a natural tunnel. Note the springboard cuts in some of the stumps, relics from the logging era. You're now in the central part of the park and it's noticeably quieter. It's a quick walk to cross Bunk Bridge and turn eastward through the forest. There a lot of old cedar stumps along this part of the trail. After passing the Hemlock Trail, continue along for 0.4 mile as you descend to another small footbridge. Pass the Red Fox Trail, which heads off south, and turn northward to the Red Fox Bridge. You'll begin seeing more people again as the trail approaches the busier nature center loops. Climb up some switchbacks from the bridge and end by hiking northward on the Old Main Trail back to the Nature Center.

Options

Shorten this long loop hike and instead take an hour to explore the Ruth Pennington Trillium Trail. This 0.35-mile barrier-free paved trail offers drinking fountains and extensive interpretive information. Benches and viewing decks add to the allure of this short trail. Walk east from the Nature Center and follow the signs for the start of the trail.

Directions

From downtown Portland, take I-5 south to exit 297/Terwilliger Boulevard. Follow the road as it curves to the right onto Barbur Boulevard. Turn right on Barbur, then right again at the next light, which is Terwilliger. Follow Terwilliger, watching for a brown and white sign that reads "Tryon Creek State Park." The park is 1 mile past the sign on the right.

From downtown Portland, you can take TriMet to access the Tryon Creek Trails. TriMet 39 picks up at Lewis and Clark College; get off at the Northwestern School of Law. The bike trail heads south into the park.

Information and Contact

Dogs are allowed on leash only. For more information, contact the Tryon Creek State Park (11321 SW Terwilliger Blvd., Portland, OR, 97219) or The Friends of Tryon Creek (503/636-4398 or 503/636-9886, www.tryonfriends.org). The Friends of Tryon Creek run the Nature Center, have paper trail maps, and can answer many questions for visitors.

4 WARRIOR POINT

BEST

Sauvie Island Wildlife Area

Level: Easy

Total Distance: 7.0 miles round-trip

Hiking Time: 3.5 hours

Elevation Change: Negligible

Summary: Hike to the northernmost tip of Sauvie Island, the largest island in the Columbia River.

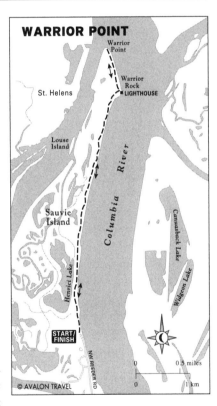

Just minutes from downtown Portland, Sauvie Island stands alone as one of the area's premier birding destinations. In winter migratory birds including sandhill cranes arrive by the flock. Springtime brings the return of the osprey, and abundant year-round resident birds like great horned owls and bald eagles contribute to the island's riches. Black-tailed deer, beaver, and raccoons also make Sauvie Island their home. Wildflowers dot the path and mushroom hunters comb trees for the elusive treat. What better way to view birds amongst this pastoral setting than by hiking the sea-level trail to Warrior Point?

Sauvie Island was discovered by explorers in 1792, and its northern end is rich with history. On the Columbia side (east) of the point sits Warrior Rock—home to the Warrior Rock Lighthouse. The original lighthouse was built in 1889 and has been rebuilt several times over the years. Sauvie Island is now home to rich farms and pastures and preserved lands managed by the Oregon Department of Fish and Wildlife. This unique hike will lead you along the Columbia River.

Walk north from the small parking area, past the information board. The path follows a fence for a short distance before making a jog left into the trees to continue north. I recommend ignoring the trail in the trees and opting for a hike along the sandy beach. When the river is low, there is plenty of shoreline to hike

Warrior Rock Lighthouse and the Columbia River

and the pretty little lighthouse beckons from the distance. The lighthouse is the first stop en route to the tip of the island. In spring, you may see dozens of fishing boats as you walk along the river or marvel at the massive container ships southbound for the Port. Along the distant northeast horizon lies Mount St. Helens, its flanks glistening with snow until mid-summer. Osprey platforms usually house nesting birds—take a look with your binoculars. As you make your way north you will pass all manner of boating detritus—large pieces of unidentifiable metal ship fragments, buoys, and a long-abandoned boat now permanently grounded high on the shore. Eagles frequently roost on the treetops to your left—if you're quiet you may even get a close-up of a mature bald eagle with its distinctive coloring.

Aside from the occasional murmur of a ship engine the dominant sounds are made by birds. Pause every once in a while and just take in the sounds—all manner of songbirds and raptors live here and you can distinguish their distinct calls as you listen in.

Approaching the 3-mile point you may have to jog left onto the trail for a short distance if the water level is rising. If so, just continue north on the wide, tree-lined path that curves gently northeast toward the lighthouse. After enjoying a break here, continue north along the beach to the tip of the island, which is right across from the town of St. Helens. Savor the views of the old pier pilings in the water off the shore and enjoy the solitude. Return the way you came.

Options
Oak Island Nature Trail is a pretty 2-mile loop on Sauvie's "island within an island." Follow the directions to Sauvie Island and once on NW Reeder Road turn left after 1.3 miles at NW Oak Island Road. Drive 4.1 miles to the end of the road and a parking area. The trailhead is north of the parking area and you may hike the loop in either direction.

Directions
From I-405/Fremont Bridge drive north on U.S. 30 W about 9.5 miles. Turn right to cross the Sauvie Island Bridge and continue on NW Sauvie Island Road 2.1 miles. Turn right on NW Reeder Road and drive 12.8 miles to the end of the road. Park in the small dirt parking area or along the west side of the road. There is an information sign and a portable restroom at the trailhead.

Information and Contact
A Sauvie Island Wildlife Area Parking Permit is required, and available for purchase at island stores ($5/day or $20/season). Island wildlife areas are open from April 16th through September 30th. During winter months, trails are closed but roads are walkable and allow good access for bird-watching. For more information, contact Sauvie Island Wildlife Area (18330 NW Sauvie Island Rd., Portland, OR 97231, 503/621-3488).

5 EASTBANK ESPLANADE LOOP

Tom McCall Waterfront Park

10-12-13

Level: Easy

Total Distance: 3.0 miles round-trip

Hiking Time: 2 hours

Elevation Change: Negligible

Summary: Enjoy architectural details, public art, and a walk across two bridges on this urban stroll.

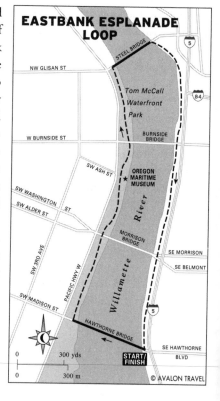

Portlanders love their city parks, and Tom McCall Waterfront Park is one of the most popular. When the Eastbank Esplanade opened in spring 2001, the park on the West Side was connected to the east bank of the Willamette via a new route—the Steel Bridge RiverWalk. Add in the new paved path down to the Hawthorne Bridge and you have the ingredients for an urban walking treat. Rain or shine, any season of the year—it's always a good time to visit the Esplanade and stroll along the Willamette River.

Walk towards the river, turn left, and head south towards the Hawthorne Bridge. One of the pleasures of walking along the Esplanade is enjoying the art and interpretive signs along the path. Before you head up the spiral walkway to the bridge deck, take a minute or two to enjoy the etching of the Willamette and Columbia River confluence adjacent to the Portland Fire Bureau's EMS station. Resume your walk south along the path, passing a bronze sculpture of former Mayor Vera Katz, who was a big booster of the Esplanade project. It's always fun to walk across Portland's bridges and the Hawthorne is no exception. You get great views of downtown and the river far below. After descending the stairs, take a moment to walk south to a viewpoint with some binoculars and interpretive signs. This area is adjacent to "the bowl"—the sloping lawn between the Hawthorne Bridge and the RiverPlace Hotel and Esplanade.

© BARBARA I. BOND

Hawthorne Bridge and the Willamette River with views of downtown Portland

From here it's a little over a mile to the Steel Bridge. As you head north you'll pass the Salmon Street Springs fountain and the vacant modernist building that housed McCall's Restaurant. The fountain is popular in spring and summer with visitors and children. Continuing north to the Morrison Bridge, note the information sign about the river near Alder Street. Cross under the Morrison Bridge and towards the Burnside Bridge. Part way up is the Oregon Maritime Museum, which includes the historic sternwheeler *Portland*. Walk under the Burnside Bridge and continue north to the Steel Bridge. Just past the Burnside Bridge is the Japanese American Historical Plaza. Take a little detour along the crescent-shaped path that goes through the memorial plaza. After returning to the path, note the stainless steel sculpture just prior to the Steel Bridge RiverWalk. The concrete bench surround is inviting and is a good place to people watch and appreciate the design of the Steel Bridge.

Cross the river on the walkway, suspended 30 feet above the Willamette River, and take in this unique view of downtown Portland. After reaching the east side of the river and turning south onto the Eastbank Esplanade, you'll travel a short distance to reach the Esplanade's most unique attribute—a 1,200-foot floating walkway—the longest in the United States. Public art and interpretive signs are featured prominently in this part of the hike. One favorite is the Echo Gate, which sits right below the Morrison Bridge. This represents Portland's mythic Shanghai tunnels and long-demolished pier buildings. Enjoy the rest of the art and take time to read the signs as you make your way south just another 0.3 mile to your starting point.

Options

You can add onto the hike or do an out-and-back to Oaks Bottom by passing up the Hawthorne Bridge and walking south past OMSI about 3 miles. Oaks Bottom Wildlife Refuge is a haven for birds—lots of them. Be sure and check out the osprey nesting platforms high above the trail and watch along the river for bald eagles and great blue heron. Bring your binoculars to take advantage of this impressive birding destination.

Directions

From East Burnside Avenue, drive south on SE Martin Luther King Jr. Boulevard. Turn right at SE Taylor, then left in 0.2 mile on SE Water Avenue. In two blocks turn right on SE Main and either use on-street parking or continue to the end at the U-Park lot.

Information and Contact

Leashed dogs allowed. There are no fees, although you may need to pay to park. Free parking is allowed along SE Main and Salmon Streets and SE Water Avenue. There is also a U-Park lot under the interstate and adjacent to the Hawthorne Bridge (free on Sunday). For a West Side treat, detour south past the RiverPlace Hotel to the Little River Café (7 A.M.–9 P.M. Mon.–Sat., 8 A.M.–9 P.M. Sun.). They dish up big Umpqua ice cream cones, a variety of café offerings, and good espresso drinks.

6 MOUNT TABOR

Mount Tabor Park

10-4-14

BEST (

Blue signs - 3 miles

Level: Easy

Hiking Time: 2-3 hours

Total Distance: 1-3 miles round-trip

Elevation Change: 250 feet

Summary: Walk to the top of Portland's Mount Tabor, one of only two extinct volcanoes in the U.S. located within city limits.

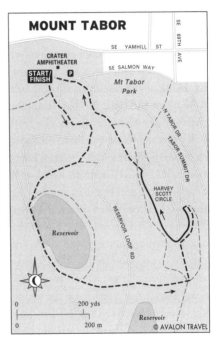

Mount Tabor Park is a Portland landmark. Nearly 100 years old, this heavily forested park is built on and around an extinct cinder cone. Walks in the park can be short or long, but the real fun comes when you reach Harvey Scott Circle at the top of the cone. This 0.32-mile paved loop has extraordinary panoramic views of the Portland area and invites you to sit on one of the benches and stay awhile. Plenty of people do just that, nearly any time of day you can find folks lounging on the benches reading, gazing across the Willamette at the West Hills and downtown Portland, or checking out the finger-pointing statue of Harvey Scott himself.

One way to explore the park is to begin at the parking lot in the northwest corner of the park. There is a labyrinthine collection of trails, so there is no straightforward way to hike in the park. That said, the trails are so short that you can just pick a direction and begin walking. As long as you take a look at the park trail map on the board, you'll be just fine. When in doubt keep heading uphill; eventually you'll reach a trail or road that goes to the top.

Still, there are some areas that are worth checking out. Hike downhill through the heavily treed canyon west to the tennis courts from the crater amphitheater. The trees are big; there is dense understory of vine maple and shade-loving wildflowers. You can also hike a couple of loops by using the recent trail markers installed by the Friends of Mount Tabor. Again start at the parking area near the crater amphitheater, off East Tabor Drive. Follow either the blue or red posts for a hike of whatever length you prefer. This will wind you down south along the reservoir and back up along the southern flanks of the 630-foot cone. When the posts run out, just keep heading uphill.

Walk south out of the lot, follow the road 0.10 mile to catch the trail on the east side of the road. The trail parallels the road curving west, and then south, down to the north end of the reservoir. You can walk along the west side of the reservoir, turning left to stay on the path 0.25 mile across the southern tip of the park. The trail will cross the Reservoir Road halfway, then begin climbing up to a trail junction in 0.12 mile. Turn left, which will

a typical Mount Tabor trail

take you to another quick junction; then turn right to wind up and around the east side of Tabor Summit Drive. Turn left on the road and walk up to Harvey Scott Circle at the top of the park. At the south end of the park is Scott's statue, pointing west. (Walk up onto the grass to the northern end of the circle and look for the USGS benchmark embedded in a chunk of cement and set into the grass.) To return to the bottom, head north from Harvey Scott Circle but don't take the stairs. Instead take the trail that begins just past the restrooms. Keep left for the steeper path, this will take you down to Reservoir Loop Road. Continue downhill on the path towards the volcano playground and lot where you began.

Options

One of my favorite things about Mount Tabor Park is the many sets of steps leading to the top. It can be a fun challenge to walk up staircase after staircase past huge Douglas-fir trees, crossing the roads and generally getting a good look at the north end of the volcano. Start at the north entrance where SE 69th dead-ends at SE Salmon Way and take a deep breath. On the way up, there are plenty of places to stop for a rest—and as you near the top the steps end for a few hundred yards so that the trail can curve upwards through a patch of grass. Otherwise, enjoy this shaded workout. Your climb ends at the north tip of SE Tabor Summit Drive/Harvey Scott Circle, conveniently next to a drinking fountain.

Directions

From SE Martin Luther King Jr. Boulevard and East Burnside in Portland, drive east on East Burnside Street for 3 miles to SE 61st Avenue. Turn right and drive three blocks to SE Belmont Street. Turn left onto SE Belmont and continue for 0.4 mile to SE 69th Ave. Turn right on SE Salmon Way and into the parking lot.

Ride the no. 15 Tri Met bus to the corner of SE 69th and SE Yamhill, then walk south on SE 69th to the park entrance. To head up the stairs, go straight ahead; for the parking lot, restrooms, and information signs, turn right and walk 0.2 mile on SE Salmon Way into the park.

Information and Contact

Dogs are allowed on leash only. For more information about Mount Tabor Park, contact Portland Parks and Recreation (SE 60th St. and Salmon St., www.portlandonline.com/parks). The website has a trail map and off-leash dog area map. A new trail map with trails corresponding to the red and blue posts is available at the main park information sign-in or through the Friends of Mount Tabor Park (503/200-4176, email at taborfriends@aol.com).

The park is open 5 A.M.–midnight and is closed to vehicles on Wednesday (the road gates at Salmon, Lincoln/Harrison, and Yamhill Streets will be closed).

2-21-15

7 POWELL BUTTE NATURE LOOP   BEST **C**

Powell Butte Nature Park

Level: Easy

Total Distance: 4.4 miles round-trip

Hiking Time: 2-2.5 hours

Elevation Change: 620 feet

Summary: Hike on one of Portland's extinct cinder cones and enjoy magnificent views of surrounding peaks including Mounts Hood, St. Helens, and Adams.

Powell Butte rises gently above the dense development of outer Southeast Portland. It may not look like much as you approach, yet the 600-acre city park offers outdoor lovers 9 miles of gentle trails in a surprisingly rich natural environment. There is a network of nearly a dozen trails that can be linked up for explorations ranging from an after-work leg-stretcher to an all-day hike-a-thon.

Walk uphill from the car park and main information sign on a short connector trail to a signed trail junction. Go straight to begin on the Mountain View Trail, which climbs steadily on a couple of switchbacks on the northeast corner of the butte. There are a couple of nice viewpoints on the way up, with benches strategi-

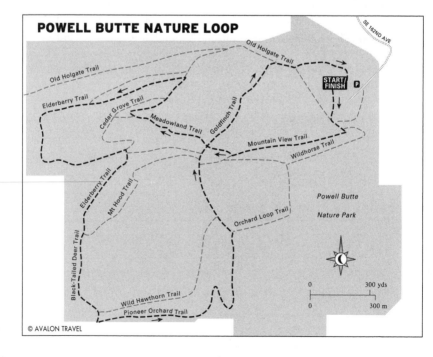

© BARBARA I. BOND

an amazing forest along a trail of volcanic butte

cally placed. As you approach the top, look on your right for a trail. Bear right and leave the main trail on a dirt track that heads across a short section of meadow. You're now on the Meadowland Trail. Watch the signs at an old road and keep left. Don't turn right on the Goldfinch Trail. Head towards the trees through the meadow filled with blooming wildflowers, but be sure to watch for nuisance plants like stinging nettle, poison oak, thistles, vetch, blackberry, and scotch broom. I saw a black-tailed mule deer as I hiked past the trees—there is a lot of wildlife on the butte. You're more likely to spot coyote or raccoon in early morning or near dusk. As you continue, the trail ducks into the forest of Douglas-fir, bigleaf maple, western red cedar, and lots of understory plants. Ferns, wild roses, and fringecup all thrive here. You will reach a "T" junction at 1.1 mile; turn right. Now you are on the Cougar Trail, which will descend slightly through pretty cedars and then out of the trees completely to yet another signed junction at 1.4 miles. Turn left on the Elderberry Trail and then pass through an open meadow with a row of large Douglas fir on the right. You're back in the forest again with its wood sorrel all along the forest floor. Keep left uphill past a grove of cedars.

At around 2 miles you will meet the junction with Cedar Grove Trail—turn right to stay on the Elderberry Trail and follow it south as it descends through the trees. You will reach another trail junction; in a short distance, keep right on the Black-Tailed Deer Trail. You are now heading towards the junction with the Pioneer Orchard Trail at the far south end of the park. There are a lot of side trails in that part of the park, most of them used by neighbors who walk in from the side streets. Ignore the junctions and continue southward until reaching the Pioneer Orchard Trail, which takes you north back up to the top of the butte.

This is one of the prettiest forested sections of trail, a cool respite on a hot summer day. Near the top of the butte, you reach the Orchard Loop Trail. Turn left for a final stroll across the open upper butte back to the start. This area was historically orchard, farmland, and then grazing land until the mid-1970s. It took until 1990 for it to be opened as a nature park. Hike to the signed Goldfinch Trail and take it all the way down to the parking lot. On the way you will pass the small house that the live-in ranger occupies.

Options

The paved Mountain View Trail leads about 0.6 mile to an accessible viewpoint near the top of the butte. Follow it up, switchback past the bench and then again at the top. There are some picnic tables and benches up here on the north side of the trail. There are lots of peaks to pick out from up here—Silver Star, Mounts Adams, St. Helens, and Hood are all visible on a clear day.

Directions

Drive east on I-84 to exit at NE Halsey Street. Go east on Halsey 1.4 miles and then turn right on NE 122nd Avenue. Drive south 2.5 miles to SE Powell /U.S. 26 and turn left. Continue on Powell to SE 162nd Avenue. The park entrance is ahead on SE 162nd. Turn right on SE 162nd and drive up the road to the parking area.

To reach the park via public transportation, take the no. 9 Tri-Met bus (Powell Boulevard).

Information and Contact

Leashed dogs are allowed. Contact Powell Butte Nature Park (16160 SE Powell Blvd., Portland, OR 97230, 503/823-1616) for information on trail closures during wet season. A trail map is available online at the website for Friends of Powell Butte Nature Park (www.friendsofpowellbutte.org).

8 BASKETT BUTTE AND MORGAN LAKE LOOP

Baskett Slough National Wildlife Refuge

BEST 🌙

Level: Easy

Total Distance: 5.5 miles round-trip

Hiking Time: 3 hours

Elevation Change: 210 feet

Summary: From hundreds of wintering Canada geese to a wide variety of waterfowl, Baskett Butte is a birding paradise.

The Willamette Valley is home to a series of wildlife refuges created to provide protection of and habitats for wintering waterfowl. In particular the preserves helps provide range land for the dusky Canada geese that winter here from the Copper River Delta up in Alaska. Baskett Slough is tucked inauspiciously between Oregon State Route 22 and 99W and is the northernmost refuge in the Willamette Valley National Wildlife Complex, with over 2,000 acres accessible year-round for birding and hiking. A collection of short trails may be linked together for an exploration that is sure to thrill the

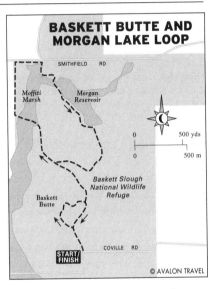

kids and challenge the birder in the group. While hiking at Baskett Butte, be sure to bring along your binoculars and field guide.

The Rich Guadagno Memorial Trail begins just past the trailhead information sign and map. Rich Guadagno was a U.S. Fish and Wildlife ranger who died on September 11, 2001 aboard United Flight 93. Take a moment to read of his dedication to the refuge. Walk northward up the wide path as it climbs up the southern flank of Baskett Butte. As you approach the turn, the grasses will eventually give way to oak trees and scattered shrubs. At the first junction, keep left and continue through the oak woodland to the viewing platform. In the early morning watch for small herds of black-tailed deer—they hang out near the trees and don't seem bothered at all by human visitors. After visiting the viewing platform and blind, return to the trail junction and follow the path as it continues up the Butte. Covered with dense trees, this area offers a surprising contrast to

hundreds of geese in the fields of Baskett Slough

the grasses in the previous stretch. The path enters a densely treed forest with a rich array of spring wildflowers. White fawn lilies nod their delicate heads, sword ferns abound, and wild roses and bleeding hearts offer some contrast to the deep greens. Watch, too, for the shiny green of poison oak. You will quickly reach a "T" junction; turn left as the trail now winds across a couple of small meadows that may have more deer roaming about.

Continue northward along the trail as it heads to Moffiti Marsh and Morgan Reservoir. You may have already noticed the raucous honking of Canada geese, in abundance in winter but also around in spring and fall. Prepare to experience the rush of air that can only accompany hundreds of pairs of wings taking flight at once. As you make your way to the water and cross between crop fields, the geese that were gleaning any leftovers will be startled into flight. Amazingly they rise nearly as one but fly in organized chaos. As you walk on the west side of the marsh, you may spot some waterfowl. Continue north until you reach the edge of the refuge and then turn right to reach the parking area and trailhead for the Morgan Lake Trail. This trailhead is austere with a small lot and information sign.

Walk southeast through the grasses to trace a path on the western edge of the reservoir. Here, as in the fields, hundreds of geese may be flocked and it's a real treat to watch them take flight. There may be other species around, too—a few types of ducks and perhaps a cinammon teal may surprise you. You will also hear the surprisingly varied call of the red-winged blackbird as you walk. Pass the water and continue south to the northern end of the butte trail, which rises gently ahead. Climb back up the butte and bear left at the trail junction to complete the loop and return to your car.

Options

To enjoy the center of the refuge without so much hiking, explore the Guadagno Memorial Trail and Baskett Butte Loop Trails by themselves. When you reach the second junction to the trail heading north to the reservoir, just bear right to make a short clockwise loop through the trees. Enjoy the lichen, fungus, and wildflowers that flourish amongst the oak.

Directions

From Portland, drive about 41.5 miles south on I-5. Take exit 260A for OR-99E/ Salem Parkway and follow the signs for the Oregon Coast and OR-22W. After crossing the Marion Street Bridge, merge onto OR-22W and drive another 12 miles to Colville Road and the refuge. You will drive along the southern border of the refuge and pass a viewing site with interpretive information and restrooms on the way to Colville Road. Turn right on Colville Road and drive about 1 mile to reach the parking area for the Baskett Butte Trail. The trailhead is on the north side of the road and has an interpretive sign and map.

Information and Contact

There are no fees. Dogs are not allowed on wildlife refuge trails. For more information, contact Baskett Slough (10995 Hwy. 22, Dallas, OR 97338, 503/623-2749, www.fws.gov/WillametteValley/baskett). A refuge map is available on the website.

9 TRAIL OF TEN FALLS BEST ☾
Silver Falls State Park

Level: Moderate **Total Distance:** 8.7 miles round-trip

Hiking Time: 4.5 hours **Elevation Change:** 900 feet

Summary: For waterfall lovers, there may be no better trail in Oregon than this popular loop that passes behind a spectacular collection of falls.

Silver Falls State Park is famous for the concentration of waterfalls along the well-known "Trail of Ten Falls." Oregon's largest state park is also home to wildlife, a dense second-growth Douglas-fir forest, and remnants of its volcanic past. The well-developed South Falls day-use area includes a historic Depression-era lodge with a nearby creek popular for swimming. The Upper North Falls also has a beautiful pool; the cool water offers perfect relief on a hot day. Although the park has over 9,000 acres, for most people who visit it is all about the waterfalls—and the best way to experience them up close is to hike the waterfall loop.

The Trail of Ten Falls is actually an amalgam of trails in the northern section of Silver Falls State Park. Bounded in part by both North and South Fork Silver Creek, the trail inscribes an irregular circle past an amazing variety of falls. Columbia River basalts covered this whole area 15 million years ago. The soft layers eventually eroded, leaving shelves, rocky lips, and pools shaped by water's tremendous forces. Now we benefit from the hard work conservation groups did during the park's formation in 1933 to give nature lovers a view of these wonders.

From the car park, cross the bridge and at the signed junction keep left on the Rim Trail. This quiet trail parallels the Silver Falls Highway for a while as it con-

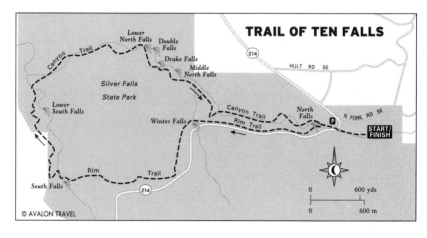

© BARBARA I. BOND

enjoying North Falls

tours along the North Fork Silver Creek canyon high above the water. There are lush spring wildflowers along the forest floor—look for bleeding hearts, oxalis, and fawn lilies in early spring. Take a moment to enjoy the North Falls viewpoint after only 0.5 mile. The next viewpoint is for Winter Falls in another 0.5 mile. For the next 1.2 miles, just enjoy the trail. You'll pass some huge old trees; be sure and take a look at the odd double-trunked tree as you wind south and then west towards the South Falls. The forest of Douglas-fir and western hemlock muffles all sounds except for the exuberant call of the tiny winter wren. Look for this little noisemaker throughout the park.

Once you reach the South Falls area, take a side trip and visit the log cabin or South Falls Lodge. After your detour, get back onto the trail and head for South Falls. After descending to the falls on the Canyon Trail, the viewing begins in earnest.

After the switchbacks, follow the trail towards the thunderous waterfall and pass right behind the falls. Continue along the Canyon Trail northward, ignoring the pretty wood bridge that would take you back to the day-use area if you turned right. What a contrast here in the canyon—bright yellow violets, yellow monkey flowers, and western red cedar all thrive down here. The next mile is along the western bank of the South Fork Silver Creek and leads to the Lower South Falls. After the stairs the trail begins a slow arc northeast towards a cluster of four falls in quick succession. Lower North Falls is the first of these, appearing after 1.3 miles. Walk towards the Hult Creek footbridge and turn left before crossing to take a short detour to view Double Falls. This unique waterfall drops twice and the total distance makes it the tallest fall in the park at 178 feet. Return to the main trail and cross the bridge to reach tiny Drake Falls, Middle North Falls, and Twin Falls over the next 0.9 mile. The nearly one mile it takes to reach North Falls will pass close to the north bank of North Fork Silver Creek. Bigleaf maples create a wonderful airy canopy and down below are violets, inside-out flowers, mossy rocks, and fairy bells. Once you reach North Falls, follow the trail behind the falls then (grunt) climb the 77 steps and return to the starting point.

Options

To enjoy several of the park's waterfalls without the long loop, try an out-and-back hike from the North Falls parking area. From the parking lot, hike the Canyon Trail west. Descend the steps to view North Falls and then continue 1 mile to reach Twin Falls. The following mile passes (or gets close to) some more waterfalls. Cross the Hult Creek Bridge and either turn right on the spur trail to view the Double Falls or continue ahead a short distance to see Lower North Falls. Return the way you came for a total of 4 miles.

Directions

From Portland, drive south on I-5 for 30 miles to exit 271 for Woodburn/Silverton/State Route 214. Follow the signs and drive east, then south, on State Route 214 for 29 miles to Silver Falls State Park. The North Falls parking lot is before milepost 27 in about 0.25 mile.

Information and Contact

A day-use ($3) or annual pass is required and may be purchased at the parking area. Dogs are not allowed on the Canyon Trail. For more information, contact Silver Falls State Park (20024 Silver Falls Hwy., SE Sublimity, OR 97385, 503/873-8681, ext. 23, www.oregonstateparks.org). A good brochure and trail map are available on the state park site. Information is also available from The Friends of Silver Falls (www.friendsofsilverfalls.net), an organization working in partnership with the state park.

10 BUCK MOUNTAIN TRAIL
Silver Falls State Park

Level: Moderate

Hiking Time: 4 hours

Total Distance: 8.1 miles round-trip

Elevation Change: 930 feet

Summary: Explore the quiet side of Silver Falls State Park on this rolling loop hike through cool, dense forest.

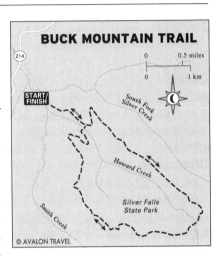

Silver Falls State Park has over 9,000 acres of land, although most visitors only see the tiny northwestern section containing the famous waterfalls. That's unfortunate, because the rest of the park is beautiful and has lots of other hiking opportunities. The Buck Mountain Loop is a wonderful way to see some of the dense fir, hemlock, and cedar forest that made this land so attractive to early settlers. Remnants from the area's logging past are scattered throughout the forest—you'll see some springboard notches on old stumps in the middle of the hike. the loud call of the tiny winter wren as you hike in the morning or near dusk watch for black-tailed deer.

From the parking lot, walk south past the "Trails" sign and past a horse's watering trough. Turn left (east) after a short distance and follow the signs to the Howard Creek Loop/Buck Mountain Trail, keeping right at the next two signed junctions to reach the loop in 0.5 mile. At the sign for the Buck Mountain Loop you can go either left or right, turn right to hike counterclockwise. Either way you will climb to the 2,200-foot-high point at the halfway mark, which is at the southern tip of the loop.

You will cross the creek and then begins a steady uphill climb. After some switchbacks, the climbing moderates (whew) as the route contours above the short west fork of Howard Creek. Here the forest is dense with second-growth trees and heavy undergrowth of vine maple, salal, and sword ferns.

Pass the Cut-Off Trail as the foliage changes to that classic mix of Oregon grape, alder, salmonberry, and vine maple. The new growth on the maples is delightful in the spring light. The trail nearly flattens out as it heads southward.

Keep left at the old road junction around 3.2 miles and check out the huge stumps on the left. Some of these old trees were logged using springboards and have notches prominently on one side. In areas with steep slope, the old-time loggers placed boards in these notches, stood on either side and wielded their long cross-cut saws. There are lots of huge ancient stumps on either side of the trail at 4.2 miles.

Now the trail descends nicely so you can really take in the quiet and revel in the shadow of the few remaining big trees. Two quick creek crossings then reach another "T" junction around 5 miles. Head left, which will take you northwest back to the start of the loop along a gentle descent on the east side of Howard Creek. Retrace your path to the car once you reach the start of the loop.

Options

Explore Silver Falls State Park on a shorter hike. On the Buck Mountain Trail, turn right at the Cut-Off Trail and loop back to the Buck Mountain Loop in 2 miles. Turn left to retrace your steps to the parking area for about a 4.2-mile hike.

Directions

From Portland drive south on I-5 30 miles to exit 271 for Woodburn/Silverton/ State Route 214. Follow the signs and drive east, then south, on State Route 214 for 29 miles to Silver Falls State Park. Keep going south past the turn-off for North Falls and milepost 27. Continue nearly 2 more miles, then turn left at the sign for Camper Registration, just before milepost 25. Follow the signs for the horse camp, which is about a mile from the main road. Turn left on a gravel road and then turn left into the parking area. Park near the trailhead for the Howard Creek Loop, which is on the south side of the lot.

Information and Contact

A day-use ($3) or annual pass is required and may be purchased at the parking area. Leashed dogs are allowed on the Buck Mountain Trail. For more information, contact Silver Falls State Park (20024 Silver Falls Hwy., SE Sublimity, OR 97385, 503/873-8681, ext. 23, www.oregonstateparks.org). A good brochure and trail map are available on the state park website. Information is also available from The Friends of Silver Falls (www.friendsofsilverfalls.net), an organization working in partnership with the state park. For a good map of the Buck Mountain Trail, use the free state park trail map or Silver Falls State Park Trail and Recreation Guide from Sky Island Graphics (available at REI, www.rei.com).

11 SECTION 36-POWDER HOUSE LOOP

McDonald Forest

Level: Easy/Moderate

Hiking Time: 2 hours

Total Distance: 4.0 miles round-trip

Elevation Change: 900 feet

Summary: Walk through a forest laboratory to see multi-aged trees and a historic building.

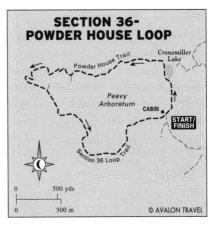

The Oregon State University Department of Forestry manages the McDonald-Dunn Forest. This is good for hikers since part of its mission is to provide recreation opportunities. There is a lot of recreating to be done on the miles of trails in the collection of trees, wildlife, and rich understory. Hikers can walk through the forest and enjoy big trees, summer wildflowers, and the rich beauty of this unique forest.

Walk around the gate from the information kiosk and take a look around. Huge bigleaf maples create an almost magical forest canopy. You'll reach the Forestry Club Cabin in a quick quarter of a mile; drinking water is available here if you need a top-off. Turn left on the path just before the cabin and you reach a quick signed "T" junction—turn right here. Now you're heading toward Cronemiller Lake and the flowers are abundant—spring beauty, fringecup, waterleaf cover the forest floor. Douglas-fir and alder fill out the canopy and thimbleberry bushes complete the dense understory. At the lake, bear left (although you can walk around the lake if you want) and at the junction take a moment to look down at the forestry demonstration area. Resuming the hike, turn left and drink in the big trees. Check out the huge Pacific yew with its mossy trunk.

Keep walking uphill to a "Y" at nearly 1.5 miles, bear right, and cross the first of two footbridges. In a short distance uphill you cross Road 500 and pass the Cap House, a historic building built in the 1930s to store dynamite. Continue on the Powder House Loop, entering an open, cut forest with lots of stumps, and some views. Keep to the trail as you cross the road several more times, winding around to head southward and back on the Section 36 Trail. At 2.25 miles you reach a junction and the high spot for the day at about 1,250 feet. Turn south and continue now on your descent, passing 1,000 feet and 2.8 miles. A huge "wolf" tree will draw your attention—it's an outsized tree that dominates its surroundings. Keep descending past an experimental series of ponderosa pine trees that originated in various locations around the country. The placards list details of the tree origins and the trees are in various states of health.

You'll keep descending on the Section 36 Trail until you return to the forestry cabin near the start of the hike. Retrace your steps from here down to the information kiosk and your vehicle.

an old-growth tree on the trail

Options

For a shorter hike amongst dense understory and immense old growth trees, take the Old Growth Trail from Lewisburg Saddle. This short trail descends slightly past huge trees and an amazing array of wildflowers that thrive in the dark, moist environment. Walk east on Road 580 for 0.4 mile and then turn left onto the trail for 0.5 mile. The trail ends back at the road, turn right for the 0.7 mile back to the saddle where you began for a total loop of 1.6 miles.

Directions

From Portland, drive south on I-5 for 67 miles and take exit 234B. Drive on OR-99E S then merge onto U.S. 20 W, following the signs for Albany and Corvallis. After 5.5 miles on U.S. 20 W turn right on NE Granger, then right on OR-99W/ Pacific Highway West. After 1.2 miles turn left at NW Arboretum Road, left again at NW Peavy Arboretum Road. Follow a short distance, keeping left at the junctions to park at the Badewitz Kiosk. The hike begins on the road after walking around the orange gate ahead.

To reach the Lewisburg Saddle, follow the directions to Corvallis. Follow the directions above and stay on NE Granger; it turns into Lewisburn Ave after 2.4 miles. Turn right at NW Sulphur Springs Road and continue 1.5 miles to the saddle and parking area. Park on the right, there is a gate ahead (east) where Road 580 begins. Bear left for the Old Growth hike.

Information and Contact

For more information, contact the Oregon State University College of Forestry (541/737-4452, www.cof.orst.edu). A visitor guide and map is available from OSU, or use Sky Island Graphics Marys Peak–McDonald Forest Recreation Guide.

5-2-15
5.25 miles

12 WOODPECKER AND MILL HILL LOOP TRAILS

BEST ☾

William L. Finley National Wildlife Refuge

Level: Easy

Total Distance: 1.1-3.3 miles round-trip

Hiking Time: 3 hours

Elevation Change: 150 feet

Summary: Be sure to bring your field guide and binoculars during this visit to this wildlife refuge, one of Willamette Valley's spectacular birding destinations.

Finley National Wildlife Refuge was established to protect remaining historic native habitats in the Willamette Valley. Native prairie and Oregon white oak savannah are two precious examples of historic habitats. The prairie on Finley's refuge is one of the last remaining examples of native Oregon prairie undamaged by farming. No matter what season you visit, Finley National Wildlife Refuge has the opportunity for varied wildlife and bird viewing from trails suited for all abilities.

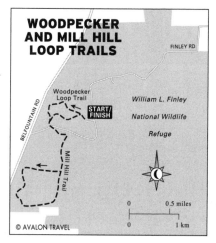

Many visitors to the wildlife refuge come to do one thing: bird-watching. However, Finley offers so much more. Whether strolling on the Homer Campbell Memorial Trail, a 1,500-foot boardwalk through a hardwood forest, or hiking the short Woodpecker Loop Trail, it's a destination that will call you back again and again. The short hikes on the refuge offer a snapshot of what the valley may have once looked like and include lots of opportunities for bird- and wildlife-watching. If you are a novice birder, be sure to bring along a friend with some real birding chops—it seems like there is another bird around every bend.

The Woodpecker Loop Trail is a short, pleasant walk through a woodland containing huge old oaks, some Pacific madrone, and lots of flowers. You can walk either direction from the trailhead; the following directions are counterclockwise. From the trailhead, turn right, crossing a bridge, and follow the trail gently uphill past a bunch of poison oak and camas lilies. There are interpretive signs along the trail. As you make your way along, you may spot

Homer Campbell Memorial Trail boardwalk

wild irises brightening the trail with their white and purple blooms, and some bright pink wild roses provide a nice contrast. A variety of birds can be seen on this short loop, along with the occasional rabbit. Watch for lazuli bunting with its bright purple feathers, nuthatches, goldfinches along the pond, and even a red-breasted sapsucker. You'll cross a boardwalk after passing the pond. Note the Ash Swale sign. Walk to a "Y" and bear right if you want to hike the 0.5-mile Inter-Tie Yrail leading south to Mill Hill. Otherwise stay left to finish the Woodpecker Loop passing some Douglas-fir trees. Douglas-fir is slowly being removed from the refuge since its dense canopy prevents the native oak from thriving.

Mill Hill occupies a small corner of the western refuge and is home to more old oaks, grasses, and abundant wildflowers. From the trailhead walk south, passing the Inter-Tie Trail junction shortly. Continue to a "T" and a sign with an arrow pointing right for Mill Hill Trail. You'll then hit the loop trail, turn right to head counterclockwise around Mill Hill. The forest is a dense mix of Douglas-fir, bigleaf maple, oak, and a lot of shiny poison oak. There are quite a few dead trees with multiple nesting holes in their trunks, and the wildflowers include hooker's fairybell, fairyslipper, and glacier lily. Continue on the loop until meeting the junction where you started, then retrace your steps north to the parking area.

Options

Finley National Wildlife Refuge has a lot of short hikes that can be linked or done separately. To explore the southern part of the refuge, head south on Bellfountain Road, then turn left to wind north, then east, on Bruce Road. You'll reach a signed trailhead for Cheadle Marsh. Hike north along the trail on the north side of the road to explore the land surrounding the dike. This out-and-back hike is 3 miles. Cheadle Marsh is open from April 1 to October 31.

Directions

From Corvallis, drive south on State Route 99W for 10 miles. The refuge entrance is signed for Finley Road. Turn right on Finley and follow the refuge road to the trailheads. You will first come to an interpretive area for the historic prairie, then the Homer Campbell Boardwalk just before the refuge headquarters. The road turns south, and on the right is the Woodpecker Loop Trailhead. Continue south, then west, for the Mill Hill trailhead. If you reach Bellfountain Road, you passed the trailhead. Turn around and backtrack about 0.5 mile to the trailhead parking area for Mill Hill.

Information and Contact

There are no fees. Dogs are not allowed on the trails of Finley National Wildlife Refuge. For more information, contact the Willamette Valley National Wildlife Refuge Complex (26208 Finley Refuge Rd., Corvallis, OR 97333-9533, 541/757-7236, www.fws.gov/willamettevalley). The refuge office has maps and other brochures.

THE COLUMBIA RIVER GORGE

© BARBARA I. BOND

BEST HIKES

The Columbia River Gorge is the lowest passage

through the Cascade Range. Protected in part by the Columbia River Gorge National Scenic Area and the Mark O. Hatfield Wilderness, the Gorge (as it is know to locals) offers a wide array of outdoor experiences for hikers of all ages and abilities. This is due in part to its close proximity to the Portland/Vancouver metropolitan area and major interstate and state highway access, but also to the rich natural beauty of the rugged Gorge cliff faces and abundant waterfalls.

Catastrophic geologic events over millions of years have shaped what we now enjoy. Rivers of lava flowed throughout Washington and Oregon, laying down deposits thousands of feet thick. The subsequent Missoula Floods, about 12,000 years ago, then sent torrents of water rushing through the river canyon scouring out any loose or soft deposits. The result is a seemingly sculpted array of cliffs, ridges, deep ravines, and endless plateaus. Standing atop the cliffs of Cape Horn gazing upriver, you can almost imagine what that might have looked like.

From Portland, the biggest contrast is the Columbia Plateau in the far eastern Gorge. Hikes in this region feature open oak and pine wood-lands, grasslands, and wildflowers that flourish in the more arid climate. The flowering season begins here when many western Gorge trails are still under several feet of snow. The Klickitat River canyon exemplifies this area with its historic Rails-to-Trails hikes and historic structures. When you just are finally worn down by winter rain in Portland, head east. By visiting the far eastern region of the Gorge you will experience a new and contrasting landscape.

In the immediate rain shadow of the Cascades, the Eastern Cascades are where the damp and lush western Gorge transitions from the arid east. Elevations in the Eastern Cascades Range are not as high as the main Cascades – mostly between 3,000 and 7,000 feet – and the region has a wider range of temperature extremes, less precipitation, and forests with predominantly Ponderosa and lodgepole pine. Hiking amongst the open canopy of a Ponderosa forest is exhilarating – the huge trees are home to a rich array of wildflowers, wildlife, and birdlife. Trails that visit locales such as Tom McCall Point or Coyote Wall will introduce you to this more open landscape. As in the western Gorge, hikes here will showcase dramatic examples of the violent geologic history in exposed layers of basalt columns and deep piles of collapsed rock and rich sediment deposits.

A majority of the Gorge trails climb away from the river to mountains and cliffs over 2,000 feet high. For many, this is the classic Gorge of scenic postcards and calendars. Winter in the western Gorge means several feet of snow at high elevations resulting in abundant waterfalls, full streams and creeks, and rich wildflower displays once the snows melt off. Hikers flock to these trails year-round to battle the elements with snowshoes and heavy rain gear. Multnomah Falls, Oregon's highest waterfall, is an iconic destination for locals and tourists alike. Dozens of other trails with waterfalls, named and unnamed, will become favorites for Portland-area hikers. Short trails such as Elowah Falls are a worthy introduction to the rich plant life of the western Gorge. For those of you seeking adventure, the long climb to Tanner Butte will leave you with a feeling of accomplishment and wonder while sitting atop the butte gazing at nearby Mount Hood.

The Columbia River Gorge is home to a collection of diverse plants, flowers, and trees unlike any in Oregon or Washington. For amateur botanists, the Gorge can provide endless opportunities to view rare and endemic species, as well as the huge number of introduced plants and flowers. Be sure to carry binoculars or perhaps take along a regional birding guide. Migratory waterfowl and songbirds make the Gorge home, adding to the richness of the hiking experience. You may also see or hear deer crashing through the brush along the Devil's Rest Trail or spy a black bear amongst the trees along Starvation Ridge. For hikers, the Columbia River Gorge really does have it all.

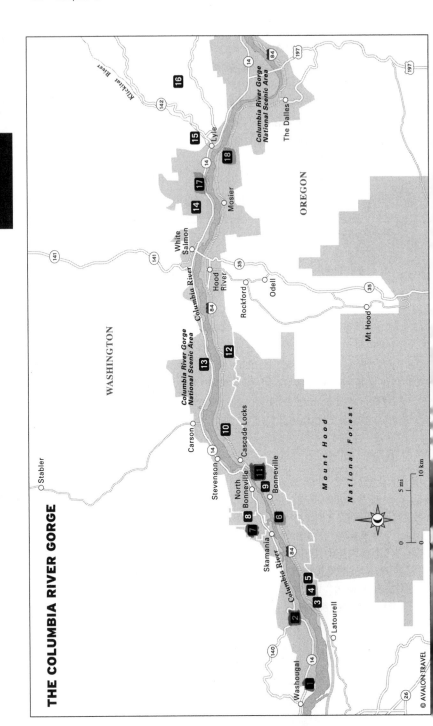

THE COLUMBIA RIVER GORGE

WASHINGTON

OREGON

*Columbia River Gorge
National Scenic Area*

*Columbia River Gorge
National Scenic Area*

*Mount Hood
National Forest*

Stabler

Washougal

Latourell

Stevenson

North
Bonneville

Bonneville

Carson

Cascade Locks

Skamania

Columbia River

Columbia River

White
Salmon

Hood
River

Odell

Rockford

Mosier

Lyle

The Dalles

Mt Hood

Klickitat River

0   5 mi

0   10 km

© AVALON TRAVEL

TRAIL NAME	LEVEL	DISTANCE	TIME	ELEVATION	FEATURES	PAGE
1 Washougal Dike Trail *1-3/-15*	Easy	7.0 mi rt	2.5 hr	Negligible		68
2 Cape Horn *4-26-14*	Moderate	7.0 mi rt	4.5 hr	1,400 ft		71
3 Wahkeena to Devils Rest	Strenuous	7.0 mi rt	4-5 hr	2,300 ft		74
4 Multnomah–Wahkeena Falls Loop	Easy/Moderate	5.5 mi rt	3 hr	1,550 ft		77
5 Larch Mountain	Butt-kicker	14.1 mi rt	7 hr	4,200 ft		80
6 Elowah and Upper McCord Creek Falls *1-24-15*	Easy	3.0 mi rt	2 hr	600 ft		84
7 Hamilton Mountain *5-30-15*	Moderate	7.5 mi rt	4.0 hr	1,950 ft		87
8 Table Mountain	Butt-kicker	10.0 mi rt	5 hr	3,650 ft		90
9 Tanner Butte	Butt-kicker	18.0 mi rt	9-10 hr	4,000 ft		93
10 Indian Point	Strenuous	8.0 mi rt	4-5 hr	1,800 ft		96
11 Eagle Creek *6-14-14*	Easy/Moderate	6.6 mi rt	4 hr	500 ft		99
12 Mount Defiance	Butt-kicker	12.0 mi rt	7 hr	4,900 ft		102
13 Dog Mountain	Strenuous	6.6 mi rt	3.5 hr	2,836 ft		104
14 Coyote Wall (Syncline)	Moderate	8.0 mi rt	5 hr	1,800 ft		107
15 Klickitat Trail	Easy	6.0 mi rt	3.5 hr	Negligible		111
16 Swale Canyon	Moderate	13.0 mi one-way	5-6 hr	1,150 ft		114
17 Catherine Creek *3-21-15*	Easy	2-3.5 mi rt	3-4 hr	125 ft		117
18 Tom McCall Point *6-20-15*	Easy/Moderate	4.0 mi rt	2.5-3 hr	1,500 ft		120

windy!!

I-31-15

1 WASHOUGAL DIKE TRAIL
Steigerwald Lake National Wildlife Refuge

Level: Easy

Total Distance: 7.0 miles round-trip

Hiking Time: 2.5 hours

Elevation Change: Negligible

Summary: This family friendly hike travels along the top of a dike paralleling the Columbia River with mountain and river views.

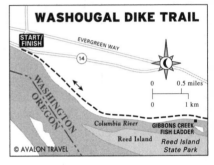

In 2006 the Pacific Northwest celebrated the bicentennial of the Lewis and Clark exploration. Vancouver dedicated Cottonwood Beach Park to commemorate a visit in 1806 by the Corps of Discovery and Captain William S. Clark. For six days, the Corps camped on the shores of the Columbia River at Cottonwood Beach. Now, more than 200 years later, anyone can walk along the dike trail and imagine what it would have been like to be an explorer in the early 19th century. This flat, scenic, and historic path offers bird-watching along Steigerwald Lake and the Columbia River in addition to fine views of Mount Hood. The interpretive viewpoints offer tips on birds, natural history, and wildflowers.

Begin your trek back in time at Steamboat Landing, heading out along the trail clearly marked by unique green trail signs. Detour at 0.1 mile to the floating walkway and viewpoint with an information kiosk that explains about the natural and cultural history of the area. Resume your walk east along the dike trail and enjoy views south of the mighty Columbia. (Unfortunately, you must use your imagination for the first mile or so of trail because it parallels an industrial park on the north.) Keep your eyes right and you'll see huge cottonwoods lining the shore of the river. After passing a couple of interpretive viewpoints with benches you'll reach the Recognition Plaza. This beautiful tribute to Clark was dedicated in 2005 and has interpretive information, a restroom, and beach access.

Your exploration continues eastward on the path as it enters the Steigerwald Lake National Wildlife Refuge. Steigerwald Lake is part of the Ridgefield National Wildlife Refuge Complex. Thankfully, the industrial park soon ends and the hike becomes markedly more peaceful. The terrain is unchanged, yet suddenly there are clusters of purple martin houses along the south side of the path; along the north side, the asphalt has given way to a complex of old barns, fields and in

period canoe and Recognition Plaza at park entrance

the distance, Steigerwald Lake. If you have binoculars you may see Canada geese, white-fronted geese, great blue heron, and other birds on or around the lake. You may even spot a heron alongside the trail if you're out early and are quiet.

Reed Island is the prominent view to the south. The trail continues for about another 1.5 miles, passing a fish ladder along Gibbon Creek just before the end. The fish ladder was constructed in the mid-1990s to return salmon to their spawning grounds up the creek from the Columbia River. The trail clearly ends at a gate marked "Private Property" at 3.5 miles. Return the way you came.

Options

In fall 2008 a new trail was under construction on Steigerwald Lake NWR. The trail will run south from a parking area along State Route 14 and east of Gibbons Creek. It will be an out-and-back with a loop at the south end near the dike trail. For updated trail information, visit the Steigerwald Lake National Wildlife Refuge website (www.fws.gov/refuges).

Directions

From Portland, drive east on I-84 for 4.9 miles to the I-205 North exit. Cross the I-205 and turn right on State Route 14 east 19.5 miles to Washougal. When you reach Washougal, turn right into a parking area on 15th Street.

To begin your exploration at the Recognition Plaza in William S. Clark Park, continue east 1 mile on State Route 14. Turn right on South 32nd Street and follow it to the parking area at the park entrance. From here just get on the trail and turn left.

Information and Contact

There are no fees. Leashed dogs are allowed. Parking is available at Steamboat Landing and there are four additional lots along South Index Street. Park hours are 7 A.M.–dusk. Services include picnic shelters and restrooms. Camping is available at Cottonwood Beach. A map may be downloaded from the Vancouver–Clark Washington Parks and Recreation Department at www.cityofvancouver.us. For more information, contact Vancouver–Clark Washington Parks and Recreation Department (360/619-1111) or Steigerwald Lake National Wildlife Refuge (360/835-8767, www.fws.gov/refuges).

2 CAPE HORN

4-26-14

BEST ◖

Columbia River Gorge National Scenic Area

Part of trail closed Feb1-July 15

Level: Moderate

Total Distance: 7.0 miles round-trip

Hiking Time: 4.5 hours

Elevation Change: 1,400 feet

Summary: Hike to tremendous viewpoints above the Columbia River and the longest rail tunnel in the Gorge.

Cape Horn is a series of lava-covered basalt cliffs high above the Washington shore of the Columbia River, 8 miles west of Beacon Rock. These geologic wonders have only recently been redis-covered as a prime hiking location due to the efforts of local conservation and hiking groups. The final result is due in late 2009—a fully realized trail system with hikes suitable for all ages and abilities. At this writing in late 2008, the trail system is a work-in-progress and well worth a visit.

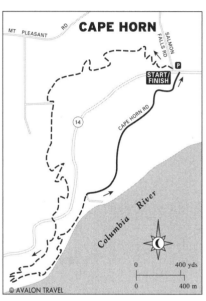

The hike begins across Salmon Falls Road. From the parking lot, follow a gravel walk put in by the county to ac-commodate hikers, to the trail. Once on the trail, head northwest through the trees. In the spring, expect stunning dis-plays of wildflowers including dramatic larkspur, some bleeding heart, and shade-loving vanilla leaf in the trees. Most of the elevation gain on this hike occurs in the first 0.75 mile; look north for fine views of Silver Star Mountain. As the trail continues gently uphill, you will pass a stunning viewpoint along the cliff edge before reaching Pioneer Point. Shortly after Pioneer Point, the trail turns northwest 0.25 mile to follow an old wagon road for 0.5 mile. Stay left at the wagon road junction until the trail ends suddenly at paved Strunk Road. Turn left and walk to the end of the road, then turn right onto a gravel road, keeping to the west-side road. You will pass an old home site that was cleared in 2008. Continue on the road towards the river (south) and in less than 0.1 mile you will reach a faint fork; keep to the leftward old road bed and pass through a field. You will turn right

looking upriver along the Columbia River

briefly near the end to skirt the trees, and then re-enter the woods on your left to pick up the trail again. Remember, just keep heading towards the river.

The trail descends for a while on some switchbacks through the disturbed forest with red alder, true firs, bitter cherry, Douglas-fir, and Oregon white oak. About 1.5 miles from Strunk Road, a viewpoint along the cliff gives a fine overview of the Cape Horn Road area below, and Phoca Rock on the river. Look upriver for stunning classic views. Continue southward to cross State Route 14 in another 0.5 mile. The sounds of the highway intrude on the peacefulness of the hike until you finally cross it (carefully). As you get back on the trail you'll cross a stream on a plank bridge then reach a four-way trail junction (unmarked). Turn left and visit the cliffs for some amazing views; check out the top of Cape Horn Falls. Return to the junction and turn left to continue the hike. This section of trail includes another stream crossing and a series of wonderful views all along the river. You will hear some falls at the cliff edge (turn around to take a look) and may catch sight of a bald eagle in the treetops below. Remember to exercise some caution along the cliffs—it's a long way down.

As you keep hiking down, the trail will cross more streams, eventually ending up above a series of switchbacks through a steep talus-covered slope. (The switchbacks were put in during the Prohibition era by industrious bootleggers who needed a way to get their wares down to their cliff-edge distribution point.) At the bottom you will have made a 180-degree turn and now head eastward towards the falls. As you hike along the talus there will be good views of two upper falls. Continue to reach the main attraction—a short section of trail that goes behind a waterfall. In winter be prepared to get drenched (carry a garbage bag for pack items and wear rain gear with a hood).

After the falls, the trail continues eastward until you are unceremoniously dumped out onto lower Cape Horn Road. Stay left to hike the road 1.3 miles to return to the trailhead at the junction of State Route 14 and Salmon Falls Road. In late 2008, the county put in a gravel path along Cape Horn Road. Walk across the street and use the path to hike back to your starting point.

Options

About 1.8 miles before Salmon Falls Road, there is room to pull over at the State Route 14 trail junction just past a guardrail along the south side of the road. If you park here, you can just do the lower section of the hike to the last waterfall. At that point, return the way you came for an out-and-back hike of about 4 miles.

Directions

From Portland, take I-84 east for 4.9 miles to the exit for I-205 North. Cross the bridge and turn right on State Route 14. Drive east 19.5 miles to Salmon Falls Road, just past milepost 26.4. Turn left on Salmon Falls Road and turn immediately right onto Canyon Creek Road. Parking is on the right in the Skamania County Transit Park and Ride lot. Note that no parking is allowed along Cape Horn Road.

Information and Contact

There is no fee, though a trailhead parking pass may be required in the future. Dogs are allowed on leash only. For more information, contact Friends of the Gorge (522 SW Fifth Ave., Ste. 720, Portland, OR 97204 503/241-3762, www.gorgefriends.org).

3 WAHKEENA TO DEVILS REST

Columbia River Gorge National Scenic Area

Level: Strenuous

Total Distance: 7.0 miles round-trip

Hiking Time: 4-5 hours

Elevation Change: 2,300 feet

Summary: Enjoy endless Gorge views and several waterfalls en route to this rocky destination.

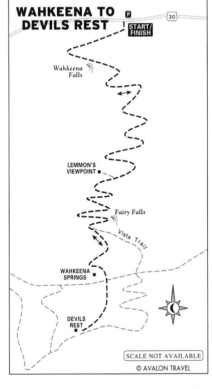

WAHKEENA TO DEVILS REST

Wahkeena Falls

START/FINISH

LEMMON'S VIEWPOINT

Fairy Falls

Vista Trail

WAHKEENA SPRINGS

DEVILS REST

SCALE NOT AVAILABLE

© AVALON TRAVEL

The Wahkeena Trail 420 is a popular destination for hikers in the Columbia River Gorge. For many, the visit begins and ends at the viewpoint right in front of the falls, near the historic Columbia River Highway. However, to really delve into the essence of this area, one must only venture 1 mile upwards on the well-marked trail. This part of the journey is along a well-traveled paved path and ends on a stone bridge dramatically sited in front of the upper Wahkeena Falls. Spray from the falls will dampen your face as you gaze upwards.

After enjoying the views, continue along the path, past a bench popular in summer, to the steep switchbacks which lead to a trail junction. Turn right for a quick detour to the second view: Lemmon's Viewpoint sits on a rocky outcrop high above the Columbia River. On a clear day, look eastward along the river to see Beacon Rock, a volcanic plug that stands nearly 850 feet high, and Hamilton Mountain; both are landmarks along the Washington side of the Columbia River. From the viewpoint, backtrack to the trail junction and then continue along the trail, which quickly crosses Wahkeena Creek on a slippery wooden bridge. You are now entering Wahkeena Canyon, a narrow gorge formed when the Columbia River basalts flowed through this area. The sides rise steeply and are green with mosses, ferns, and other opportunistic plants. In the spring, the water rushes through this, narrowing to the squeeze below which signals the start of the dramatic falls.

As the trail parallels the creek, you will cross under a huge downed tree, caught by the rocks. Keep watch as you ascend to the next creek crossing—there are always trees in various stages of being blown down—sometimes precariously perched against the rocky canyon walls. The next creek crossing is via a ford, where the Forest Service has strategically placed logs and wood to allow safe passage. This replaces a bridge that was split in two when a huge fir tree was blown down one winter.

Now the trail begins climbing in earnest, passing beautiful red cedars. As the trail levels for a short distance, the rush of water forewarns hikers of the upcoming Fairy Falls. Along the trail, note the thimbleberry bushes on the left. In the spring and summer they are home to many small animals and birds. Sharp-eyed hikers may see hummingbirds here. Cross in front of the falls on a log bridge and, after marveling at the view, continue ascending.

The trail levels out near a trail junction. You can take a short detour and visit the Wahkeena Springs by turning right and walking about 50 yards. The springs originate here on the right as evidenced by the pool of water, which immediately begins flowing downhill to feed the creek and falls below. Surrounded by huge cedars and Douglas-fir, it is a beautiful spot. When you're done taking it all in, return to the trail junction.

Relax for the next 0.5 mile while you walk past some huge Douglas-fir and spindly vine maple and watch for the devil's club which grows in boggy areas. Beware the long needles on both the top and bottom of the large leaves and along the thick stalk. Continue past the junction with the Vista Trail (which comes in on the left), and in a short distance is the signed trail on the right to Devils Rest.

Now begin climbing again on long steep switchbacks to a plateau offering dramatic views along the western edge. The trail meanders through the magnificent forest, crossing two bridges and eventually climbing steeply for a short section. Finally, you reach the junction for the side trail up to the collection of moss-covered rocks that is Devils Rest. Although there are no views at the moment, you will feel a definite sense of accomplishment.

Return the way you came.

Options

You can extend this hike by taking an alternate return from Devils Rest. Descend from the rocks to the main trail and turn right to head east to the Foxglove Trail. When you reach the trail junction, turn right on the trail southward to meet up

along the Wahkeena Trail

with the Angel's Rest Trail 415. You are now at a decision point: turn left and hike another 2 miles to the Angel's Rest viewpoint, or turn right (west) to hike past Wahkeena Springs and then on to the Wahkeena Trail, which reaches the trailhead in 1.6 miles.

Directions

From Portland, drive east on I-84. Take exit 28/Bridal Veil and bear right; continue to the stop sign. Continue ahead after the stop and park at the Wahkeena Falls parking area. Parking is available on both sides of the highway.

Information and Contact

There are no fees. Leashed dogs are allowed. In the summer, restrooms are available at the picnic area. For more information, contact Columbia River Gorge National Scenic Area (541/308-1700, www.fs.fed.us/r6/columbia) or Mount Hood National Forest, Hood River Ranger District (541/352-6002). For maps, try USGS Multnomah Falls or Geo-Graphics Trails of the Columbia Gorge.

4 MULTNOMAH-WAHKEENA FALLS LOOP

BEST ◖

Columbia River Gorge National Scenic Area

🏠 ✈️ 🎿 🏄 🐕 🚶

Level: Easy/Moderate

Total Distance: 5.5 miles round-trip

Hiking Time: 3 hours

Elevation Change: 1,550 feet

Summary: Hike to the airy viewpoint at the lip of Multnomah Falls — Oregon's highest waterfall and most popular tourist destination.

Multnomah Falls has been attracting attention since before Lewis and Clark noted it in their journals in the early 1900s. The 620-foot waterfall is the tallest in Oregon and one of the tallest in the United States as well. As such, it attracts millions of visitors each year. You only have to see the logjam of cars trying to get into the parking lot on a sunny July day to verify that fact. Still, it's so beautiful that I visit many times a year and never really tire of that thundering sound of water crashing down above the Benson Bridge.

From the lodge area, head up towards the first viewing area, directly below the bridge. This is where you'll see wedding parties posing for photographs, families with out-of-town guests, and just about every sort of visitor imaginable. And good for them, they're all enjoying one of Oregon's natural wonders. The water from high on Larch Mountain careens over a multilayered lip of Columbia River basalts to create this spectacle.

MULTNOMAH-WAHKEENA FALLS LOOP

© AVALON TRAVEL

SCALE NOT AVAILABLE

After taking it in, begin the hike by turning right on the paved path and beginning the winding trail upwards. The trail takes you past rich foliage that includes lots of poison oak—so beware. The trail was closed for a time in the late 1990s so that the protective mesh fence could be erected to protect visitors from rockfall. When you cross the amazing Benson Bridge, be ready to get wet. The next section of trail up to the switchback is always damp from spray. Continue up past the switchback and begin the serious climbing. The first 0.5 mile is really the warm-up for the second 0.5 mile, which is where it gets steep and sustained. Be comforted by the fact that each weekend, hundreds of folks do this 1-mile ascent in flip-flops. You're probably better prepared, so you're going to enjoy it a lot more.

Just when you feel you can't climb any further, you wind up at the top of the trail, above the falls. Continue as the trail makes a sharp turn and descends to meet the 0.1-mile side trail down to the viewpoint. Turn right and head down. The view from the platform is tremendous. The pretty creek just drops over

Multnomah Falls and Benson Bridge

that lip of rock and the water freefalls hundreds of feet. It's quite a sight any time of year. I took my children up to the platform when they were in preschool and I still remember their look of awe at the water's plunge below.

After marveling at the falls, turn right back onto the Larch Mountain Trail and continue ahead another 0.8 mile. First cross the bridge across Multnomah Creek, pass the closed Perdition Trail, and hike up past "Dutchman" Weisendanger and Ecola Falls. This succession of falls upstream along Multnomah Creek is amazing and really provides you with the quintessential Pacific Northwest view. At the junction with Wahkeena Trail 420 turn right and begin a steep-ish climb northwesterly along a broad ridge. Just when you think the climb reaches a particularly strenuous point, the trail levels out and you begin to contour west along a steep slope. I often hear or see flickers or other woodpeckers along here. The big Douglas-fir provide lots of trunk for them to mine for bugs.

This is such a pretty part of the trail—it's often quiet, and in spring there are lots of flowers blooming. You'll pass the steep trail up to Devil's Rest at 3 miles. Another few steps takes you past the Vista Trail off to the right. Continue ahead to drop into a beautiful basin with big Douglas-fir, lots of moss-covered vine maples, and devil's club. You pass the junction with the Angel's Rest Trail 415 at mile 3.3.

If you want a pretty detour, turn left after 100 yards and check out Wahkeena Springs. There is a pretty pool of water on the right surrounded by big cedars. Return to the Wahkeena Trail and turn left to continue downward. The trail descends a few switchbacks, passing the Vista Trail junction. The trail then turns to descend along Wakheena Creek, continuing on more switchbacks to Fairy Falls. Right in front of the falls you'll cross a log footbridge, then pass a bench. This is a good spot from which to watch hummingbirds in the spring. Continue down the canyon carved by the creek. This canyon and its undulating walls of layered basalt flows are so characteristic of the Columbia River Gorge and its unique geology. You'll see some huge cedars growing here, along with a number of big downed trees that sometimes seem to clog the narrow canyon. Cross the creek ford, hike a short distance further downhill, and then cross a small footbridge. Continue ahead to the viewpoint, or turn right down the paved path to Wahkeena Falls. Just after the bench and before the bridge take a look up at the top of the falls—it's a view that is usually obscured from the trailhead. Cross the spray-covered bridge and descend 0.25 mile more to the bottom. Walk across the creek, then continue ahead at the sign to hike the 0.6-mile Trail 442, a connector trail, back to the Multnomah Falls parking area. This pretty trail goes by a rocky cliff with a year-round seepage—look for the strings of moss that always seem to be growing. Thimbleberry, poison oak, ferns, and wildflowers grow along here, too.

Options

Of course some folks will really only want to visit Multnomah Falls and the upper viewing platform. Due to the crowds, try to plan your visit in early morning or in the evening. Parking at the Wahkeena parking area just west of Multnomah Falls is another way to avoid the crowds. Use the 0.6-mile connector trail to walk over to the falls and back. Round-trip distance for this hike is 3.2 miles.

Directions

From Portland, drive east on I-84 to exit 28/Bridal Veil. Follow the Historic Columbia River Scenic Highway east past the Wahkeena Falls parking area. The Multnomah Falls Lodge area is in 0.5 mile and has a lot of parking. If it's full, drive back west to the Wahkeena parking area and walk over.

Information and Contact

There are no fees. Leashed dogs are allowed. For more information, contact the Columbia River Gorge National Scenic Area (541/308-1700, www.fs.fed.us/r6/columbia) or Mount Hood National Forest, Hood River Ranger District (541/352-6002). For maps use USGS Multnomah Falls or Geo-Graphics Trails of the Columbia Gorge. There are restrooms, a gift shop, water fountains, a snack bar, a restaurant, and more at the highly developed Multnomah Falls parking area. The snack bar has soft-serve ice cream and a coffee cart serves espresso drinks in the summer. Seasonal restrooms are also available at the Wahkeena picnic area.

5 LARCH MOUNTAIN

BEST ◖

Columbia River Gorge National Scenic Area

Level: Butt-kicker

Total Distance: 14.1 miles round-trip

Hiking Time: 7 hours

Elevation Change: 4,200 feet

Summary: This trail up an extinct volcano takes you through some of the prettiest scenery in the Gorge: multiple waterfalls, huge old-growth trees, and views of five Cascade peaks.

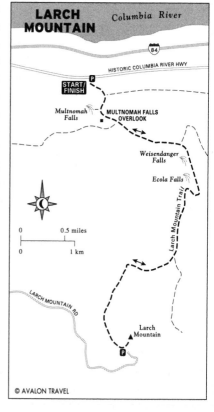

The Columbia River Gorge has so many stellar hikes that sometimes merely excellent ones get neglected. Larch Mountain Trail 441 is a hike that suffers from that fate. The lower 1-mile paved trail up to Multnomah Falls sees more visitors annually than just about any other Gorge location. However, few venture all the way to Sherrard Point even though it's along a well-graded trail beside Multnomah Creek with lots of scenic features. Waterfalls, narrow canyons, mossy bowls, wildflowers, big trees—it's all here with the bonus of fantastic views at the top. Deer may be spotted in early morning and a wide variety of birds make their home in the dense forest along the trail. You will likely see downy woodpeckers, flickers, or hear the loud call of the grouse. Steller's Jay may accompany you with a mocking call, particularly near the picnic area at the top of the mountain. A couple of options exist for making this hike shorter or longer depending upon your taste. Don't want to hike 14 miles? Get someone to meet you at the Larch Mountain picnic area and catch a ride back to the bottom. Want to do more? Start at the Wahkeena Falls Trailhead for an additional 2 miles of hiking.

After gawking at the magnitude of Multnomah Falls' 621-foot drop, get onto the paved trail and begin the steady climb up. The trail has heavy growth most of the way up, and it's best to keep an eye out for poison oak. This lower trail is so heavily impacted by tourism that it's important to keep to the paved trail. The trail switchbacks up to a high point above the falls and then back down again to meet the side trail to a viewpoint. Turn right if you want to check out the view down to the parking area and lodge. If not, keep going straight ahead. The pavement ends, you'll cross Multnomah Falls on a stone footbridge and then turn left to continue up alongside Multnomah Creek. This is a good spot for picnics. During the next 0.5 mile you will pass a succession of small waterfalls along the creek. Dutchman Falls is near the basalt overhang Dutch-

Weisendanger Falls on Multnomah Creek

man Tunnel, followed by the more dramatic Weisendanger Falls. Weisendanger is popular for photographers and you may recognize it from numerous postcards and Pacific Northwest calendars. Ecola Falls are the last named waterfall on this trail. A couple of quick switchbacks and then a short distance along the trail brings you to the Wakheena Trail junction (but it's possible the sign may be down). Several hundred yards up is a footbridge across the creek. You can see the remnant logs from the old bridge just upstream and below this footbridge. This is a really nice spot for photographing the mossy green of the creek banks and swift-flowing waters.

The next 2 miles pass through some of the most beautiful forest in the region. Dense trees, thick understory rich with maidenhair ferns, sword ferns, and vine maples all blend together to make this a hiking wonderland. You'll pass a couple of trail junctions as you pass through Multnomah Basin. The high water trail leads to a plateau with some old roads. If you visit this area you'll find yourself above some steep cliffs leading north back to the old highway. There are some old rock climbing spots along here including Cougar Rock. Passing the Franklin Ridge Trail junction at 3 miles, continue through the thick forest. Two more footbridges bring you to back to the west side of the creek. You'll climb steeply and jog left after the first bridge, pass a nice camp spot, and then continue through the forest of increasingly big trees. There are some huge Douglas-fir trees in the area. Cedar, true fir, and hemlock fill in the gaps and many tree limbs seem weighted down with thick moss. In some of the wetter areas along the creekbank you may spot a grove of huge devil's club, with its profusion of needle-like thorns.

Suddenly around 4 miles you pop out of the thick trees to cross a rock slide. The sun can seem blinding after the time spent in the shady forest. It doesn't last long, though; soon you head back into the trees as the ascent continues. The Multnomah Creek Way Trail junction is near the 5-mile point. Bear grass begins to appear, and often this area has dozens of striking blooms in summer. An old sign announces the 2 miles remaining and you'll shortly cross a dirt road. Continue the climb on the trail across the way to reach the picnic area. At the picnic area, head across and left to pick up the paved trail to Sherrard Point. This viewpoint on the craggy 800-foot summit spire of the old volcano offers views in all directions. The nearby Washington Cascade peaks are all there to the north, and you can pick out Silver Star and its collection of peaks and ridges, too. Mount Hood to the south is the closest and most dramatic mountain view; in addition, look in the distance southwest for the sharp profile of Mount Jefferson. Return the way you came unless you arranged for a shuttle.

Options

With access from the Larch Mountain Road in summer, one can do this hike one-way as an ascent or descent. Either way, arrange for a shuttle and pick your poison: ore quads from the climb up or aching knees from the steep, rocky descent. Either way it is 7.1 miles and 4,200 feet of elevation change by the time you're done. If you opt for the descent, give your knees a break by using a pair of trekking poles. Northwest Forest Pass ($5) is required to park at the Larch Mountain picnic area.

Directions

From Portland, drive east on I-84 to exit 28/Bridal Veil. Follow the Historic Columbia River Scenic Highway east past the Wahkeena Falls parking area. The Multnomah Falls Lodge area appears after 0.5 mile and has a lot of parking. If it's full, drive back west to the Wahkeena parking area and walk over on the 0.6-mile connector trail.

Information and Contact

There are no fees. Leashed dogs are allowed. For more information, contact the Columbia River Gorge National Scenic Area (541/308-1700, www.fs.fed.us/r6/columbia) or Mount Hood National Forest, Hood River Ranger District (541/352-6002). For maps, use USGS Multnomah Falls or Geo-Graphics Trails of the Columbia Gorge. There are restrooms, a gift shop, water fountains, a snack bar, a restaurant, and more at the highly developed Multnomah Falls parking area. The snack bar has soft-serve ice cream and a coffee cart serves espresso drinks in the summer. Go ahead—you've earned it.

6 ELOWAH AND UPPER McCORD CREEK FALLS

John B. Yeon State Scenic Corridor

1|24|15

Level: Easy

Hiking Time: 2 hours

Total Distance: 3.0 miles round-trip

Elevation Change: 600 feet

Summary: Enjoy solitude and scenery on this short hike to two beautiful waterfalls in Yeon State Scenic Corridor.

Elowah Falls is one of the Columbia River Gorge's most beautiful falls. In less than 1 mile, you reap the reward—an up-close view of water rushing over a basalt rim to a basin below. This often-overlooked hike will thrill waterfall fans and anyone looking for a short hike with big payoff. Elowah Falls was named by a committee of outdoor organizations in the early part of the 20th century. A wooden bridge over McCord Creek offers a stunning viewpoint right in front

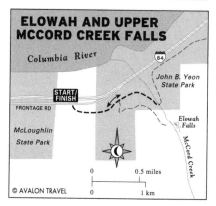

of the falls. After heavy rain, the spray from the falls will soak you as you gaze upwards from the bridge. A trail also goes to Upper McCord Creek Falls, which is the nearest waterfall neighbor. McCord Creek is named for an Oregon pioneer who built an early "fish wheel" at the mouth of the creek. Common birds along the trail include woodpeckers, steller's jay, and ruffed grouse.

The trailhead is at the end of the parking lot near an information sign. Follow the trail a very short distance to a trail junction and keep left for Gorge Trail 400. You will do most of the climbing in this first 0.5 mile or so to Elowah Falls. As you head east along the trail you'll see lots of different kinds of ferns, thimbleberry, salal, and wildflowers in spring. In some areas the ground is covered with a virtual blanket of licorice ferns. At 0.4 mile is an old wood sign marking the trail junction with the spur to Upper McCord Creek Falls.

For Elowah Falls, keep left. Some sections of the trail wash out in wintertime, so use caution as you cross muddy sections. The trail makes a curve to the right as you approach the steep-sided bowl with the falls and bridge. This section of the trail is like entering an outdoor wonderland, complete with its own multi-hued palette of greens. Mossy rocks and old blowdown are covered with many variet-

© BARBARA I. BOND

hikers soaked from Elowah Falls spray

ies of plants, mosses, and fungi. Downed trees covered with thick green mosses criss-cross the creek and trail. The rocky basalt cliffs that make up the bowl are covered with lichen and mosses, and seem like they must never dry out completely. You'll likely hear the falls first, then see the glistening surroundings soaked by the spray. Visit the bridge for an intimate view of this beauty.

On the way back to the trailhead, continue ahead at the junction with the Upper McCord Creek Falls Trail. This somewhat rocky trail will ascend a few switchbacks before entering a cliffside route complete with guardrail. The views here are fantastic—look across the Columbia River at Beacon Rock, Hamilton Mountain, and Table Mountain. As you turn right on the trail you will hear an increasingly loud thunder of water crashing down as Elowah Falls comes into view. The water cascades over the top of the cliffs into the misty pool below. Take a moment and check it out—you were just down there. Continue a short distance to a wonderful view of the Upper McCord Creek Falls, a short twin fall. To return to the parking lot, retrace your steps to the trail junction and turn left.

Options

If you are in the mood for a leg-burning uphill training hike, from the trailhead turn right onto the Nesmith Point Trail 428 and make the steep ascent to one of the highest points in the Gorge. The trail climbs 4.5 miles to a spur road; turn right and continue about 0.3 mile to the viewpoint. Take a well-deserved break then prepare for the knee-busting descent nearly 5 miles back to the trailhead. This is a popular training hike for mountain climbers in the spring.

Directions

From Portland, drive east on I-84. Take exit 35 and turn left and follow signs to the frontage road. Take the frontage road east to Yeon State Scenic Corridor. Parking and the trailhead are on the right.

Information and Contact

There are no fees. Leashed dogs are allowed. There is an information sign at the west end of the lot. The trail to Elowah Falls is maintained by the Forest Service. For more information, contact Columbia River Gorge National Scenic Area (541/308-1700, www.fs.fed.us/r6/columbia) or Mount Hood National Forest, Hood River Ranger District (541/352-6002). The Upper McCord Creek Trail is in the state park. For information on John B. Yeon State Scenic Corridor call 800/551-6949. For maps use USGS Multnomah Falls or Geo-Graphics Trails of the Columbia Gorge.

I'd go back again !! ☺

7 HAMILTON MOUNTAIN
Beacon Rock State Park

5-30-15   7.87 miles

Level: Moderate

Total Distance: 7.5 miles round-trip

Hiking Time: 4.0 hours

Elevation Change: 1,950 feet

Summary: A visit to this popular Washington State Park is complete with a historic and geologic landmark and beautiful waterfalls.

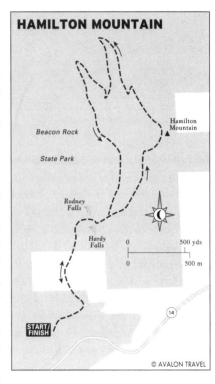

HAMILTON MOUNTAIN

© AVALON TRAVEL

Beacon Rock State Park is named for the distinctive monolith towering 850 feet above the Columbia River. The rock is all that remains of an ancient volcano—scoured clean by the Ice Age Floods. Lewis and Clark noted Beacon Rock as "Castle Rock" in their journals in 1805. In the early part of the 20th century, Henry J. Biddle purchased the landmark for only a dollar, hoping to protect it from development. He then embarked on a multi-year project constructing a one-mile trail into the rock with handrails and endless switchbacks. His heirs eventually gave the rock to the Washington State Park System so that everyone could enjoy Biddle's foresight.

The hike to the summit of Hamilton Mountain is nearly perfect. It offers just enough elevation gain to be a workout, yet can also be hiked by your intrepid fourth grader. The dense forest of Douglas-fir, red alder, maple, and thick underbrush foliage creates an atmosphere of endless green and shadow.

Start your hike beside the stone restrooms at the north end of the parking area. As you begin your ascent, note the huge stumps on either side of the trail. The trail doesn't waste any time establishing a steep ascent. In spring or early summer, the wildflowers can be a welcome attraction or distraction. Bleeding heart, vanilla leaf, goat's beard, and inside-out flower are a few varieties you may see. Numerous ferns dot the forest floor along the early part of the hike. In the trees, listen

south cliffs of Hamilton Mountain

for ruffed grouse and woodpeckers. After nearly 1 mile the trail flattens out a bit and you reach the first of two waterfalls. You can get a nice view by turning right onto the signed spur trail that leads to a viewing platform. It's worth it stopping for a look if you haven't seen Hardy Falls before.

Retrace your steps (yes, uphill a short distance) to the main trail and turn right. You'll now drop down into a small canyon created by Hardy Creek. Keep left on the trail before descending to the footbridge and take a moment to visit the Pool of the Winds. It's an impressive narrowing that concentrates the force of the creek as it heads for the drop to the creek below. Return to the main trail, cross the bridge, and climb up out of the canyon on a steep, sometimes muddy set of steps. The trail begins climbing again as the forest canopy opens up a bit and you catch an occasional view south of the river and Oregon scenery. In less than 0.5 mile you will reach a decision point—left fork for difficult or right fork for more difficult. Have no fear—the right fork is the most common route to the summit and allows you to scramble up the south flank of the mountain while enjoying stunning views of the Columbia River.

Continue through the forest on long switchbacks up to a nice viewpoint about halfway up the 1.8 miles to the summit. Once you reach the top, turn right on the summit ridge for the true summit, with no views although you may see a bald eagle circling above. To complete the loop, retrace your steps the short distance, then continue across a beautiful ridge with great views of nearby Cascade peaks

. use!

and Table Mountain just east. After 0.9 mile turn left onto an old road which descends 1 mile to reach Hardy Creek. At the start of the road you may notice a signed trail on the right.

For a shady option in summer, turn onto the short Dons Cutoff Trail; the thick forest eliminates open travel along the gravel road. It will drop you at another old road; turn left then follow it a short distance to Hardy Creek. At Hardy Creek, turn left on the trail past the picnic table. The Hardy Creek Trail climbs along the drainage to meet the Hamilton Mountain Trail in 1.1 miles. At this trail junction, turn right to reach the trailhead in about 1.5 miles.

Options

If you want to enjoy some stellar river views but don't want to hike all day, then the 1-mile trail to the top of Beacon Rock may be for you. Park in front of the monolith along State Route 14. The trail is to the west of the main parking area and is well marked. Follow the trail up, up, up to the top of the rock. Once on top, take a deep breath and enjoy the views—you've earned it.

Directions

From Portland, take I-84 east to exit 44 at Cascade Locks and cross the Bridge of the Gods ($1 toll). Turn right on State Route 14. Drive 7 miles west to Beacon Rock State Park and turn right, following the sign for the lower picnic area parking lot.

Information and Contact

Leashed dogs are allowed. Beacon Rock State Park (www.parks.wa.gov) contains several hiking trails, picnic areas, and camping. There is a daily fee of $5 with a collection box at the parking area. An information sign has a map and there are restrooms nearby.

8 TABLE MOUNTAIN

BEST ◖

Columbia River Gorge National Scenic Area

Level: Butt-kicker

Hiking Time: 5 hours

Total Distance: 10.0 miles round-trip

Elevation Change: 3,650 feet

Summary: Get your heart rate up on this early season Gorge loop hike on the Washington side – views from the top are predictably excellent.

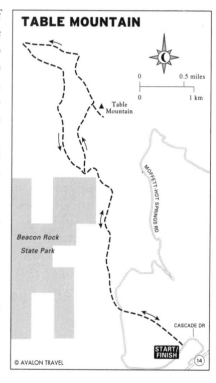

Table Mountain is part of a string of peaks just east of Beacon Rock State Park. While no official trail goes to the top, local mountaineering group The Mazamas maintains a popular, and challenging, route upwards to the flat summit. In late spring this is a rite of passage for aspiring mountaineers. The steep Heartbreak Trail climbs about 1,700 feet in 1.5 miles, making it a heart-pumping leg-burner. With hard work comes a great reward though—after the grueling up and down you can repair to the Bonneville Hot Springs Resort for a swim and soak.

Hike west from the lot on the gravel road for a short distance then turn right on the Dick Thomas Trail. You won't find this user trail on any maps. This connector trail to Carpenter Lake will take you northwest nearly a mile to join an old road. Keep an eye on the trail—there are a lot of rough-skinned newts crossing the trail in the spring. The trail begins climbing gently right away, crosses Carpenter Creek on some logs, and then meets up with the old road.

Turn right and begin hiking northward to the Pacific Crest Trail junction. The road actually parallels this trail in many spots and the dense canopy keeps it cool even when the sun is out. Ignore the two trail junctions you come to, just keep left and you'll stay on the main trail. Once you reach the Pacific Crest Trail, turn left and continue for 1 mile to the junction with the Heartbreak Trail, marked

view of Table Mountain from the ridge of Hamilton Mountain

by a couple of signs aptly labeled with breaking hearts. Turn right and begin the march up through the trees.

Breathe deep this first 0.5 mile up—it's steep and sustained. When you stop to catch your breath, take a look around. A variety of wildflowers flourish along the trails. Watch for bleeding heart, and violets in the forest; on the upper mountain look for glacier lilies after the snows melt. The trail is more moderate about halfway up, and then begins another steep uphill slog through a talus slope. Ascending the slope, you may wander off the trail occasionally. Continue upwards and when you reach the top head left to pick up the trail as it leaves the rocky slope and reenter the trees at the top of the ridge. Often along this section there are a lot of downed trees and washouts. Once on the ridge, take a look to the east when you can—and continue northward. This is the final push to the top.

You'll reach the nearly flat summit at mile 4, turn right and wander about 200 yards to a good resting place and viewpoint. Take your lunch here or retrace your steps and head north along the summit. At the extreme north end of the summit is the trail that leads down the north ridge to rejoin the Pacific Crest Trail. There are a lot of nice spots along the summit for lunch—pick the one you like most and hang around a bit. I've seen bald eagles from the summit and in good weather the views of surrounding mountains is inspiring.

When you're ready, head north down the steep ridge trail. Work your way down about 0.5 mile and join an old road that curves around westward to rejoin the Pacific Crest Trail. Turn left onto the Pacific Crest Trail and head south to the car. In 0.5 mile you'll reach the junction where you began the steep climb up Heartbreak Ridge; retrace your steps from there to your vehicle.

Options

There really is no other way to get to the top of Table Mountain. However, for an alternative way to enjoy this area you can take a short hike to Gillette Lake on the Pacific Crest Trail. Start at the Bonneville Trailhead and hike 0.5 mile easterly on the Tamanous Trail. When you reach the junction with the Pacific Crest Trail, turn north and hike 2 more miles to the lake. To reach the trailhead turn left on State Route 14 from the bridge crossing. The trailhead appears on the right after 1.5 miles, marked by a large sign. A Northwest Forest Pass ($5) is required to park.

Directions

From Portland, take I-84 east to exit 44 at Cascade Locks and cross the Columbia River on the Bridge of the Gods toll bridge ($1 or $0.75 with coupon book). Turn left on State Route 14 and drive about 2 miles to the second right turn. Turn right onto Hot Springs Road (on the left will be Dam Access Road) and immediately go under the railroad trestle, then turn right onto East Cascade Drive. Follow this as it curves north (signed) to the Bonneville Hot Springs Resort. Drive up to the hotel and turn left to park in the auxiliary lot on the west side of the hotel.

Information and Contact

There are no fees. Leashed dogs are allowed. The parking area is available due to an agreement between The Mazamas and the Bonneville Hot Springs Resort. Please be respectful of the resort property, and do not enter the premises in hiking boots or make loud noises early in the day. For maps use USGS Bonneville Dam, although the Table Mountain trails are not on the map.

9 TANNER BUTTE   BEST **C**
Columbia River Gorge National Scenic Area

Level: Butt-kicker

Hiking Time: 9-10 hours

Total Distance: 18.0 miles round-trip

Elevation Change: 4,000 feet

Summary: You have to earn the views from Tanner Butte's rocky summit. But it's worth the sweat and blisters to sample the solitude, rhodies, tiger lilies, and bear grass along this Gorge classic.

Tanner Butte is one of the highest points on the Oregon side of the Columbia River Gorge. If it were easier to get to, you would find crowds gawking at Mount Hood from the bare summit. As it is, just the determined get there so it remains a special place. The views of Hood and the Southern Washington volcanoes are wonderful, as is the peaceful quiet at the top. Experience the Hatfield Wilderness as few get to— from a place that's both remote and still rather wild.

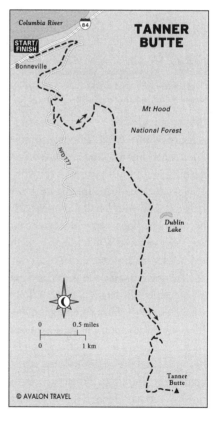

The hike really begins after a mandatory 1.9 mile warm-up on Forest Road 777. The road has been closed since the late-1990s. I drove it in 1997 and had to get help to clear a downed tree on the way down. At any rate, the hike up to the trailhead is a climb. An old sign marks the start of Tanner Butte on the left.

Hike up on a quick switchback to a crossing of the creek—your last chance for water until you pass the side trail to Dublin Lake in 4.3 miles. Brace yourself, because you are going to ascend steep switchbacks for the next couple of miles. The trail goes through thick trees and brushy understory of several species of ferns, Oregon grape, salal, and wildflowers in early summer. For a short distance, the trail follows the power lines and there are some good views west to the distinctive

© BARBARA I. BOND

Mount Hood and Tanner Butte

ridge of Munra Point. The steep trail zigzags up to a spot just south of Wauna Point before moderating at around 2,700 feet and turning southward. You'll be heading south until you reach the side trail up to Tanner Butte.

Not much happens for the next two miles to the junction with the Dublin Lake Trail on your left at 4.3 miles. Still, even in late summer there is vanilla leaf on the forest floor—its wide leaves capturing the thin sunlight filtering through the heavy canopy. Watch too for pinedrops and some clasping twisted-stalk—the red berries are a nice contrast to all the forest green. If you need water, you have to hike down 0.4 mile to the lake. There hasn't been much trail work up here as evidenced by the large number of downed trees you have to go around or climb over. Most of the hard climbing is done by this point, and over the next few miles there are only a couple of steep sections as you make your way to an old logging road. There are a lot of Pacific rhododendron lining the trail now, mixed in with bear grass and the occasional tiger lily. The open rocky areas have some Columbia columbine, Indian paintbrush, wild roses, and lupine. The trail (road) is really brushy in spots—I found myself wishing for long pants and shin guards. At about 1 mile before the side trail to Tanner Butte is a good view of the little unnamed butte to the east. Continue south and catch some glimpses of the bare summit as it extends east and away from the trees.

Just when you can't take any more crashing through the brush, the side trail appears—the old sign for the spur trail is on the ground now—but the trail gets just enough use to be obvious. There are some steep switchbacks through thick huckleberry, pink mountain heather, and then lupine as the foliage thins near the top. Some small fir and hemlocks dot the rocky upper butte. Continue the walk through some rocks and you're on top of the summit. Enjoy the five volcano views—you've earned them. There is a benchmark on top. In summer 2008 there were some prominent avalanche tracks on the slopes of the ravine just north of the summit. Retrace your steps when you're ready to return.

Options

There is no short way to get to Tanner Butte. However, you could do it as a two-day trip with an overnight at Dublin Lake.

Directions

From Portland, drive east on I-84. Take exit 40 for the Bonneville Dam and turn right at the stop sign, then quickly left. Park at the Toothrock Trailhead at the end of the road. Make sure you do not leave anything valuable in your vehicle. You can also pull out next to a water tower on the right, about 0.1 mile before the trailhead parking area. Just turn around and park on the side of the road. (This is the old road you are going to hike to the trailhead, so it is important that you do not block the gate.)

Information and Contact

There are no fees. For more information, contact the Columbia River Gorge National Scenic Area (541/308-1700, www.fs.fed.us/r6/columbia) or Mount Hood National Forest, Hood River Ranger District (541/352-6002). For a map, use USGS Tanner Butte or Geo-Graphics Trails of the Columbia Gorge.

10 INDIAN POINT

Columbia River Gorge National Scenic Area

Level: Strenuous

Total Distance: 8.0 miles round-trip

Hiking Time: 4-5 hours

Elevation Change: 1,800 feet

Summary: Ascend through dense forest to a rocky outcrop with tremendous views.

The Columbia River Gorge offers nearly limitless opportunities for hiking, rock climbing, and scrambling amongst the maze of basalt ridges and dense forest. The Herman Creek Campground, outside Cascade Locks, is one place to start a challenging hike ending in an exposed scramble on a narrow spit of rock called Indian Point. The amazing viewpoint will reward you with a unique perspective and sense of accomplishment.

Begin on the Herman Creek Trail 406 by hiking towards the junction with the Gorton Creek Trail 408. This trail wastes no time in beginning to climb, ascending through thick trees and moss-covered boulders. At the trail junction, in 1.4 miles, turn left onto the Gorton Creek Trail. Notice how quiet it gets as the forest becomes dense with Douglas-fir, cedar, and hemlock—the heavy canopy keeps this area in shade year-round. You will pass some huge old-growth trees as you climb and occasionally an owl or woodpecker will break the silence. Wildflowers of wood sorrel, fringecups, vanilla leaf, and queen's cup dot the forest floor. As you ascend, look northward for the occasional view of Mount St. Helens across the Columbia River. In another 2.6 miles you will reach the junction with the Ridge Cut-Off Trail. Continue past the junction about 20 yards and look on the left for an unmarked trail. This is the unmaintained trail down to Indian Point. Turn left down the trail. Descend on the narrow, sometimes overgrown trail that leads out to the outcrop of rock. Approaching the rocky point, the trail levels off and you

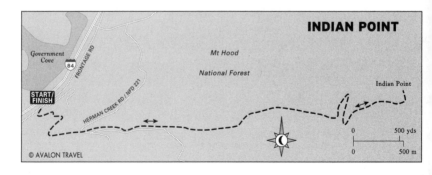

INDIAN POINT

Government Cove

FRONTAGE RD

84

HERMAN CREEK RD / NFD 221

Mt Hood

National Forest

Indian Point

START/ FINISH

0   500 yds

0   500 m

© AVALON TRAVEL

© BARBARA I. BOND

view of Indian Point with Wind Mountain in the background

will pop out of the trees. Note the impressive expanse of vertical rock to your left across a deep chasm. Ahead, the route leads to the end of Indian Point.

Scramble along towards the point, and remember to pay attention to the narrow spots with airy drop-offs. Once you reach the band of broken rock, scramble carefully out to the base of the spire of rock. This is a wonderful place to end your adventure and just soak up the incredible views all around. On a clear day, you may see Mounts St. Helens and Adams to the north, and closer in to the northeast are great views of Wind and Dog Mountains.

Options

For an 8.3-mile loop hike, take the Herman Creek Trail to the Nick Eaton Trail junction in 1.5 miles. Turn left onto the Nick Eaton Trail and ascend the steep trail to the junction with the Ridge Cut-Off Trail 437. Turn left, hike to the junction with the Gorton Creek Trail, and follow the directions to Indian Point. Return on the Gorton Creek Trail to complete the loop back to the Herman Creek Trailhead.

Directions

From Portland, drive east on I-84. Take exit 44 and drive through Cascade Locks. Drive to the stop sign and continue ahead onto the frontage road towards Oxbow Fish Hatchery (there is a sign). Pass Oxbow, and turn right at the sign for the Herman Creek Campground. Follow the road to the parking area (signed).

Information and Contact

A Northwest Forest Pass ($5) is required. Leashed dogs allowed, although caution should be exercised out on the point. In the summer restrooms are available at the campground. For more information, contact the Columbia River Gorge National Scenic Area (541/308-1700, www.fs.fed.us/r6/columbia) or Mount Hood National Forest, Hood River Ranger District (541/352-6002). For maps use USGS Mount Defiance or Geo-Graphics Trails of the Columbia Gorge.

6-14-14   *6:01*
Tunnel Falls   *15,13 miles*

11 EAGLE CREEK

BEST **C**

Columbia River Gorge National Scenic Area

Level: Easy/Moderate

Total Distance: 6.6 miles round-trip

Hiking Time: 4 hours

Elevation Change: 500 feet

Summary: A hike up Eagle Creek always has something to offer, rain or shine: wildflowers in spring, year-round waterfalls, rocky ledges, and dramatic views into the narrow canyon.

The Eagle Creek Trail 440 is arguably the most popular Columbia River Gorge hiking trail and is one of the oldest. Records indicate that the trail was established around 1915. Eagle Creek's popularity may be due to the allure of the many waterfalls or the immense diversity of spring wildflowers. No matter—a hike along this beautiful creek really does have something for everyone. Part of the draw is the imperceptible elevation change and the diversion of the natural beauty. Whether you opt for the long or short outing, Eagle Creek is always a satisfying hike. If you visit in the fall, you get to wit-

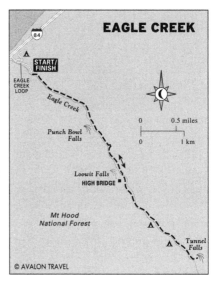

ness Pacific Northwest nature-in-action and watch salmon struggling upstream as they head towards their spawning grounds.

The trail begins with a pleasant walk upstream along the creek. Cross the wooden footbridge and meander below some crumbly cliffs. The trail begins climbing gently as you approach 0.5 mile and the first of several waterfalls—Metlako Falls. Take a detour to the viewpoint behind the big tree, then return to the trail and turn right to continue south. If you enjoy wildflowers, in spring or early summer there are a lot to see. Tiny popcorn flower, fringecups, pink and yellow monkeyflowers, and anemone thrive here. In the shade of the forest you'll spot lots of big Douglas-fir, tall bigleaf maples, and western hemlock. In the shady spots, vanilla leaf carpets the forest floor.

You'll reach a sign directing you down a side trail for Punch Bowl Falls at 1.8 miles. Take the side trail down some steps to this idyllic pool of clear water. The

Punch Bowl Falls

cliff walls are covered with mosses and lichen, and in the distance the falls spill over the lip high above. Back on the main trail you'll pass a viewpoint for Upper Punch Bowl Falls. Wind around to cross the creek on the Fern Creek Bridge at 2.6 miles and continue through the trees to High Bridge at 3.3 miles. This is a popular destination and you may see the bridge covered with happy hikers on sunny mid-summer days. Retrace your steps to the trailhead.

Options

For a longer hike that only gains about 1,000 feet of elevation over 6 miles head for Tunnel Falls. The trail goes behind Tunnel Falls, emerging on the other side on a cliffside trail with cable handlines permanently in place. Turn the corner after the cliffs and reach creekside in a short distance. This is a great spot to hang out and just enjoy the scenery. From this point, turn around and retrace your steps to the trailhead. From the High Bridge continue along the trail, past the Wilderness Boundary to the stunning Tunnel Falls.

Directions

From Portland, drive east on I-84 to exit 41/Eagle Creek. Turn right at the stop sign to the parking lot. There is parking near the stone bathrooms immediately on your left; additional spots can be found further down the road. It's 0.5 mile to the trailhead from the upper lot.

Information and Contact

A Northwest Forest Pass ($5) is required. Self-issue passes ($5) are available at the main parking area adjacent to the restrooms. For more information, contact the Columbia River Gorge National Scenic Area (541/308-1700, www.fs.fed .us/r6/columbia) or Mount Hood National Forest, Hood River Ranger District (541/352-6002). For a map, use USGS Tanner Butte or Geo-Graphics Trails of the Columbia Gorge.

12 MOUNT DEFIANCE

BEST C

Columbia River Gorge National Scenic Area

Level: Butt-kicker

Total Distance: 12.0 miles round-trip

Hiking Time: 7 hours

Elevation Change: 4,900 feet

Summary: Make no mistake – this is one of the harder hikes in the Gorge, with a reputation for hard mileage and tough elevation gain. But the views, wildflowers, and sense of accomplishment will make it worth every sweaty step!

As you drive east along I-84, it's easy to marvel at the cliffs that rise thousands of feet above the Columbia River. A hike to the top of Mount Defiance allows you the smug satisfaction of glancing up at those towering cliffs and knowing you've conquered one of the big ones. Mount Defiance is the highest point in the Columbia River Gorge and some folks think reaching its summit is nearly as hard as climbing Mount Hood. Regardless of the myths surrounding the feat, a climb to the top rewards you with stunning views of the Columbia River, nearby Washington peaks such as Wind and Dog Mountains, and surrounding Cascade volcanoes.

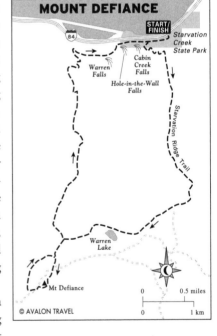

Walk west from the parking lot to a trailhead sign and the path that is going to lead you up, up, and up. The short warm-up lasts only 0.3 mile, take a deep breath and turn left at the Starvation Ridge Trail 414 on the left, which is marked by an old sign. The trail wastes no time in beginning to climb, quickly passing the cut-off trail and then rising to 1,200 feet and a nice viewpoint in less than a mile. The trail now steadily rises along the ridge and alternates between forest and the ridge. You may see or hear deer within the trees and, on rare occasions, spy a black bear ambling along near dusk. Around 4 miles the trail flattens for about 0.75 mile, enjoy this flat stretch for the last 1,000-foot push to the top. Turn right at the trail junction with the Mitchell Point Trail and then pass the Wilderness boundary marked with a sign. Lots of huckleberries grow near pretty Warren Lake, visible just south of the trail. Continue ahead around the lake and meet the Mount Defiance Trail at 5 miles. Turn left for the last 0.7 mile to the summit.

After enjoying the tremendous Mount Hood views and views north to the other peaks, walk south off the summit a short distance and curve rightward on a short 0.7-mile trail that winds around the west side of the summit and allows great views down to Bear Lake. Turn left at the junction, pass the Mitchell Point Trail junction in less than a mile and then power down the Mount Defiance Trail for the next 4 miles. Some sections are steep as it goes down. The bottom mile or so has its rewards. After negotiating the tough last 0.5 mile around the power lines—where the trail is just lined with thick, glossy, ready-to-ruin-your-week poison oak—you get to enjoy a series of waterfalls. Warren Falls, Hole-in-the-Wall Falls, and Cabin Creek Falls refresh you after the monotony of the descent and take your mind off your sore knees. Trudge the last 0.3 mile along the highway back to your car—you did it!

Options

For a short dose of natural splendor without the climb, visit Starvation Falls. From the parking lot, walk past the restrooms on the paved, accessible trail to the falls. The falls are lovely, and a nice information sign explains the history of the name. There are picnic tables and a paved path the whole way, and you can make a very short loop north back to the parking lot.

Directions

From Portland, drive east on I-84 to exit 54 for the Starvation Creek State Park. The trailhead is on the west side of the parking lot, marked with a sign. There is plenty of parking.

Information and Contact

There are no fees. Leashed dogs are allowed. For more information, contact the Columbia River Gorge National Scenic Area (541/308-1700, www.fs.fed.us/r6/columbia) or Mount Hood National Forest, Hood River Ranger District (541/352-6002). For maps use USGS Mount Defiance or Geo-Graphics Trails of the Columbia Gorge. There are restrooms, drinking fountains, and interpretive signs at the park.

13 DOG MOUNTAIN
Columbia River Gorge National Scenic Area

Level: Strenuous

Total Distance: 6.6 miles round-trip

Hiking Time: 3.5 hours

Elevation Change: 2,836 feet

Summary: Dog Mountain may be Washington's most popular spring hike. Join the throngs who come to view stunning flower-covered meadows and beautiful Columbia River Gorge vistas.

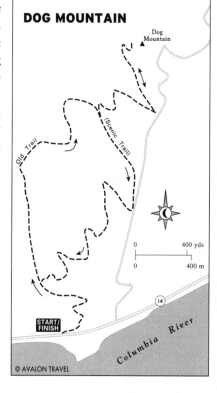

If you drive along Washington's State Route 14 on a spring weekend, you will witness an overflowing parking lot just east of milepost 53. A hike up the Dog Mountain Trail quickly illustrates the attraction. Depending upon your energy level and goals, you can enjoy a heart-pounding ascent to the former site of a fire lookout or hike up part way to enjoy Gorge views and wildflower displays.

One of the great things about Dog Mountain is that from the 125-foot trailhead, you have choices. The most popular route may be an out-and-back hike up the easternmost trail and including the summit loop. For now, start hiking on the trail past the vault toilet at the east end of the lot. The trail takes off uphill right away; be aware that it is overgrown with lots of dark green poison oak. You may want to wear long pants. Scattered along the lower trail are also lots of flowers like the tiny blue-eyed Mary, bleeding heart, wood sorrel, and the ubiquitous Oregon grape. A variety of ferns grow here—watch for wood ferns and licorice fern growing on tree trunks. The trail ascends nearly 700 feet and reaches the first signed trail junction in 0.6 mile. This is your first decision point. The old trail on the left climbs 1.6 miles through the forest before meeting the rerouted trail at 2,000 feet. If you choose to go right, you'll enjoy river

BARBARA I. BOND

view of the summit meadow and trail

views and a lookout point in just 1 mile. My preference is to ascend the old trail on the left and head up through the dense forest. It just feels better climbing in the shade.

The trail climbs steeply through the forest, which features some big Douglas-fir trees. Vine maple fills out the canopy and there are lots of shade-loving plants thriving along the forest floor. Look for abundant vanilla leaf with its wide triangular leaves and single flower. The trail flattens for a moment or two, then pushes on upward to the signed trail junction. Turn left here and emerge from the trees into the first of the upper meadows. This is what you came for. Puppy Dog Mountain, a prominent viewpoint at 2,505 feet, is surrounded by brilliant yellow balsamroot displays mid-spring. The views from Puppy Dog are incredible—you can see for miles along the Columbia River. Across the way on the Oregon side are some familiar landmarks including the antenna farm atop Mount Defiance.

From Puppy Dog the trail forks—go to the right around the back side of the summit for a loop. For the direct route go straight ahead northward and follow the trail along the west side of the upper mountain. A short trail reaches the final summit trail in 0.3 mile, turn right onto the summit trail for the final few hundred yards to the top. The summit has a west-facing meadow below some thick trees. Explore a bit in the trees and you can see Mounts St. Helens and Adams to the north. Enjoy your break in this amazing place—but be aware that ticks are plentiful up here and along the trail. Check all your gear, yourself, and your companions thoroughly. For a partial loop hike, return to the trail junction below Puppy Dog Mountain and stay left for the eastside trail. This route takes you down past wildfower displays to a viewpoint 0.6 mile from the junction. The flowers around this little viewpoint are incredible—balsamroot, buttercups, desert parsley, and shooting stars. From here it is only 1.6 miles back to the car.

Note: Poison oak, ticks, and rattlesnakes are hazards on this hike. If you are exposed to poison oak, wash the area thoroughly with Tecnu, Tecnu Extreme, or Fels-Naptha soap. Tecnu products are available at most outdoor stores.

Options
To enjoy great views and wildflower displays, opt for a 1.6-mile hike up to the viewpoint along the east-side trail. To reach the viewpoint, turn right at the first signed trail junction then relax and enjoy the scenery. This creates a 3.2-mile out-and-back trip with about 1,400 feet of elevation gain.

Directions
From Portland, drive east on I-84 to exit 44 at Cascade Locks. Cross the toll bridge ($1, or $0.75 if you have a coupon book) and turn right on State Route 14. Follow State Route 14 12 miles east to the trailhead.

Information and Contact
A Northwest Forest Pass ($5) is required. Leashed dogs are allowed. For more information, contact the Columbia River Gorge National Scenic Area, (902 Wasco Ave., Ste. 200, Hood River, OR 97031, 541/308-1700, www.fs.fed.us/r6/columbia).

14 COYOTE WALL (SYNCLINE)
Columbia River Gorge National Scenic Area

Level: Moderate

Total Distance: 8.0 miles round-trip

Hiking Time: 5 hours

Elevation Change: 1,800 feet

Summary: This challenging hike traverses through oak and pine woodland to reach stunning views of the Columbia River Gorge before descending along cliff tops of the basalt wall.

For those who venture eastward from Portland, the rewards are many. Coyote Wall sits east of White Salmon River on the Washington side of the Columbia River. The ponderosa pine and Oregon white oak define the locale as Eastern Cascade and firmly in the rain shadow. This makes Coyote Wall a wonderful winter outing for anyone needing a drier outdoor option. In spring, early wildflowers brighten the forest floor and fill the green meadows. Look for rock doves and canyon wrens and listen for woodpeckers amongst the ponderosa pine. Coyote Wall is a downwardly folded section of Columbia River basalt

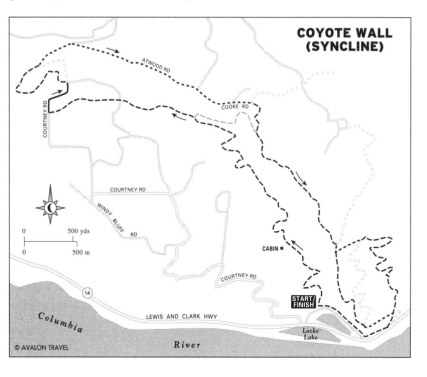

hiking along the top of a large meadow

with a vertical west face and gently sloping east side. The circumnavigation of the wall is a great early season outing.

From the parking area at Courtney Road, head eastward across the road, duck around the gate, and begin walking on the old roadbed. The basalt columns of Coyote Wall loom impossibly tall up ahead as you approach the southwestern corner. The rock is covered with moss, crustose lichen glows brightly, and the piles of fallen rock attest to its instability. After a short distance, turn left and pass a United States Forest Service sign and small gate to enter the woods. Note that the trail passes through private property, so stay on the main trail. The trail begins climbing right away through the oak forest. The understory is rich with wildflowers; in the spring, grasswidows' bright purple petals trumpet the change of season. The trail climbs steadily and curves northwest for the most part, occasionally zigzagging back and forth. It's these eastward views of the 2,000-foot wall of basalt that motivate you to continue hiking. From here, it's not at all obvious how the trail will ascend to any point above the cliffs without some rock climbing, but don't worry! Keep hiking and enjoy the eastward views up the Columbia River. The trail crosses several small streams, and passes huge boulders coated with mosses and small meadows littered with more purple grass widows. The forest floor also may have glacier lilies, prairie stars, and along the streams bright yellow violets.

The trail is easy to follow for the first couple of miles. Keep to the obvious main trail, ignore any forks—particularly those marked "closed" with piles of sticks or branches. As you wind through the forest you'll pass a dilapidated cabin across a stream on the left. The trail continues northwesterly, curving gradually more westward. At 2.5 miles or so the trail flattens and then descends slightly, passing through a stretch of thick conifers. Continue to stay on the main trail, ignoring any old roadbeds or faint mountain bike trails. A concrete foundation sits broken and forlorn adjacent to a hunter's camp on the right. Continue past the foundation through the sometimes-close brush and in a few hundred yards bear right on the trail.

The trail dips southwesterly for a short distance then suddenly dead-ends on a gravel road around 2.9 miles. Note the gated fence across the road. Turn right on this road and travel a winding path upward towards an amazing viewpoint and the westernmost point of the hike. Gorge views from here are downriver and include major landmarks such as Mount Defiance and Dog Mountain. Turn northeast, following the road as it climbs and then turns back eastward. The road continues ahead; just ignore any junctions or driveways. You will gradually head back into the forest. The road becomes a trail once more, narrowing and contouring above a steep drop-off to the south. Keep going and again ignore the junctions. Pass the junction with a Forest Service road on the left. A narrow and nearly hidden trail on the right will take you to a trail that contours along the edge of the cliffs. If you're not afraid of heights, you can descend this way for dramatic views.

Back on the main trail, at around 5.5 miles you will enter a large meadow as the descent begins in earnest. For the next couple of miles, just continue to keep to the trail along the cliff edge to nearly reach the bottom. Enjoy the wildflowers and amazing views. It's rewarding to see the forest below where you just were hiking. Near the end of the descent the trail begins to wind a bit, as you approach the wall the trail takes one last turn east, wandering through a highly eroded section criss-crossed with mountain bike trails. It then drops abruptly to the road, passing a United States Forest Service sign identical to the one at the start.

Turn right on the road and pass the tip of the wall as you walk back westward towards the start. Down on the left is Locke Lake, which sometimes has a variety of ducks and Canada geese paddling around. Often there is blooming desert parsley amongst the dark basalt.

Note: There is a lot of poison oak throughout this area. In case of poison oak exposure, carry Fels-Naptha soap or Tecnu Extreme in your vehicle and wash carefully afterwards. You may also want to carry a change of clothes.

Options

For a 5- or 6-mile out-and-back hike, go around the gate and follow the old roadbed around the tip of Coyote Wall. After passing the end of the wall, continue to the trail sign on the left. Head up onto the trail and ascend to a viewpoint along the cliff edge. There are lots of braided trails here, just bear left westward towards the cliff edge and upwards whenever you have a choice. You can continue climbing as long as you want. When you are done enjoying the views and wildflowers, return the way you came.

Directions

From Portland, drive 60 miles east on I-84. Take exit 64, turn left, and cross the bridge to White Salmon and State Route 14. Drive east on State Route 14, past Bingen, about another 3 miles. At Courtney Road, turn left, and turn immediately left into a parking area that will accommodate about 20 vehicles. There is also some limited parking across the road near the gate.

Information and Contact

There is no fee (but be advised that there may be a fee in the future). Leashed dogs are allowed. For more information, contact the Columbia River Gorge National Scenic Area (541/308-1700, www.fs.fed.us/r6/columbia) or Mount Hood National Forest, Hood River Ranger District (541/352-6002). This trail system is still under development by the Forest Service and there is a management plan currently in process; check with the Forest Service for current conditions and any trail restrictions or permanent closures. For a map, use USGS White Salmon although the trails are not on the map.

15 KLICKITAT TRAIL   BEST ◖

Columbia River Gorge National Scenic Area

🏃 🚴 🪂 🌸 🛶 ⚙️ 🐴 👥

Level: Easy   **Total Distance:** 6.0 miles round-trip

Hiking Time: 3.5 hours   **Elevation Change:** Negligible

Summary: Hike a short and scenic section of the Klickitat Trail, complete with mineral springs and historic buildings.

Residents of metro Portland are likely to say "huh?" when you tell them you've been hiking on the Klickitat Trail. Better known amongst Gorge aficionados and Washington residents, the Klickitat Trail (KT) has not yet become a standard hike for many. Enjoy the trail with the locals, and you won't regret the scenic drive out east for a hike that provides a snapshot of local history along with natural beauty.

The mile 16-13 section of this trail is a study in contrast. At the start the wide, flat trail borders a section of Yakama Nation land that is methodically being restored. The Yakama Indian Nation co-manages the Klickitat River, which is still home to stocks of native steelhead. Please stay on the trail for about the first 0.2 mile to respect Native American land. The trail winds through alders and becomes a narrow path for a short distance. Red twig dogwoods flower in spring and wildflowers abound, including wild lilac and the northwestern saxifrage that grows on rocky outcrops. There are several species of desert parsley along the

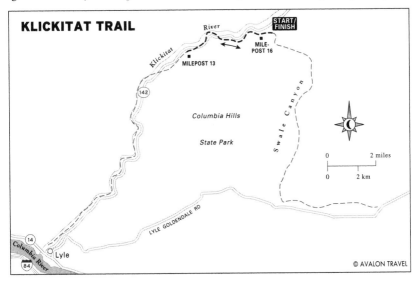

© BARBARA I. BOND

hiker looking across Klickitat River

trail—keep an eye out for the Piper's desert parsley with its distinctive "salt and pepper" flowers. Watch for bald eagles, osprey, northern flicker, and spotted to-whee overhead. Deer frequent the areas around the Klickitat Trail, and you may see signs of beaver along the river's edge.

In less than a mile you will reach Klickitat Springs—note the standpipe gushing mineral water to your right. It's worth a walk over to check out the water and take a taste if you are inclined. In the early 20th century, local entrepreneurs bottled and attempted to sell the mineral water. The buildings that were constructed to support the efforts are long gone. One building remains. A short distance west and across the river is the distinctive dry ice factory, which closed in 1957 and is now home to flocks of Vaux's swifts.

This section of trail is very wide; continue along the path westward as you head to the downed trestle and turnaround spot. Tiny white flowers of Whitlow grass dot the path in places and bright yellow gold stars offer a contrast. The trail continues past a swimming area near the split in the river near lots of hazelnut trees and rushes.

About 2 miles in, there is a flat area near the river that was an old home site. While using caution to avoid poison oak, take a look at the irises, grape hyacinth, and asparagus growing—testament to the human influence here. Continue to your turnaround at the spot where the old bridge was removed and there is a nice section of beachfront. This rails-to-trails hike follows a section of the old Lyle–Goldendale railway corridor. As you hike, keep an eye out for old railroad spikes and other artifacts. Retrace your steps to the trailhead.

Options
For a 3-mile one-way hike, drop one of two cars off in Klickitat at the Klickitat Railroad Park trailhead. Then hike the Klickitat Trail for 3 miles along the river north from the Pitt Trailhead. The Pitt trailhead is 10 miles north of Lyle on State Route 142.

Directions
From Portland, drive 60 miles east on I-84. Take exit 64, turn left and cross the bridge to White Salmon and State Route 14. Turn right on State Route 14 and drive 11 miles to Lyle and State Route 142. Turn north and drive 13 miles to the town of Klickitat, then continue another 3 miles to the Klickitat River Bridge. Turn right onto Horseshoe Bend Road and cross the bridge. Continue a few hundred yards east until Horseshoe Bend Road meets Schilling Road. Turn right and park at the parking area on the right. This is the trailhead.

Information and Contact
There are no fees. Dogs are allowed on leash only. Ticks, poison oak, rattlesnakes, and private property necessitate strict enforcement of the leash requirement. The Klickitat Trail Conservancy (www.klickitat-trail.org or info@klickitat-trail.org) has up-to-date information on trail closures and current conditions as well as a detailed topographic map. Washington State Parks information is available at 509/767-1159. Seasonal trail closure information is also available from the Washington State Department of Natural Resources (www.dnr.wa.gov).

16 SWALE CANYON

Columbia River Gorge National Scenic Area

Level: Moderate

Total Distance: 13.0 miles one-way

Hiking Time: 5-6 hours

Elevation Change: 1,150 feet

Summary: Enter the wild and rugged Swale Canyon while hiking over train trestles along the Klickitat Trail.

The Klickitat Trail is a wonderful example of a cooperative-management multi-use path along an old rail line. The complete trail is 31 miles and stretches from Lyle to Uecker Road (near Warwick). The first 13 miles are largely along the Klickitat River, and are managed by the United States Forest Service. The remainder of the trail, including the remote Swale Canyon, is managed by Washington State Parks in partnership with the Klickitat Trail Conservancy. The hike from Wahkiacus to Harms Road is the most isolated section of the Klickitat Trail and will introduce you to the wild beauty of the eastern gorge.

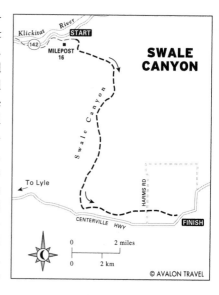

Looking eastward at the start of the Swale Canyon hike, it is hard to imagine a remote hike. Never fear: Once you get past the first couple of miles, the scenery begins to change and the canyon indeed starts to feel quite wild. The last parcel of private property is about 2.9 miles from Schilling Road. You won't need to worry about navigation challenges here—just keep following the trail as it criss-crosses Swale Creek for the next dozen miles. The trail climbs almost imperceptibly in spots; by the time you reach the Harms Road trailhead you will have climbed over 1,000 feet. Walk across Schilling Road to the trail, which is wide, flat, and nicely graded. Just think of this first section as your warm-up—stretch out those muscles and prepare for some great scenery. Notice the cottonwoods growing creekside and the native black hazelnut trees. These hazelnuts are edible, but the squirrels seem to get them first. You'll cross the first of nearly a dozen old trestles—these were built in 1903 when the Lyle–Goldendale rail line was completed. Use care

an old train trestle in Swale Canyon

on the trestles—some have broken ties and all have the potential to catch your foot and send you tumbling.

The huge ponderosa pines dotting the hills remind you quickly that this is the eastern Cascade region. Oregon white oak and a smattering of bigleaf maple make the canyon home, but it's the ponderosas that get your attention with their tall, stately, mottled trunks and long needles. I've also been told that they give off a faint sweet odor in spring. As you meander down the trail, look up at the hillside—you'll catch several varieties of desert parsley including lots of pungent yellow blooms and the distinctive purple flowers of the Columbia desert parsley.

As the trail continues winding southward, the canyon narrows. Occasionally you will hike over the deposit from rock and mud slides. Imagine the rush of water, rock, and mud that made this debris pile. Steller's jays may be chattering at you as you walk, and if you look above the canyon you may catch sight of a magnificent bald eagle on a snag or circling high. After more trestle crossings, and particularly past trestle no. 5, there are some nice spots nearer the creek where you could stop for a longer break or lunch. Just remember that the right-of-way for the trail extends 30 feet on either side—don't venture further.

Continuing southward, you may hear frogs as you walk closer to the creek through a section with the eastern cliffs closing in and rugged side canyons to the west. In spring, some of the inlet creeks create small waterfalls as they drop into Swale Creek. By the time you reach this section, you may have noted some marker signs with numbers. These are the old railroad mile markers and begin in Lyle. With only about 3 miles to go, the creek becomes more scenic as it flows over a series of rocky benches and narrows. Suddenly the trail leaves the canyon behind and enters the rolling hills that mark the remaining miles to the Harms Road trailhead. Here you will pass through some gates; be sure to leave them as you find them. Enjoy the wildflowers amongst the meadows that lead to the end. Cross one last trestle to the parking area.

Options

To experience some of Swale Canyon's beauty, venture along the trail from Harms Road. The trailhead is located on the west side of Harms Road. Walk around the gate, across the trestle, and continue west along the creek. The trail makes a sharp right turn north in about 2.5 miles—this is a good turnaround point. Retrace your steps to the trailhead for an out-and-back loop.

Directions

From Portland, drive 60 miles east on I-84. Take exit 64, turn left and cross the bridge to White Salmon and State Route 14. Turn right on State Route 14 and drive 11 miles to Lyle and State Route 142. Turn north and drive 13 miles to Klickitat, then continue another 3 miles to Klickitat River Bridge. Turn right onto Horseshoe Bend Road and cross the bridge. Continue a few hundred yards east until Horseshoe Bend Road meets Schilling Road. Turn right and park at the parking area on the right. This is the trailhead.

To drop a vehicle at the Harms Road trailhead or do the short option, follow the directions to Lyle. Turn north, then east, on the Centerville Highway nearly 15 miles to Harms Road. Turn left and drive 0.5 mile and park on the right of the road. The trail leading to Swale Canyon is on the west side of the road, marked with a sign.

Information and Contact

There is no fee. Dogs are allowed on leash only. Ticks, poison oak, rattlesnakes, and private property necessitate strict enforcement of the leash requirement. The Klickitat Trail Conservancy (www.klickitat-trail.org or info@klickitat-trail.org) has up-to-date information on trail closures and current conditions. Seasonal trail closure information is also available from the Washington State Department of Natural Resources (www.dnr.wa.gov).

17 CATHERINE CREEK *& Coyote Wall* BEST C
Columbia River Gorge National Scenic Area

2.08 Min.
4.28 miles

Level: Easy

Total Distance: 2-3.5 miles round-trip

Hiking Time: 3-4 hours

Elevation Change: 125 feet

Summary: Wildflower enthusiasts flock to Catherine Creek each spring to enjoy the amazing wildflower displays.

Flower lovers have long known when and where to go to catch the spring wildflower displays in the Columbia River Gorge. The Catherine Creek area has a split personality. On the south side of the road is a wheelchair-accessible paved trail with two loops that wind around old oaks and pines that mark a landscape liberally sprinkled with dozens of wildflowers from mid-winter through early summer. This trail provides visitors with an informative and scenic alternative to the slightly more strenuous option. As you wind along the path, a series of informational signs explain the flowers and natural history, and an occasional bench invites you to linger and drink in all the beauty. If you hike north of the road, the path follows along old roads and introduces you to Catherine Creek up close. It also passes a natural arch in a basalt wall, and an old homesite complete with a collapsed cabin and the remains of a corral.

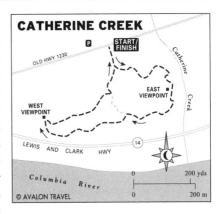

The Catherine Creek Universal Access Trail begins at an information sign just across the street south of the parking area. From the sign, walk ahead a short distance on the wide path to an immediate junction; the loops are both less than 1 mile and are easily covered in a longer loop or figure eight. Turn left for the 0.65-mile east loop which quickly reaches a bench and north-facing view of Catherine Creek; the view includes wildflower-covered meadows and a waterfall. Enjoy the miner's lettuce growing around a small grove of Oregon white oak along the way. Common and meadow-death camas, bi-colored cluster lily, and the ever-present grass widows add color to the somewhat dry grassland. The bench offers an opportunity to take a break and drink in the dramatic views east up the Columbia River.

After continuing along the loop as it turns westward, you will cross a small

view east from above Catherine Creek

bridge and reach the junction with the 0.75-mile west loop trail. Walk west along the loop, enjoying the change of scenery as you now gaze downriver along the Columbia. The trail leads you mostly through open meadow, although the occasional ponderosa pine towers above all. You will quickly reach another viewpoint with a bench. The information signs point out how this area has come to be such a collection of diverse species of flowers. Continue along the trail as it loops back eastward. When you reach the trail junction, the signs will direct you back north to the trailhead.

North of the road is a trail that allows more exploration of this natural wonder. Hike northward along signed Forest Road 020 for a short distance and drop downward towards Catherine Creek. On the immediate left is a small ridge. Take a moment to note all of the flowers scattered throughout the mossy rocks. The bright yellow of frittilaria is a highlight along with delicate prairie stars, licorice ferns, and western saxifrage. As you approach the creek, bear right on road "021" and cross the creek on a wobbly wooden bridge. Ahead on the right is the rib of basalt with the arch high above. Continue north, approaching first the old corral and then the collapsed cabin. The corral is surrounded with bigleaf maple trees. Some large ponderosa pines are scattered throughout this modest woodland. Note the pile of talus on the right, just below the arch. Look in the meadow along here for some small blue-eyed Mary, buttercups, and more saxifrage. The trail gently ascends the hillside and crosses under some power lines around 0.8 mile. Continue up bearing northeast, and follow the trail until you have made a U-turn and are heading back south towards the blocky basalt ridge with the arch. The trail crosses just east of the arch, you can take a spur to explore the narrow ridge if you want. Careful, there are some very narrow spots with a long fall to the ground below. Continue to view the arch up close at 1.4 miles. You could turn back here and retrace your steps for a slightly longer hike.

From the arch, the trail winds along for another 0.5 mile as it drops down through flower-covered meadows, crosses a couple streams (in the spring) and takes you eventually southward to the road. Turn right to return to your vehicle.

Options

There are several options for hiking Catherine Creek. A round-trip hike to the arch and back is a little under 3 miles; a one-way loop hike to the arch continues back down to the road for a 2-mile hike. If you opt for only the Universal Access loops, the distance is about 1.5 miles with some variation depending on which loops you choose. For a more exploratory trip, grab a map and wildflower guide and take more time to explore the area north of the arch. With a little luck you may identify dozens of wildflower species. There are over 90 species blooming from February through July. To return, just head back towards the river to reach the road and your vehicle at the trailhead.

Directions

From Portland, drive 60 miles east on I-84. Take exit 64, turn left, and cross the bridge to White Salmon and State Route 14. Drive east on State Route 14, past Bingen. At milepost 71 and the junction with County Road 1230, turn left. You will pass Rowland Lake immediately on the right once you turn off State Route 14. Drive on County Road 1230 for 1.4 miles to the parking area on the north side of the road and park along the road. Walk south across the street to the signed trailhead for the Universal Access loops.

Information and Contact

There are no fees. Dogs are allowed on 6-foot leashes only. For more information and for a map of the Catherine Creek Universal Access Trail, contact the Columbia River Gorge National Scenic Area (541/308-1700, www.fs.fed.us/r6/columbia). For another map, use USGS Lyle.

6-20-15

18 TOM McCALL POINT
Columbia River Gorge National Scenic Area

BEST **C**

Level: Easy/Moderate

Hiking Time: 2.5-3 hours

Total Distance: 4.0 miles round-trip

Elevation Change: 1,500 feet

Summary: This short hike to a high point offers stunning views of the Columbia River and Cascade volcanoes, and is a Gorge classic for spring wildflower displays.

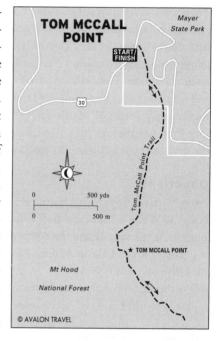

Tom McCall Point is a 1,722-foot viewpoint high above the Rowena Overlook and the Columbia River Historic Highway. The trail leading to the top is one of two trails on The Nature Conservancy's Tom McCall Preserve. In the spring, the Tom McCall Point Trail quickly delivers hikers through oak and pine woodland and dozens of wildflower varieties to the viewpoint. Tom McCall, Oregon's 30th governor, was a conservationist and left a legacy of environmental protections for Oregonians. McCall spent many hours exploring and enjoying the wildflowers in the Rowena Crest area. To honor him, The Nature Conservancy named the trail after him in 1983.

The trail begins from the south side of the Rowena Overlook entrance road. Walk along the gravel path through an open grassy meadow liberally sprinkled with spring wildflowers. Showy balsamroot, delicate light pink prairie stars, purple grass widows, and Columbia desert parsley all vie for your attention. The trail is flat and wide for the first 0.5 mile or so until it jogs east, then back south, through some scattered oak and pine trees. Here you will want to start watching for poison oak—it grows alongside the trail for the rest of the hike.

You will reach an old Nature Conservancy sign (due to be replaced Spring 2008) warning visitors of the trail's attendant dangers including ticks, rattlesnakes, and the three-leafed menace—poison oak. Take a moment here to read The Nature

© BARBARA I. BOND

view across the Columbia River from Tom McCall Point

Conservancy's preservation guidelines—they are a little different than the typical Forest Service or State Park rules. Properties such as this one are managed for conservation, not recreation. As such, visitors are asked to follow the guidelines in order to promote that goal.

Continue along the trail, which alternates through short sections of shrubby oaks and across meadows to reach a viewpoint along the eastern edge of the cliffs marked by three old posts. Glacier lilies, oaks toothwort, and the occasional Indian paintbrush break up the monotony of the climb. From here the breathtaking views look upriver, east along the Columbia and northward towards the Washington town of Lyle and the Klickitat River.

The sometimes-steep march upwards continues through some larger oaks and a few more narrow switchbacks across now-open meadows to end up on a large open area marked only by a small plastic post. Most folks will want to stop here and enjoy the views and perhaps have a picnic lunch or at least a break.

Go longer by following the path southward once more as it drops down a slight slope then climbs past some large pines along a fence line. If you go another 0.5 mile you reach a series of small viewpoints along the eastern edge of the plateau. You may hear the ruffed grouse in spring or the rhythmic sound of frogs. The views eastward along the river are wonderful. Return the way you came.

Options

There is also an option for a lovely hike that includes wildflowers, great views, and no steep climb. Across the road at The Nature Conservancy's information sign begins the Plateau Trail. This 2-mile "lollipop" loop crosses the rocky meadow to circle a small pond. Lots of birds congregate around the water, and you may see and hear the distinctive cry of the red-winged blackbird, along with songbirds and the occasional hawk.

Directions

From Portland, drive 66 miles east on I-84 to exit 69/Mosier. Take exit 69/Mosier to drive east along the Old Columbia River Scenic Highway to the Rowena Overlook on the right. The preserve is on both sides of the road. There is a sign on the left, just past a fence and gate, announcing the Tom McCall Preserve. The information board includes a map and guidelines for the preserve.

Information and Contact

There are no fees. Dogs are not allowed on Nature Conservancy lands. For more information, contact The Nature Conservancy's Oregon, Columbia Plateau Office, 541/298-1802. Read The Nature Conservancy's guidelines for visitors at www. nature.org; search for "guidelines." For groups larger than 10, please contact The Nature Conservancy's main office at 503/802-8100. A map is on the information board at the trailhead, or use USGS Lyle. In case of poison oak exposure, carry Fels-Naptha soap or Tecnu Extreme in your vehicle, and wash carefully afterwards. You may also want to carry a change of clothes.

MOUNT HOOD

BARBARA I. BOND

BEST HIKES

The region surrounding Mount Hood is a diverse

environment covering a huge geographic territory. Most of Mount Hood is a part of the Cascades ecoregion and in many ways it defines Oregon. For Portland-area hikers, the lands surrounding Mount Hood provide hundreds of miles of hiking opportunities. Although the alpine meadows and rocky expanses of Mount Hood are the ultimate hiking environs for some, this mountain region offers much more.

East of the mountain is the open forestland that sits in the rain shadow of the Cascade crest. Here ponderosa pine, grand fir, and vine maple forests encompass both wilderness and non-wilderness hiking areas. The Badger Creek Wilderness, east of the mountain, provides solitude and quiet for hikers or backpackers seeking to get away from the urban forest of Mount Hood's flanks and the dissonance of city life. Further afield and southward is the Clackamas River. Popular with river rats, the Clackamas also offers hikers dramatic waterfalls and towering trees along nearby trails. The nearby Bagby Research Area has historic hot springs and offers a lower-elevation hike amidst immense Douglas-fir trees and pretty streams and creeks. The short hike to Bagby Hot Springs is a wonderful outing for children of all ages and can introduce beginners to the splendor of the outdoors.

Moving west from Mount Hood, you'll come upon some Old Cascade lower-elevation peaks in the Salmon–Huckleberry Wilderness. This densely forested wilderness is surprisingly easy to get to and offers trails of wide-ranging appeal. A hike along the very popular Old Salmon River Trail won't be the same as the steep ascent of Hunchback Mountain – yet they both wind through old-growth trees, carpets of spring wildflowers, and the aura of magic that this forest possesses.

Mount Hood's southern region is highly developed and easily accessible for hikes of nearly any length. The historic Barlow Pass has a trailhead for the Pacific Crest Trail, which stretches from Mexico to Canada and bisects Mount Hood's western slopes. Deer wander quietly through the trees near the trail as hikers visit stunning viewpoints or hike the short trail to Twin Lakes. These pretty lakes often serve as a testing ground for hikers expanding their range to include short backpacking trips. Lakes and waterfalls are abundant and lure locals and tourists who bask in their natural beauty. Tamanawas Falls and Mirror Lake have that unique combination of easy access, short hikes, and stunning scenery that you'll recognize from numerous postcards, calendars, and book covers.

Finally, there is the penultimate hiking of Mount Hood, the subalpine and alpine meadows of the wilderness surrounding its timberline. Mount Hood's famous Timberline Trail circumnavigates the mountain providing wildflower lovers, photographers, and backpackers access to some of the most pristine areas of the mountain. Many Portland-area visitors seek out the rustic elegance of Mount Hood's Timberline Lodge, midway up the mountain's south side. From here hikers can experience the wonder of the mountain by hiking the Timberline Trail to the flower-dense Paradise Park – one of the mountain's most splendid collections of alpine wildflowers.

Mount Hood's alpine trails range in difficulty and length, yet offer even young hikers an opportunity to view some of Mount Hood's most rugged glacial features up close. Or you may choose to spend the day with a picnic lunch at Lost Lake – gazing across the water at the unforgettable view of Mount Hood. Whichever you choose, there is no question that for high-value recreation, Mount Hood is the place to visit.

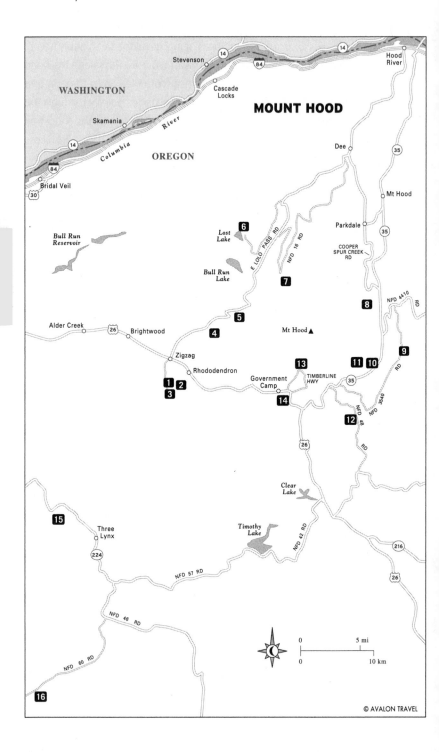

TRAIL NAME	LEVEL	DISTANCE	TIME	ELEVATION	FEATURES	PAGE
1 Old Salmon River Trail	Easy	5.0 mi rt	2.5 hr	150 ft		128
2 Devils Peak Lookout	Butt-kicker	11.8 mi rt	6-7 hr	3,410 ft		131
3 Salmon Butte	Strenuous	9.5 mi rt	4.5 hr	3,020 ft		134
4 Horseshoe Ridge-Zigzag Mountain	Moderate	6.4 mi rt	3.5 hr	2,000 ft		137
5 Ramona Falls	Easy/Moderate	7.3 mi rt	3.5 hr	1,100 ft		140
6 Lost Lake	Easy	3.2 mi rt	2 hr	Negligible		143
7 Vista Ridge-Cairn Basin	Moderate	8.7 mi rt	4.5 hr	1,700 ft		146
8 Tamanawas Falls	Easy	3.8 mi rt	2 hr	400 ft		149
9 Lookout Mountain	Easy	2.5 mi rt	1.5 hr	500 ft		151
10 Gumjuwac-Badger Creek Loop	Strenuous	11.7 mi rt	6 hr	2,800 ft		154
11 Gnarl Ridge	Strenuous	11.7 mi rt	6.5 hr	2,700 ft		156
12 Palmateer Point-Twin Lakes	Moderate	9.2 mi rt	4.5 hr	1,500 ft		159
13 Timberline Trail-Paradise Park Loop	Strenuous	12.5 mi rt	6.5 hr	2,900 ft		161
14 Tom Dick and Harry Mountain	Moderate	6.6 mi rt	3 hr	1,400 ft		164
15 Clackamas River Trail	Moderate	7.8 mi one-way	4 hr	600 ft		167
16 Bagby Hot Springs	Easy	3.5 mi rt	2 hr	Negligible		170

1 OLD SALMON RIVER TRAIL
Mount Hood National Forest

Level: Easy

Total Distance: 5.0 miles round-trip

Hiking Time: 2.5 hours

Elevation Change: 150 feet

Summary: The Old Salmon River Trail – widely known for wildflowers, old-growth trees, and the wonder of the nearby Salmon River – may be one of the prettiest forest hikes in Mount Hood.

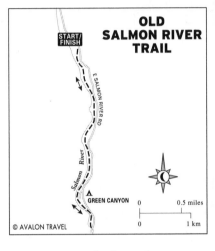

The Salmon River winds its way down the southern flanks of Mount Hood, providing miles of recreation, diverse wildlife habitat, and spawning grounds for native salmon. Deer wander the early mornings, squirrels scale trees, and ducks glide through the river while belted kingfishers and American dippers call overhead. It's a delightful site for hikers—miles of trails both easy and challenging and all amongst mature trees, rich understory, and wildflowers galore. Hiking the Old Salmon River Trail 742-A is really popular for those wanting to enjoy a rich outdoor experience on a wide, flat trail.

The trail begins on the west side of the road and heads to the right and downhill to cross a footbridge surrounded by huge sword ferns and trees dripping with moss. Licorice ferns thrive in this damp forest, and you might see some skunk cabbage in the boggy areas. Trillium bloom early in the spring, followed by wood sorrel and bunchberry blooms. Cross another stream on a plank bridge, walk up some stairs, and check out what is probably one of the biggest western red cedars you've ever seen. The trail continues along the river, providing lots of different views of the rushing waters. In the spring, the river is especially high, fast, and cold. (Be advised: A friend of mine almost lost her dog along this trail when the water-loving animal excitedly decided to go for a swim and got swept away by the fast-moving waters.)

As the trail winds along the river, it passes some huge nurse logs coated with thick mosses and with lots of tiny trees and flowers growing in their moist rotting bark. Just before the mile marker, you cross another bridge. Along the

© BARBARA I. BOND

a hiker takes a break near the Salmon River

stream bank, look for the pretty pink flowers of Scouler's corydalis. The flower almost looks like a giant bleeding heart, and it is very distinctive because it grows in long clusters at the top of the plant. You'll then pass a nice camping spot. Salmonberry's pretty pink flowers brighten up the shaded forest. Continue along the river for almost 1 mile; you'll then see some stands of alder that have filled in disturbed areas over the years. Then trail leads up to the road for a short distance, passing a small rock wall that's popular with rock climbers. The trail is marked with a sign on your right, and as you enter the forest once more, you'll pass a huge stump on the right, then cross a stream just below a huge washout. At the 2-mile point, you'll pass to the west of the Green Canyon Campground. There are numerous side trails from the campground to the river trail. The campground has bathrooms and picnic tables. As you're passing the campground, check out the river—there is a small waterfall on the other side, and some small rapids add to the beauty. The trail continues another 0.3 mile or so.

The trail climbs back up to the road to end at the Salmon River West Trailhead. This sometimes rugged trail leads along the north shore of the Salmon River and enters the Salmon–Huckleberry Wilderness. If you decide to check it out, fill out a self-issued permit at the station across the street and to the left of the bridge at the trailhead. About 0.5 mile in are some rocky benches right above the river that make a nice lunch spot. Return the way you came.

Options

To explore a bit of the Salmon–Huckleberry Wilderness, continue southeast along the Salmon River Trail 742 from the west trailhead. The trail mostly follows the river for the first couple of miles. You pass the Wilderness boundary in about 2 miles, then reach the Rolling Riffle Camp in 0.3 mile. There are huge Douglas-fir, western red cedar, and western hemlock all along the trail; watch for fairy slippers in the spring. The sunny, rocky outcrops along the way sport pretty blooms of stonecrop and blue-eyed Mary.

Directions

From Portland, drive east on U.S. 26 for 36 miles to Salmon River Road/Forest Road 2618. Turn right and drive 2.6 miles to the signed trailhead.

Information and Contact

A Northwest Forest Pass ($5) is required. Leashed dogs are allowed. For more information, contact Mount Hood National Forest Zigzag Ranger District (70220 E. Hwy. 26, Zigzag, OR 97049, 503/622-3191, www.fs.fed.us—choose "Oregon" and "Mount Hood" from the drop-down menus). For current conditions, stop by the Mount Hood Information Center (24403 E. Welches Rd., Ste. 103, Welches, OR 97067, 503/622-5560). For maps, use the USDA Forest Service Salmon–Huckleberry, Bull of the Woods, Opal Creek Wilderness map.

2 DEVILS PEAK LOOKOUT
Salmon-Huckleberry Wilderness

BEST ☾

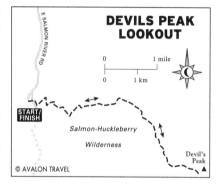

Level: Butt-kicker

Total Distance: 11.8 miles round-trip

Hiking Time: 6-7 hours

Elevation Change: 3,410 feet

Summary: The Salmon-Huckleberry Wilderness is known for big trees, steep trails, and great views. This hike takes you up to the long upper ridge of Hunchback Mountain to Devils Peak Lookout.

The Green Canyon Campground is aptly named. Surrounded by the dense old-growth forest in the Salmon River drainage—it's like entering a wonderland of mossy tree trunks, lichen-coated branches, and thick carpets of sword ferns. The dense forest provides plenty of cover for the ubiquitous deer and squirrels. The Green Canyon Way Trail 793A probably doesn't get as much attention as some of the other trails in the area—its steep, narrow track and over a dozen switchbacks probably scares most folks off. Yet, the 3.5 miles up a broad west ridge of Hunchback Mountain takes you through some of the most beautiful forest around. If you enjoy the deep silence of the forest and a good workout, this is the hike for you.

Walk across the road to the signed trailhead. Right away you can tell this is a special place, the forest is dark and cool, and if you look up, all you'll see is the thick canopy of the big Douglas-firs that dominate here. Sword ferns seem bigger than usual and wood sorrel, mosses, Oregon grape, and vine maples fill in the understory. Take a deep breath—you'll be ascending over 2,000 feet in the first 2.5 miles. The trail passes numerous downed trees as it begins the first of several sets of switchbacks of the ridge. As you ascend, check out the huge nurse logs littering the forest floor. Near 2,700-foot elevation, the thick trees being to thin and the forest opens up to allow more light. The trail traverses a short, open slope then re-enters the trees as it continues upwards. Some of the old trees along this trail have blazes carved at just above eye level into their trunks.

At around 3,200 feet you round the corner of a knob of rock to traverse across an open steep slope. There are a lot of mushrooms growing happily on the forest floor, and on the tree trunks you may spot more old blazes. The trail narrows across a rocky exposed section for a very short distance, drops down a moment, and then resumes the upward march along the steep slope. You'll reach the upper ridge in 3.4 miles at an unmarked "T" junction. Turn right onto the Hunchback Mountain Trail.

The Hunchback Mountain Trail 793 rolls along the upper mountain like a crazed roller coaster—over downed trees, through aster- and paintbrush-filled meadows, and across steep slopes. Woodpeckers nest in old snags along the trail here; look for their nesting holes in the trunks of dead trees. There are a few points when you can see Mount Hood peeking through the trees on your left. The forest is full of huge Douglas-fir and the trail keeps climbing past vanilla leaf,

the lookout perched atop its rocky summit

© BARBARA I. BOND

huckleberry, and pine drops. Pacific rhododendron and bear grass round out the blooms. A small wooden sign on a tree lets you know there is water on the north side of the trail about 0.2 mile before the lookout. You know you're close when you pass the Cool Creek Trail coming in from the left. Continue climbing to the lookout, perched atop a rocky high spot with stellar views of Mounts Hood and Jefferson. The lookout is maintained by volunteers and can be used for overnights. In winter, it is a welcome respite from the wind and cold. Take a moment to sign the journal that usually sits on the small table in the lookout. Return the way you came.

Options

You can also get up to the lookout on the Cool Creek Trail (no. 794), which is just outside the wilderness boundary. The trail climbs a heart-thumping 3,200 feet in 3.9 miles. Watch for chanterelles in the forest on your way up. When you reach the junction with Hunchback Mountain Trail, turn left to reach the lookout. The trailhead for this alternate hike is past the junction with Salmon River Road. Just before Rhododendron, turn right on Still Creek Road and drive nearly 3 miles to the trailhead on the right. Parking is along the wide part of the road before the trailhead.

Directions

From Portland, drive east on U.S. 26 for 36 miles to Salmon River Road (Forest Road 2618). Turn right and follow it for about 4.5 miles to the Green Canyon Campground on the right. Parking is available in the day use area in the campground. The trailhead is across the road.

Information and Contact

Leashed dogs are allowed. For more information, contact Mount Hood National Forest Zigzag Ranger District (70220 E. Hwy. 26, Zigzag, OR 97049, 503/622-3191, www.fs.fed.us and choose "Oregon" and "Mount Hood" from the drop-down menus). For maps, use the USDA Forest Service Salmon–Huckleberry Wilderness or Green Trails Government Camp (no. 461). For current conditions, stop by the Mount Hood Information Center (24403 E. Welches Rd., Ste. 103, Welches, OR 97067, 503/622-5560).

3 SALMON BUTTE

Salmon-Huckleberry Wilderness

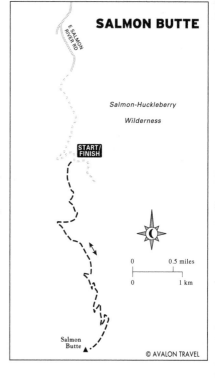

Level: Strenuous   **Total Distance:** 9.5 miles round-trip

Hiking Time: 4.5 hours   **Elevation Change:** 3,020 feet

Summary: Salmon Butte is one of the best hikes for Mount Hood views and early summer rhododendron blooms amidst steep drainages and dense forest.

The Salmon–Huckleberry Wilderness has nearly 45,000 acres of sharp ridges, deep ravines, and dense forestland. The rich understory and thick canopy contribute to the magical feeling one gets when exploring the trails. Wildlife is common here and you are as likely to find other hikers on this trail as mule deer. In summertime, the bright pink of rhododendron blooms offer a wonderful contrast to the dark quiet of the surrounding trees. Salmon Butte is a small, rocky summit southwest of Mount Hood. For some reason it is not as popular as nearby wilderness trails, yet the well-graded trail climbs through some of the most beautiful scenery in the area. The trail begins on a wide rocky track past a picnic table and garbage can. However, that track quickly narrows to a duff-covered trail that leads to summit views of surrounding peaks.

Walk across the road to the signed trailhead and begin the southward ascent. At first the trail is fairly level, but soon it begins a steady, gentle climb. Aside from the occasional two or three switchbacks and a steeper finish to the top, this trail climbs so gradually that you may never really notice the elevation change until you turn around and look back. The first mile has a lot of blowdown you have to climb under, over, or go around. The trail passes through an odd stand of trees with lots of downed logs showing blackened bark and a forest floor nearly bare save a thick carpet of needles. It's quite a contrast to the lush green understory to come. Once through this section, the forest returns to its typical riches—salal, oxalis, several varieties of ferns, rhodies, and Oregon grape cover the ground. Around 1.5 miles the trail makes a sharp turn left to cross a sunny corner of the ridge before ducking back into the trees. Keep an eye out for the distinctive white and red of candystick that grows in mature forests and has no chlorophyll. Ground-hugging manzanita lines the trail for a short distance before the shade-loving foliage once again takes over.

thick rhododendron and forest

The trail passes through some wet areas between miles 2 and 3, evidenced by the many stream crossings and the tall, intimidating devil's club. The trail continues its march upwards until a break for a viewpoint appears at 4 miles. Here, a sign on a tree on the right side directs you onto the old road that leads to the summit. However, on the left there is a spur to a nice view.

Continue on the old roadbed, which takes a turn to climb the east flank of the upper butte and then make a 180-degree turn for the final push upwards. From the open summit, enjoy the stellar Mount Hood views and surrounding peaks, as well as the wildflowers in early season—you may even see some bear grass in bloom on the eastern side of the summit. Return the way you came.

Options

The Salmon–Huckleberry Wilderness has other wonderful hiking trails. For something different, visit the Old Salmon River Trail. There are multiple access points along Salmon River Road. For trail access to both the old trail and the Salmon River West trailhead, park near the bridge just south of the Green Canyon Campground.

Directions

From Portland, drive east on U.S. 26 for 36 miles to Salmon River Road (Forest Road 2618). Turn right and drive 6.5 miles to the trailhead. Park in the small lot on the left; the trailhead is on the right.

4 HORSESHOE RIDGE-ZIGZAG MOUNTAIN

BEST (

Mount Hood Wilderness

Level: Moderate

Total Distance: 6.4 miles round-trip

Hiking Time: 3.5 hours

Elevation Change: 2,000 feet

Summary: Enjoy great views and a five-volcano vista from a small summit on the upper ridge of Zigzag Mountain.

Mount Hood, Oregon's highest mountain, is known as a quiet volcano. It wasn't always so: During the Old Maid eruptive period in the late 1700s, the Sandy River drainage was filled with rock and sand deposits. Lewis and Clark noted that the Sandy River seemed full of "quicksand"; subsequently, the river channel has deepened as the river flows washed away the loose debris. The Old Maid Flat surrounds the upper Sandy River drainage and is the starting point for a number of popular hikes.

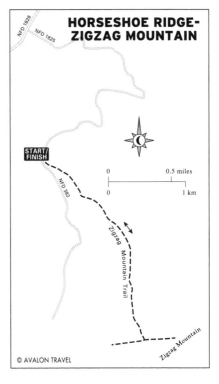

The Horseshoe Ridge Trail 774 begins in the Old Maid Flat just south of the Sandy River. Most hikers will want to skip the first two miles of trail and begin where the trail crosses Forest Road 380 at 2,800 feet. The trail begins heading uphill immediately through the fire-damaged second-growth forest. The forest is thick with rhododendron and their beautiful blooms are a highlight of early summer. Ascend a few steep switchbacks, then cross the road, jog right, and pick up the trail across the way. As you pass the self-issue permit station, take a moment and fill one out. Enter the wilderness around 1 mile.

As the trail climbs, there is a lot to take in. Wood sorrel, twisted stalk, vanilla leaf, and a lot of devil's club create a lovely atmosphere. You may see deer or squirrels or hear the tapping of woodpeckers. (Sometimes you can even spy them busily climbing a tree trunk while they hunt for bugs in the bark.) There are some old cedar stumps along with a mix of true fir as you climb higher. Nearing 4,200 feet, the trail opens up and flattens out for a bit. The terrain is now distinctly alpine with bear grass, fir trees, whitebark pine, and mountain hemlocks filling in. Huckleberry and thimbleberry bushes line the trail as it traverses across a rocky slope with good views. Purple gentian and penstemon are a welcome contrast to the green bushes and gray rock. You might see the bright orange of tiger lilies and some Indian paintbrush with the bear grass and huckleberries.

Three miles up you'll reach the old wooden sign marking the junction with the Zigzag Mountain Trail 775. The

Mount Hood from Zigzag Mountain

view across the gently sloping ridge northward foreshadows what's to come—it's only getting better. Mount Hood looks stunning rising up behind the forest of alpine trees. Turn left and wander along the Zigzag Mountain ridge for about 0.2 mile. You'll notice a rocky high point on the left of the trail; make your way over to a good lunch spot and enjoy the views from this nearly 4,900-foot perch. On a clear day, Mount Hood's landmarks stand out: the Reid Glacier, Zigzag Glacier, and Illumination Rock, to name a few. The Palmer lift is obvious on the right horizon along the ridge. Mounts Adams, Rainier, St. Helens, and Jefferson round out the panorama looking counterclockwise from Mount Hood. It's a mountain lover's delight. If the huckleberries are ripe, enjoy the bounty—there are a lot of bushes with the small but sweet berries. Return the way you came.

Options

Hike to Cast Lake to enjoy lunch. Pass the rocky viewpoint and continue on the Zigzag Mountain Trail another 1.5 miles to the junction; a side trail travels 0.5 mile down to the lake. Return the way you came for a total 10.4-miles round-trip.

Directions

From Portland, drive east on U.S. 26 for 37 miles. Turn left on East Lolo Pass Road and drive 4 miles to Forest Road 1825, signed Campgrounds and Trailheads.

Turn right on Forest Road 1825 towards Riley Horse Camp. Following the signs for Riley, turn right on Forest Road 380 and drive 2.1 miles to the trailhead. You will pass Riley Horse Camp, cross Lost Creek, and drive to a wide spot on the road to park. The trail crosses the road here; the trailhead is on the left side of the road heading uphill. There is only room for about three or four vehicles.

Information and Contact

Leashed dogs are allowed. For more information, contact Mount Hood National Forest Zigzag Ranger District (70220 E. Hwy. 26, Zigzag, OR 97049, 503/622-3191, www.fs.fed.us and choose "Oregon" and "Mount Hood" from the drop-down menus). For maps, use Geo-Graphics Mount Hood Wilderness and/or Green Trails Government Camp (no. 461). For current conditions stop by the Mount Hood Information Center (24403 E. Welches Rd., Ste. 103, Welches, OR 97067, 503/622-5560).

5 RAMONA FALLS

BEST C

Mount Hood National Forest

Level: Easy/Moderate

Total Distance: 7.3 miles round-trip

Hiking Time: 3.5 hours

Elevation Change: 1,100 feet

Summary: Visit one of Mount Hood's spectacular waterfalls on this popular hike along the Sandy River.

The power of Ramona Falls really isn't evident until you are staring up at it from the wooden footbridge at its base. The wide fan of water cascades over the basalt wall in dozens of shimmering rivulets-, making it an incredible destination. The trail to the falls is a jumble of contrasting images—dry, eroded riverbank; hemlock, lodgepole, Douglas-fir, and red alder forest; the milky waters of the glacier-fed Sandy River; and the cool, dark forest surrounding the falls and creekside return trail.

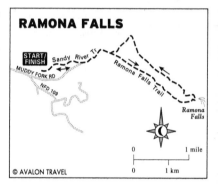

The Sandy River Trail 770 goes eastward south of the river 1.2 miles to cross Sandy River on a wooden bridge. Along the way, the trail meanders closer to the river in places and then ducks into the trees only to emerge again near the river. Note the places where washouts have taken out the trail. As you hike, look west occasionally to really get an impression of the erosion that takes place when the snowpack thaws and the water level is high. Drop down to the river channel to cross the Sandy on wooden bridges, which are installed every spring or early summer by the Forest Service. After climbing up out of the channel, turn right and hike the 0.2 mile to the trail junction with the Ramona Falls Trail 797. There is a big information sign here with a map, and a trail sign points out the loop. It's also the Pacific Crest Trail junction. I suggest you bear right and go counterclockwise around the Ramona Falls Loop. In a few yards, you will pass a Wilderness Permit box on the right; please fill out a permit. The trail continues to the falls as it climbs gently. After the ascending traverse, the trail turns left at the Pacific Crest Trail junction (southbound) and then drops to the basin with the falls. Walk through a stock gate and enjoy a long break at the wonderful viewpoint of this treasure. The trail climbs gently another 800 feet as it approaches the falls.

hikers cross the Sandy River channel

After your break, continue past the falls on the footbridge and take a quick left at the "Y" to complete the loop. This northern part of the loop is a contrast to the dry riverside trail. You meander across the creek a couple of times as the trail goes west and parallels a layered cliff band to the north. The creek keeps this stretch cool and wildflowers here last into mid-summer. Maidenhair ferns add to the rich green of the forest floor and mid-level vine maples filter the sunlight along the creek. After another creek crossing on a simple log footbridge, you'll pass another permit box and in a short distance reach the trail junction where you began the loop. Retrace your steps along the Sandy River Trail to the car.

Options

Want to get up into extreme alpine country? Take a long out-and-back up to Yocum Ridge. From Ramona Falls, cross the footbridge and bear right at the "Y." Continue another 0.5 mile to reach the Yocum Ridge Trail 771. The trail climbs, sometimes very steeply, nearly 5 miles to its official end around 6,400 feet and below one of Mount Hood's most technical climbing routes. This has long been one of my favorite Mount Hood hikes—the wildflowers and views of the mountain's north side are tremendous.

Directions

From Portland, drive east on U.S. 26 for 37 miles. Turn left on East Lolo Pass Road (Forest Road 18) and continue for 4 miles. Turn right on Forest Road 1825 signed Campgrounds and Trailheads. (This has one paved lane going in each direction.) Stay right on the bridge going over the Sandy River and keep left at the next two junctions to reach the Ramona Falls Trailhead in 2.4 miles. There is a huge parking lot.

Information and Contact

A Northwest Forest Pass ($5) is required. Leashed dogs are allowed. For more information, contact Mount Hood National Forest Zigzag Ranger District (70220 E. Hwy. 26, Zigzag, OR 97049, 503/622-3191, www.fs.fed.us and choose "Oregon" and "Mount Hood" from the drop-down menus). For maps, use Geo-Graphics Mount Hood Wilderness and/or Green Trails Government Camp (no. 461). For current conditions, stop by the Mount Hood Information Center (24403 E. Welches Rd., Ste. 103, Welches, OR 97067, 503/622-5560).

6 LOST LAKE

BEST

Mount Hood National Forest

Level: Easy

Total Distance: 3.2 miles round-trip

Hiking Time: 2 hours

Elevation Change: Negligible

Summary: Lost Lake, nestled amongst old growth trees with postcard views of the Mount Hood, is one of the premier scenic hikes in Mount Hood National Forest and one that the whole family can enjoy.

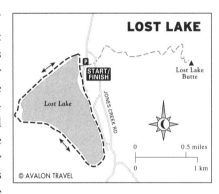

Lost Lake may indeed seem "lost" when you are driving there the first time. The labyrinth of forest roads seems endless until you suddenly come upon a sign with a Lost Lake arrow. Near the end of the 19th century, a couple of brothers from Hood River were said to have discovered the lake, which was then rediscovered by a party of 12 who set out to find this gem. Modern explorers of any type can now enjoy the natural wonders of this discovery. Begin your hike on the lakeshore trail just across from the camp store. This hike follows a counterclockwise loop around the perimeter trail, but you can hike the lake trail in either direction. (The shoreline is not equidistant but is described in approximately 1-mile segments.)

Turn right onto the trail and walk north a very short distance before the trail turns westward. The trail crosses a footbridge over the lake outlet and it becomes immediately obvious why this is such a popular destination. The views from the northern part of the trail are amazing—at least on a clear day. Viewpoints are scattered about along this end of the lake, some with wooden benches. You'll also pass some stairs that go up. Walk past the old-growth cedars and take a moment to drink in their massive girth—these are really big trees. The trail crosses a boggy spot on a long wooden boardwalk—the first of many throughout the loop. These raised sections protect the fragile ground beneath.

As you walk along the trail, the trees tower over head—stately Pacific silver fir, western hemlock with their droopy branches, and ponderosa pines with their easy-to-recognize bark. The trees are just part of the wonder of this trail; they provide such a rich habitat that woodpeckers, jays, sparrows, deer, squirrels, and

© BARBARA I. BOND

looking southward across Lost Lake

chipmunks all call this forest home. Keep an eye out for pileated woodpecker (easy to recognize with their large size and the males' red-crested heads), Townsend's warbler, and mountain chickadee, just to name a few forest species. In the cavities of dead trees, you may find Vaux's swift.

The forest floor adds another level of complexity to this fun hike. Wildflowers bloom throughout the summer months. The contrast of vanilla leaf, queen's cup, false Solomon's seal, and inside-out flowers break up the deep greens and in the wet spots you are likely to spot devils' club and smell the skunk cabbage.

During the second mile you will pass a private cabin on the right. Please respect the No Trespassing signs. The trail winds around southwesterly to then head southeast along the western shoreline. Here you will find yourself right down at the waterline. Take a look east across the lake at Lost Lake Butte; there is a steep 2-mile trail to the top if you want to do more. The trail crosses a rock slide, then heads back into the cool, dark forest. As you round the southern tip of the lake, you will pass a pavilion and then a trail sign for the old growth interpretive trail. Finally, the trail winds northward along the eastern shore with many access points from various camping loops that also offer opportunities for swimming. There are numerous boardwalks along the eastern shore with accessible and barrier-free docks for fishing. Finish up after walking on another boardwalk and going up some steps.

Options

Lost Lake Butte can be reached by taking a 2-mile trail that climbs nearly 1,300 feet to the small summit. The path travels mostly through a forested area, but you can get some fine views from the top by exploring a bit. The trailhead is on the right as you head towards the exit on the road and it is marked with a sign.

Directions

From Portland, drive east on I-84 to exit 62 in Hood River. Head right, following the Highway 30 business route for 1 mile before turning right on 13th Street. Follow signs to Odell through several dogleg turns before reaching a bridge over the West Fork of the Hood River. From here, head right again, passing Tucker Park, then continuing 6 miles to the abandoned lumber mill at Dee. Veer right again, cross the Middle Fork of the Hood River, then follow signs for 14 miles to Lost Lake.

Alternatively, from Portland drive east for 37 miles on U.S. 26. At Zigzag, turn left onto East Lolo Pass Road (turns into Forest Road 18 in 4 miles) and drive 10.5 miles to Lolo Pass. Turn right on Forest Road 1810 and take this road for 5.5 miles, at which point it turns into Forest Road 18 once more. Drive ahead to Lost Lake Road/Forest Road 13 and a stop sign. Turn left (signed) for Lost Lake. From here, follow the signs to the entrance.

Information and Contact

Leashed dogs are allowed. For more information, contact Mount Hood National Forest, Hood River Ranger District (6780 Hwy. 35, Parkdale, OR 97041, 541/352-6002, www.fs.fed.us and choose "Oregon" and "Mount Hood" from the drop-down menus). Lost Lake Resort and Campground are not managed by the Forest Service. For hiking information, directions, and trail maps visit http://lostlakeresort.org. There is a day-use fee ($7), payable at the entry kiosk. From there, follow signs to "day use area," and turn right at the second junction to roadside parking near the small camp store. A second parking area is located across the outlet stream, past the store.

7 VISTA RIDGE–CAIRN BASIN   BEST ◖

Mount Hood Wilderness

🏕 🥾 🛫 🎒 🌼 🦌 👫

Level: Moderate   **Total Distance:** 8.7 miles round-trip

Hiking Time: 4.5 hours   **Elevation Change:** 1,700 feet

Summary: This short yet rugged alpine hike provides great access to flower-filled meadows with views of the ridges, glaciers, and pinnacles on Mount Hood's north side.

There is no shortage of beauty on Oregon's highest peak. In fact, you can find a spectacular alpine hike just about anywhere near timberline on this dormant volcano. Visiting the north side of Mount Hood will expose you to a part of the mountain with unique geologic formations, rushing waters from glacier-fed creeks, and a real adventurous feel. The hike loops through Cairn Basin, passes the historic stone shelter, and returns through Eden Park. A 1922 camping party from Hood River named the two alpine meadows, Vista Ridge, and Cathedral Ridge as they explored the northwest corner of the mountain. Now you can lead your own exploration though this special place.

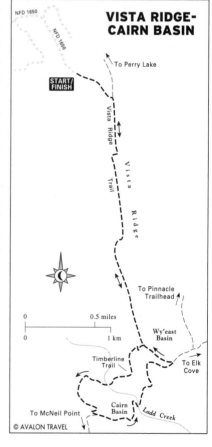

Start out on the Vista Ridge Trail 626 by hiking 0.2 mile up the old rock-strewn roadbed from the parking area to the junction with the recently restored Old Vista Ridge Trail marked by a wooden sign on a tree. Volunteers from portlandhikers.org have cleared this trail. A wilderness map and self-issue permit station are ahead. Fill out a permit and continue along in the dense forest of fir, hemlock, and pine. Huckleberry bushes line the trail and wildflowers bring color to the green landscape. At this elevation you will see avalanche lilies right after the snow melts. Wild strawberry and lupine also thrive here and will accompany you for most of the hike. While on Vista Ridge, watch for deer and a variety of squirrels, chipmunks, or pika. There are usually a wide variety of birds flitting amongst the tall trees before you break out of the forest—gray or scrub jays, woodpeckers, or mountain chickadee.

Mount Hood from Cairn Basin

The trail climbs steeply in spots the next 0.5 mile or so, then makes a zigzag to continue southward towards the Timberline Trail 600. Continue up through the forest gaining 1,300 feet to meet the signed trail junction on the right for Eden Park. You are now beginning to see glimpses of Mount Hood ahead through the thinning trees; keep going straight ahead 0.3 mile more to reach the junction with the Timberline Trail. At the signed junction, turn right for Cairn Basin. (If you have a moment, it's worth a little side trip in the opposite direction: Turn left to hike east a short distance for a glimpse of the stunning basin below the ridgeline to Barrett Spur, a rocky ridge between the Ladd and Coe Glaciers. After enjoying the views, retrace your steps to the signed junction to continue on to Cairn Basin.)

Once you are back heading west on the Timberline Trail, the trees thin even more as you head towards Cairn Basin. You may see lots of pink mountain heather, western pasqueflower, lupine, and gnarled whitebark pine. Early-season hikers may see a carpet of avalanche lilies. You'll drop down a moment before traversing across the loose, ashy soil characteristic of these glacial basins. Look north for views of Mounts St. Helens, Adams, and sometimes Rainier along the horizon. Glance east for a moment for a good open view of Mount Hood, too. The bright red of Indian paintbrush is interspersed among the small trees. Cross below a boulder field; then descend to cross Ladd Creek. You will likely find a log to walk across, use caution just the same. Look around the channel carved by the runoff; it's an impressive reminder of the fragility of this landscape. Ascend the bank on the other side, heading towards the shelter. You'll now cross a series of meadows as you descend towards the Cairn Basin rock shelter. After exploring the shelter, continue past it to a pretty meadow-always a good lunch spot—before heading to Eden Park. In a short distance is the signed trail junction; turn right to Eden Park. If you go straight ahead, you will eventually reach Timberline Lodge.

The 1.5-mile return trail through Eden Park drops you down to the boggy meadows past a rock slide and countless Indian paintbrush and pink mountain heather. On the way down you get a nice clear view down to the thick green meadows criss-crossed by tiny streams and ringed by trees. If there are hikers down there, you can easily see them as they make their way along the trail. Once you reach Eden Park, note that this is a particularly fragile area; try to stay on the main trail despite the numerous side trails. As you head east, you will again descend slightly to cross Ladd Creek (there is no footbridge) and then climb back up the other side to wind uphill through the trees back to the junction with the Vista Ridge Trail. As you contour along just prior to the trail junction, you have open views north and may see Laurance Lake in the near distance. At the signed junction, turn left and hike 2.5 miles back to the trailhead.

Options
To enjoy a shorter hike, use the Old Vista Ridge Trail 626A to visit the tiny Perry Lake. This trail takes off north from the signed trailhead near the wilderness information sign. There are a few hundred feet of climbing to be done during the first 0.5 mile. The forest through here has some big trees and even though much of the blowdown has been removed, you should still be prepared to climb over a few downed trees. Around 1.4 miles the trail takes a sharp turn east to continue gently up and down towards Perry Lake, which is at the end of an old road. The round-trip total for the lake visit is about 5.4 miles.

Directions
From Portland, drive east on U.S. 26 for 37 miles. At Zigzag, turn left onto East Lolo Pass Road and drive 10.5 miles, continuing as it turns into Forest Road 18. Drive 3.3 miles to the junction with Forest Road 16, then turn right and drive 5.5 miles. At the signed junction with Forest Road 1650, turn right and drive to the trailhead at the end of the road. The parking lot is small and fills up on nice weekends.

Information and Contact
Leashed dogs are allowed. For more information, contact Mount Hood National Forest, Hood River Ranger District (6780 Hwy. 35, Parkdale, OR 97041, 541/352-6002, www.fs.fed.us and choose "Oregon" and "Mount Hood" from the drop-down menus). For maps, use Green Trails 462 Mount Hood, Geo-Graphics Mount Hood Wilderness Map, or USGS Mount Hood—North. The Geo-Graphics map has a good road map on the 1:125,000 recreation map; the 1:30,000 wilderness map is for trails.

8 TAMANAWAS FALLS
Mount Hood National Forest

Level: Easy

Total Distance: 3.8 miles round-trip

Hiking Time: 2 hours

Elevation Change: 400 feet

Summary: Hike along the roaring East Fork Hood River and Cold Spring Creek to view a spectacular waterfall.

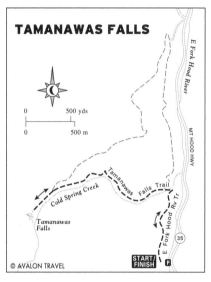

The Mount Hood National Forest has many waterfalls worthy of a visit. On a hot summer day, there is nothing better than a short hike to a spray-filled bowl to experience the best of what nature has to offer. The hike to Tamanawas Falls takes you up close to a roaring waterfall in a beautiful forested setting. A classic curtain waterfall, the water falls nearly 100 feet before splashing on the rocks below. Tamanawas Falls plunges over a basalt rim crashing to a dramatic splash pool in a mossy bowl along Cold Spring Creek.

The trail begins west of the parking area and almost immediately crosses the milky waters of the East Fork Hood River, home to salmon, trout, and ducks, as well as belted kingfishers. After a wooden footbridge is a sign for the East Fork Hood River Trail 650. Turn right on the trail and head north along the river 0.5 mile to the junction with the Tamanawas Falls Trail 650A. Turn left on the trail. Enjoy the riches of the forest as you make your way west to the falls. Huge Douglas-fir, stands of smaller lodgepole pine, and western white pine fill in the canopy. The forest floor has carpets of delicate twinflower interspersed with vanilla leaf, wintergreen, and Oregon grape. Some spindly rhodies and abundant vine maple make for a complex forest with a beautiful mix of verdant green. Along the ridge trail you may spot deer or hear elk crashing through the forest.

The trail winds along, dropping downhill a bit to cross Cold Spring Creek on a second footbridge. Pass a huge boulder that blocks the trail by going around on the left, and continue upstream along the rushing waters of the creek. As you pass, you will see lots of small rocky falls as the creek heads downhill.

Plenty of wildflowers bloom along the trail and even in late summer you can see bright pink penstemon, purple asters, and occasional columbine. The trail stays right and climbs to a "Y" at 1.5 miles, just before the boulder field. Keep left for the 0.4 mile to the falls. You will make a quick switchback or two through a field of huge boulders. Note the ruined bridge below on the creek—the trail was rerouted. The last 100 yards or so lead to the northern side of the bowl and a tremendous view of the loud falls. Return the way you came. Note that there is a lot of rock at the bottom of the cliffs that make up the walls of the bowl. Please don't sit below the cliffs and be sure to watch for rockfall.

© BARBARA I. BOND

approaching the falls

Options

You can hike a longer loop by retracing your steps to the junction nearly 0.5 mile from the falls. Turn uphill and walk up some switchbacks to gain the ridge. You will pass a signed junction for Elk Meadows, keep right on the Elk Meadows Trail 645 to continue about 1.25 miles northerly towards Polallie Campground. You will descend to reach the East Fork Trail just west and above Polallie Trailhead. Turn right and hike the East Fork Trail 1.6 miles back to the trailhead where you started. The loop total is about 5.6 miles.

Directions

From Portland, drive east on I-84 to exit 64. Turn right and follow signs for Highway 35 and Mount Hood. Follow Highway 35 for 28 miles to the pullout between mile marker 73 and 72 for the East Fork Trailhead. There is a trailhead sign with map, portable restroom in summer, and parking for at least 20 vehicles.

Information and Contact

A Northwest Forest Pass ($5) is required. Leashed dogs are allowed. For more information, contact Mount Hood National Forest, Hood River Ranger District (6780 Hwy. 35, Parkdale, OR 97041, 541/352-6002, www.fs.fed.us and choose "Oregon" and "Mount Hood" from the drop-down menus). For maps, use Green Trails 462 Mount Hood.

9 LOOKOUT MOUNTAIN
Badger Creek Wilderness

Level: Easy

Hiking Time: 1.5 hours

Total Distance: 2.5 miles round-trip

Elevation Change: 500 feet

Summary: This short trail leads to a former mountaintop lookout site with unobstructed views of Mount Hood and several other Cascade volcanoes. Add in rich displays of purple lupine and Indian paintbrush, and you have a dream destination.

The Badger Creek Wilderness is a mid-elevation gem tucked along the eastern border of the Mount Hood National Forest. Just inside the wilderness is the High Prairie Trail 493; it's short and sweet. Climbing just 500 feet from the flower-filled start at High Prairie and ending on Mount Hood's nearest-neighbor peak, it's a wonderful introduction to the Badger Creek Wilderness. Badger Creek is home to rich forests of cedars, true fir, mountain hemlock, and lodgepole pine.

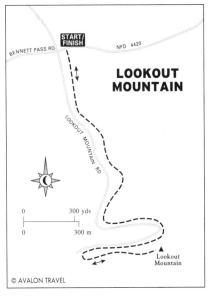

The trail enters the wilderness at the trailhead at the northern edge of High Prairie. Following an old road that's now a pleasant trail, you walk through beautiful flower-filled meadows as the trail gently climbs. During the first 0.7 mile, the trail climbs almost imperceptibly through the fir and hemlock trees. Purple asters, hellebore, and silvery snags accent the green of the forest. It's quite a contrast to the deep red volcanic rock that most of the mountainside is made of. As you climb southward towards the summit ridge, you reach an open area around 0.8 mile where the road continues to the left and the trail heads south and steeply uphill. Keep going straight uphill, glancing west for some increasingly good views of Mount Hood through the trees. The trail reaches the top of the ridge; continue to the edge of the gray rock for a magnificent viewpoint. Then backtrack to the trail, which now turns eastward up the final 0.3 mile to the top. The trail heads up through the thinning trees atop the west summit

© BARBARA I. BOND

Mount Hood from Lookout Mountain

ridge. There are a lot of huge weathered snags along here, and some brilliant lupine blooms.

Pass a campsite and then reach a clearing with a trail sign to the summit. On the summit are two old foundations-a fire lookout and a storage barn—dating back to the 1930s. Pink mountain heather, whitebark pine, and buttercups add color to this beautiful viewpoint. You'll want to pause and marvel at the impressive sight of Mount Hood. The dense forest of the Badger Creek Wilderness lies to the south as does Badger Lake, and in the distance, Mount Jefferson. When you descend the ridge you can also explore some rock outcrops or just enjoy more views along the south side of the ridge. Retrace your steps back to the car.

Options

Just below the east face of Lookout Mountain is Senecal Spring. It's a water source if you need it, or just a short diversion before hiking back to your car. Turn left on the Divide Trail 458 as you come off the summit. Turn in a short distance onto the spur trail 458C to the springs. Return the way you came and descend back to your car at High Prairie.

Directions

From Portland, drive east on U.S. 26 past Government Camp to Highway 35. Turn on Highway 35 towards Hood River. Drive 13.5 miles east to Dufur Mill Road/Forest Road 44 and turn right. Drive on Forest Road 44 for 3.8 miles and turn right on Lookout Mountain Road/Forest Road 4410. Drive on the gravel Forest Road 4410 for about 5 miles to a "T" intersection with Bennett Pass Road. Turn left and drive 150 yards to the trailhead on the left. There is a vault toilet and room for at least a dozen vehicles. A Northwest Forest Pass ($5) is required.

Alternatively, drive east from Portland on I-84 to exit 64/Hood River. Follow the signs for Mount Hood and drive south on Highway 35 for about 25 miles to Dufur Mill Road/Forest Road 44. Follow this road to a "T" intersection and turn left; continue 150 yards to the trailhead. This is a longer drive but includes a long stretch on the interstate, which some may prefer.

Information and Contact

A Northwest Forest Pass ($5) is required. Leashed dogs are allowed. For more information, contact the Mount Hood National Forest, Barlow Ranger District (780 NE Court St., Dufur, OR 97021, 541/467-2291, www.fs.fed.us, search for "Barlow Ranger trail conditions"). For maps, use USGS Badger Lake, USDA Forest Service Columbia Wilderness and Badger Creek Wilderness, or Green Trails 462 Mount Hood. If you are exploring any trails heading east/southeast, use Green Trails 463 Flag Point.

10 GUMJUWAC-BADGER CREEK LOOP

Mount Hood National Forest and Badger Creek Wilderness

Level: Strenuous

Total Distance: 11.7 miles round-trip

Hiking Time: 6 hours

Elevation Change: 2,800 feet

Summary: Expect lots of solitude hiking through old-growth trees within the quiet wilderness southeast of Mount Hood.

The Badger Creek Wilderness would be more popular if it wasn't in the shadow of nearby Mount Hood. Still, the mid-elevation wilderness offers hikers and backpackers a chance to travel quiet trails through ponderosa pine woodland, true fir, and subalpine meadows.

The Gumjuwac Trail 480 begins climbing quickly and doesn't let up for the first mile and 1,000 feet of gain. The trail switchbacks up a steep slope through huge, old trees until reaching a nice viewpoint after another 0.5 mile. After breathing deep, continue through the trees to the saddle at 2.4 miles. Cross the road and continue on the trail to the left of the old sign with the history of the name "Gumjuwac." There is a trail sign on a tree as the trail resumes. The trail wanders a bit through some meadows and washout areas and is littered with downed trees. Descend through alternating forest and meadows to the signed junction with the Badger Creek Trail 479. This is the main trail in the wilderness. Turn right and cross the creek on a nice wooden footbridge and begin a very scenic 2-mile hike to Badger Lake, which is stocked with rainbow trout.

The trail passes through stands of huge old cedar, crosses a couple of springs, and winds upstream along Badger Creek. There are wildflowers even in late summer and you might even find a ripe huckleberry or two. Both deer and elk travel the forest of Badger Creek Wilderness on trail towards Badger Lake. Listen for woodpeckers, gray jays, and scrub jays among the big trees. This is a moist forest and the forest floor is covered with green; note that the trail can be overgrown in places. A side trail on the left offers a short detour for a view of this pretty lake from the dam at the northwest corner.

© BARBARA I. BOND

Badger Lake

   Resume hiking west on the Badger Creek Trail 0.2 mile to the signed junction with the Divide Trail. Turn right and hike uphill to reach the Gumjuwac Saddle. This trail climbs steeply for 0.75 mile then crests around 5,400 feet. The trail then continues 1.25 miles more to the saddle. From the saddle retrace your steps.

Options

For a straight out-and-back, turn around at Gumjuwac Saddle. You get to enjoy the fine views of Mount Hood on the way up and still have some energy when you get back down. The round-trip distance is 5 miles and has an elevation gain of 1,700 feet.

Directions

Drive east from Portland on I-84 to exit 64/Hood River. Follow the signs for Mount Hood and drive south on Highway 35 for about 28 miles to the small trailhead on the left just before the bridge over the East Fork Hood River. There is room for two or three cars.

Information and Contact

Leashed dogs are allowed. For more information, contact the Mount Hood National Forest, Barlow Ranger District (780 NE Court St., Dufur, OR 97021, 541/467-2291, www.fs.fed.usand search for "Barlow Ranger trail conditions"). For maps use USGS Badger Lake, USDA Forest Service Columbia Wilderness and Badger Creek Wilderness, or Green Trails 462 Mount Hood.

11 GNARL RIDGE   BEST ◖

Mount Hood National Forest

🏕 🦌 ✈ 🌿

Level: Strenuous   **Total Distance:** 11.7 miles round-trip

Hiking Time: 6.5 hours   **Elevation Change:** 2,700 feet

Summary: Gnarl Ridge offers amazing views of Mount Hood's upper southeast corner.

The southeast corner of Mount Hood is home to glacier-fed creeks, sharp ridges, subalpine meadows, and stunning views of Oregon's highest mountain. This is the land of the dwarfed and misshapen pines that adapt to survive high winds and heavy winter snow. This hike really shows off a wide range of terrain—from flower-filled meadows to silty, roaring creeks that rush down highly eroded channels.

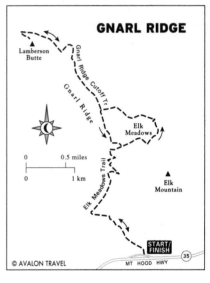

The nearly flat first 1.1 mile of the trail follows Clark Creek upstream to a wooden footbridge. Enjoy hiking past more huckleberry bushes than you can imagine; in late August, they are loaded with tasty berries. Brilliant blue lupine, lodgepole pine, and hemlock round out the beautiful surroundings. At the bridge is a self-issue permit box; fill out a permit and then cross the creek to continue 0.5 mile to the junction with the Newton Creek Trail. A trail sign on the right gives trail mileage to the Elk Meadows perimeter—another 1.5 miles to go. Continue ahead on the Elk Meadows Trail 645 0.1 mile to the crossing of Newton Creek. Although the milky water rushes impressively down the highly eroded channel from the glacier above, there is no permanent footbridge. Trail crews trimmed down logs to make a decent temporary footbridge for a easier crossing. It's still wise to use caution crossing glacier-fed creeks, as they are very cold and usually filled with rocks and debris. Climb up away from the creek and begin an ascent of long switchbacks through some really large Douglas-fir, tall silver snags, thimbleberry bushes, and lots of wildflowers. Pass yet another set of signed trail junctions and hike ahead to the perimeter trail at about 2.9 miles.

Turn right and head around the meadows, now evident on the left through the
trees. Avoid any side trails that wander
into the meadow—they destroy this
fragile landscape. There is a main trail
in a short distance to the shelter. Stay
on the perimeter trail and continue
around to the junction with the Gnarl
Ridge Cutoff Trail 652A at mile 4.2.
Follow this up to the Timberline Trail
600 marked by a sign and turn right
towards Cloud Cap. Follow the classic
round-the-mountain trail 1.5 miles as
it winds in and out of forested areas,
crosses a dry creek bed, and enters the
cool wonder of subalpine and alpine territory. The trees thin and become bent
from the harsh life at 6,000 feet. Flowers are smaller and more fragile and the

Elk Meadows and Mount Hood

thin soil supports less growth. The rich duff of the forest becomes a sandy, rocky
trail as the landscape opens up to views of the mountain ahead. Deer and elk
may be seen from the trails around Elk Meadows, and look for pika among the
rocks on the upper trails. Gray jays seem to congregate in the trees along the
lower section of Gnarl Ridge. The Newton Clark Glacier fills the SE corner of
the upper mountain.

Continue along Gnarl Ridge to an open, flat spot with thick old whitebark
pines that are misshapen from years of harsh conditions. You'll pass Lamberson
Butte just as you enter the flat at 6.6 miles. To reach a nice viewpoint near the
top of the butte, make a hairpin turn left onto a very faint trail. Use care because the trail is covered with loose rock, scree, and talus. Enjoy the views and
descend carefully back to the Timberline Trail. Reverse your path back to the
Gnarl Ridge–Timberline Trail junction. Turn left and follow the Gnarl Ridge
Trail 1 mile down to the Elk Meadows Trail. You emerge at a trail junction you
passed on the way to the perimeter trail. Turn right on the Elk Meadows Trail
and return to the trailhead.

Options

For an incredibly beautiful route, take the perimeter trail all the way around Elk
Meadows. From the Elk Meadows/perimeter trail junction, hike the perimeter

trail counterclockwise, ignoring any trail junctions. Retrace your steps back to the trailhead for total distance of 7.2 miles.

Directions

From Portland, drive 45 miles east on U.S. 26 past Government Camp to Highway 35. Turn left on Highway 35 and drive 8 miles to the Clark Creek Sno-Park on the left. (A landmark on the right is the turnout for Teacup Nordic Area.) Turn in and drive about halfway around and park. The trailhead is on the left. There is a vault toilet.

Information and Contact

Leashed dogs are allowed. For more information, contact Mount Hood National Forest, Hood River Ranger District (6780 Hwy. 35, Parkdale, OR 97041, 541/352-6002, www.fs.fed.us and choose "Oregon" and "Mount Hood" from the drop-down menus). For maps use Green Trails 462 Mount Hood.

12 PALMATEER POINT-TWIN LAKES
Mount Hood National Forest

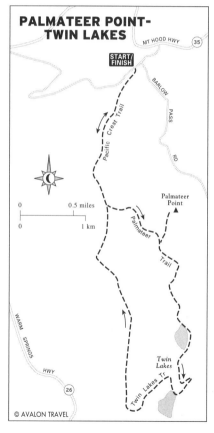

Level: Moderate

Total Distance: 9.2 miles round-trip

Hiking Time: 4.5 hours

Elevation Change: 1,500 feet

Summary: Visit historic Barlow Pass while hiking to a magnificent Mount Hood viewpoint, then continue on to serene Twin Lakes for a bonus stop on this alpine adventure.

Samuel Barlow was an Oregon pioneer who created the road around Mount Hood that's still in use today. Barlow Pass, on the Mount Hood loop, was Barlow's path over the Cascade Crest. It's still a popular meeting place for outdoor enthusiasts and an important starting point for the Pacific Crest National Scenic Trail. The hike to Palmateer Point and Twin Lakes begins on the Pacific Crest Trail through luscious subalpine terrain. In summer lupine, penstemon, and lilies thrive amongst the lodgepole pine and mountain hemlock. Huckleberry bushes are abundant; if it's late summer you may even find a ripe berry or two. Deer can often be found on the trail or in the nearby woods, while gray jays and the squawking call of Steller's jay may accompany your hike.

From the trailhead, enter the big trees and hike south along the Pacific Crest Trail for 1.78 miles to a signed trail junction. You'll climb steadily for about the first 1.4 miles, before descending from an elevation of around 4,500 feet to turn left on the Palmateer Trail 482. In mid-summer, penstemon and lupine line the trail. The trail heads eastward for 0.9 mile, passing through beautiful, flower-filled meadows to a side trail to Palmateer Point. Turn left and ascend for the views—Mount Hood starts showing up off the north side of the point. Looking eastward as you cross to the north side, you see the dense forest and ridges of the Badger Creek Wilderness. The little summit is mostly open and has some scattered lupine, mountain heather, and yarrow.

When you've soaked in the view, descend back to the trail and continue south to reach Twin Lakes. First you drop down to cross Palmateer Creek. There is no footbridge, but helpful hikers usually lash some logs together. From the creek drainage ascend once more, passing meadows filled with flowers, lots of bear grass, and even more huckleberries. Less than 0.5 mile from the creek, the trail jogs right a short distance to meet the Twin Lakes Trail 495 junction. Turn left to head south to the upper lake. There is a sign noting Bird Butte Summit's 4,560 foot elevation on a tree. Descend through the trees to the north side of Upper Twin Lake and keep left to continue along the east shore and reach Lower Twin Lake. Contour across the west of a butte for about 0.5 mile; the trail then makes a dogleg, ending at the 0.9-mile lakeshore loop trail. The lake has camping spots and is a good spot for a swim or picnic. You'll wind around the north side and back to the Pacific Crest Trail. After ignoring a couple of trail junctions, turn north onto the Pacific Crest Trail for the 4-mile return.

Options

For a day on the water, take the Pacific Crest Trail south to the trail junction for Lower Twin Lake. Turn left and make your way 0.7 mile down to the lake; hike the lakeshore trail if you want to find just the right spot for relaxing. Retrace your steps to the trailhead when you are done, for a total hiking distance of about 9.4 miles.

Directions

From Portland, drive 45 miles east on U.S. 26, past Government Camp, to Highway 35. Turn left on Highway 35. Drive about 2.5 miles to Forest Road 3531 at Barlow Pass. Turn right and drive a short distance to the well-marked trailhead.

Information and Contact

A Northwest Forest Pass ($5) is required. For more information, contact Mount Hood National Forest, Hood River Ranger District (6780 Hwy. 35, Parkdale, OR 97041, 541/352-6002, www.fs.fed.us and choose "Oregon" and "Mount Hood" from the drop-down menus). For maps, use Green Trails 462 Mount Hood and Mount Wilson 494.

13 TIMBERLINE TRAIL– PARADISE PARK LOOP

BEST 🄲

Mount Hood Wilderness

🏕 ✈ 🌿 🐾

Level: Strenuous

Total Distance: 12.5 miles round-trip

Hiking Time: 6.5 hours

Elevation Change: 2,900 feet

Summary: Paradise Park, on the west side of Mount Hood, may be the most well-known hiking destination in Mount Hood National Forest, and deservedly so. The alpine meadows here have fantastic wildflower displays after the snowmelt.

Mount Hood is considered by many to be Portland's playground. Miles of trails in the national forest and wilderness give hikers a huge range of opportunity. Mount Hood is also home to one of Oregon's most famous WPA-era lodges—Timberline Lodge. It's a great starting point for your hike on the mountain.

The Timberline Trail encircles Mount Hood and also parallels the Pacific Crest Trail in some sections. The hike to Paradise Park proceeds west along the Timberline/Pacific Crest Trail and it really follows the

timberline. You'll see subalpine fir, western hemlock, and whitebark pine along the trail as it meanders near 6,000 feet in elevation amongst an alpine wonderland. The stark beauty of the alpine zone isn't for everyone, but for those who feel the call of the wide-open vistas and airy ridges of timberline, this hike is for you.

Walk up along the right side of Timberline Lodge to catch a paved road 0.2 mile to the signed junction for the Pacific Crest Trail. The sign boldly announces "Canada 550"! Turn left (but rest assured that this hike will not go quite that far today). Still, you may catch some Pacific Crest Trail thru-hikers on their way north. They are recognizable by their (usually) grimy visage, extremely fit and healthy glow, and big backpacks. For today, hike west and then northwest on the Pacific Crest Trail towards Paradise. The first 1.2 miles is a gentle descent to the

Wilderness Boundary and across Little Zigzag Canyon. Check out the flowers already along the trail. From the start it's a bounty of lupine, both broadleaf and the wonderful dwarf varieties. In summer you can really see the flanks of Mount Hood for what they are—crumbling, barren, rock-strewn—but the flowers don't seem to notice. Asters, phlox, and Indian paintbrush are also abundant. Watch for Clark's nutcracker, and even ravens, as you make your way along the first few feet of the Pacific Crest Trail. Other forest birds to watch out for include thrushes, warblers, jays, and the mountain chickadee with its easily recognizable black cap.

There is a self-issue permit box, map, and information sign after you climb back out of Little Zigzag Canyon. You are back in the forest now, and although right near timberline, the forest is full of good-sized trees. A short distance later, the trail to Hidden Lake shoots off downhill on the left. The duff is thick along the trail and odd-looking pine sap appears in places. Approaching Zigzag Canyon around 2.8 miles is a nice viewpoint before the trail makes a sharp left turn. It's quite a sight gazing at the scoured gray rock of the canyon. Across the chasm, the rim has fir and hemlocks that seem startlingly green. The trail drops down into the canyon and crosses the Zigzag River. Pink monkey flowers cover the rocky banks near the river. There is no bridge; walking upstream usually leads to a safe crossing on rocks. In early summer, the runoff can be treacherous, though, and is higher in the afternoon on hot summer days. This is a good place to filter water if you didn't bring much along. Ascend the other side of the canyon past huckleberry and ground-hugging queen's cup, and around 3.7 miles meet up with the trail junction to Paradise Park. Turn right and begin a 2.6-mile journey past some of the most spectacular flower displays around. The trail heads up towards the upper canyon and then turns back westerly to zigzag through Paradise Park. With the mountain rising up ahead, you pass fields of lupine and asters, glacier lilies with their nodding yellow blooms, and bear grass. Trees occasionally dot the otherwise multicolored landscape. Midway along the Paradise Park loop, you will pass the remains of a rock shelter before winding around to continue north through beautiful, open meadows with stunning views of the mountain. Watch for the cartoonish seed heads of western pasqueflower amongst the purple lupine. You'll head back through a forested area to meet the Pacific Crest Trail junction at 6 miles. Turn left and follow the Pacific Crest Trail back to Timberline Lodge in about 5.4 miles. The reverse hike has just as many great views and you may see some of the flowers you missed on the way out.

Options

The Pacific Crest Trail can seem long after the amazing wildflowers and open meadows of Paradise Park. You can still catch a ton of alpine wildflowers and stunning mountain views by just hiking around Timberline Lodge. Hike up the paved access road behind the lodge to the Pacific Crest Trail–Timberline Trail junction. Turn left and take a relaxing stroll as far as you want—the wildflower displays begin almost immediately. Repair to Timberline Lodge afterwards and drink in some of that historic ambiance. If you must have a destination in mind, head to the wilderness boundary at 1.2 miles.

Directions

From Portland, drive 44 miles east on U.S. 26. Just past Government Camp, turn left at the signed turnoff for Timberline Lodge. Follow the Timberline Access Road 6 miles to Timberline Lodge.

Information and Contact

Leashed dogs are allowed. For more information, contact Mount Hood National Forest Zigzag Ranger District (70220 E. Hwy. 26, Zigzag, OR 97049, 503/622-3191 or www.fs.fed.us and choose "Oregon" and "Mount Hood" from the drop-down menus). For maps use Geo-Graphics Mount Hood Wilderness and/or Green Trails Government Camp (no. 461). For current conditions stop by the Mount Hood Information Center (24403 E. Welches Rd., Ste. 103, Welches, OR 97067, 503/622-5560).

14 TOM DICK AND HARRY MOUNTAIN
Mount Hood National Forest

Level: Moderate   **Total Distance:** 6.6 miles round-trip

Hiking Time: 3 hours   **Elevation Change:** 1,400 feet

Summary: Great views of Mount Hood and surrounding peaks await on this lovely alpine hike.

The Mount Hood National Forest gets a lot of visitors for a reason: its spectacular scenery near a major urban center. The Mirror Lake Trail, which leads to its namesake lake and to the top of Tom Dick and Harry Mountain, is a very popular hike. The short hike into the lake yields immediate gratification to those seeking an idyllic alpine setting. The real payoff comes when you invest in another 1.8 miles of mostly uphill hiking to reach the western edge of Tom Dick and Harry Mountain. The views of nearby Mount Hood

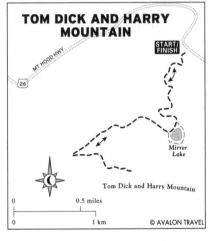

TOM DICK AND HARRY MOUNTAIN

Mirror Lake

Tom Dick and Harry Mountain

0   0.5 miles

0   1 km

© AVALON TRAVEL

will take your breath away and on a clear day it's easy to see some Cascade neighbors including Mount Jefferson and Mounts Adams and Rainier.

Cross Camp Creek on the bridge from the parking area and enter the deep forest typical of the western Mount Hood National Forest. After passing the picnic table and garbage can on the left, you begin the climb to the lake on a wide dirt trail surrounded by dense second-growth forest. This part of the forest has many huge cedar stumps with springboard cuts in them. They are remnants from logging days of old.

Halfway to the lake, you will cross another bridge and continue the gradual climb to reach the northern lakeshore trail junction in 1.5 miles. Continue ahead as the trail climbs past the western shore on the way to Tom Dick and Harry Mountain. (Note that along the shore are many fenced areas and clear paths marking camping spots. This area is so heavily used that restoration efforts are underway. Please respect all closures around the lakeshore.) Pass the sign and trail junction for the lake loop and continue on the trail as it heads west and across some rock slides that give great views of Mount Hood. The

© BARBARA I. BOND

Mirror Lake and Mount Hood

forest gradually becomes more alpine with thinner trees and changing canopy as you climb. The trail reaches a huge rock pile where a sharp turn east signals the real climbing is about to begin.

As the trail begins to approach the west ridge of the mountain, it becomes more rocky, bear grass and rhododendron dot the forest floor, and whitebark pine appear. The final 100 yards switchback up to the now-evident ridgetop, as you push upwards glance left at the Mirror Lake basin and up at Mount Hood's heavily forested lower flank. Once you reach the top of the ridge, pick your spot and take a break with some of the best views in the area. In spring and fall, you can continue southeast along the ridge for a short distance, but don't venture on in summer months due to nesting peregrine falcons.

After soaking in the view, return the way you came.

Options

A short option is to hike the trail to Mirror Lake and circumnavigate the lake on the 0.4-mile lakeshore trail. From the parking area, turn left at the first lakeshore trail junction and hike the lakeshore clockwise. On the western shore is a popular photography site where you can get a nice reflection of Mount Hood when the water is still. The trail on the west side of the lake passes through a boggy area; a two-plank boardwalk leads to the main trail junction. Turn right to get back to the parking lot.

Directions

From Portland, drive 40 miles east on U.S. 26. The trailhead is on the south side of U.S. 26 at milepost 51.7, 1 mile west of Government Camp. The main parking lot and an overflow lot are further east on U.S. 26.

Information and Contact

A Northwest Forest Pass ($5) is required. Leashed dogs are allowed. For more information, contact Mount Hood National Forest Zigzag Ranger District (70220 E. Hwy. 26, Zigzag, OR 97049, 503/622-3191 or www.fs.fed.us and choose "Oregon" and "Mount Hood" from the drop-down menus). For maps, use Geo-Graphics Mount Hood Wilderness and/or Green Trails Government Camp (no. 461). For current conditions, stop by the Mount Hood Information Center (24403 E. Welches Rd., Ste. 103, Welches, OR 97067, 503/622-5560).

15 CLACKAMAS RIVER TRAIL
Mount Hood National Forest

Level: Moderate

Total Distance: 7.8 miles one-way

Hiking Time: 4 hours

Elevation Change: 600 feet

Summary: The Clackamas River Trail offers hikers a year-round low-elevation trail with scenic overlooks and numerous waterfalls.

The Clackamas River cuts a swath through the far southwest corner of the Mount Hood National Forest. Originating south of Mount Hood on Ollalie Butte, the Clackamas travels miles to drain into the Willamette River. Along its course, there are numerous recreation opportunities. Hikers will enjoy this exploration of the Clackamas River and its numerous waterfalls, stream crossings, and dramatic cliffs. This is a wonderful outing in mid-winter, even with a little snow on the trail. In spring the trail is flush with a huge variety of

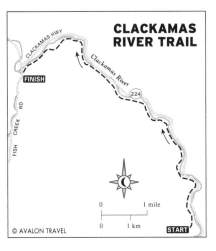

wildflowers. The recommended hike is a one-way trek requiring a car shuttle from the end point of Fish Creek Campground to the Indian Henry trailhead.

Begin walking up the trail from the Indian Henry trailhead parking area. From this southern trailhead you will trace a lazy path northwest along the river channel and then finish with a curve southwest to the Fish Creek trailhead. The forest here, high above the river, is dense and lots of blowdown litters the forest floor. A footbridge crosses a ravine at 0.6 mile, passing the first of many small waterfalls along the trail. The heavy rainfall and thick loamy forest floor create ideal conditions for wildflowers, and you will see a great variety including snow queen and bleeding heart. Shelf fungus and witch's butter also stand out amongst the greenery.

As you continue northward, a series of rocky cliffs line the trail; note the occasional balancing rock perched above. The trail will reach a tunnel of sorts—more like a deeply notched section that goes behind the waterfall around mile 1.7. After enjoying the water display and the numerous saxifrage and sedum growing in the rocks, including the trail passes even more cliffs, which are moist and green in the spring. There are some huge trees along the trail; check out the big western red cedars and Douglas-fir.

In another mile or so, at 2.9 miles, there will be a little spur trail on the right leading to a bench above the river at The Narrows. This is a wonderful place for a snack or a break. Once back on the trail, wind up to the ridge crest and then cross two more streams on the way to the junction with the side trail to Pup Creek Falls at 4.3 miles. Just prior to the side trail, you will have to ford Pup Creek. There are usually logs upstream to make it easier in the spring when there is more water flowing. To view the stunning waterfalls, take this short trail and enjoy the 100-foot falls and dramatic basalt bowl.

the amazing Pup Creek Falls

© BARBARA I. BOND

Back on the trail, you will cross another stream (there is no bridge) and then begin a rocky descent on switchbacks which traverse a steep slope. The trail then passes through a flat area with huge old cedars and some rhododendrons. After yet another stream crossing and more descending, you will pass through a small meadow past some power lines and then begin the descent to the trailhead. With only 0.3 mile to go, the trail changes to an old roadbed as it leads down to the Fish Creek trailhead.

Options

You may want to just visit Pup Creek Falls on an out-and-back hike of 7 miles. Start from the Fish Creek trailhead to avoid the ford of Pup Creek. Hike 3.5 miles until you reach the short side trail to the falls.

Directions

Drive east from Portland on I-84 and take exit 6 to head south on I-205. Drive 8.5 miles to exit 12A/Estacada. Follow the signs to Estacada for about 18 miles.

To reach the Fish Creek Campground, continue southeast on State Route 224 for 16 miles to Forest Road 54. Turn right, cross the bridge, and take the first right into the campground to park.

To reach the trailhead at Indian Henry Campground, continue another 6 miles south and turn right onto Forest Road 4620. The parking area appears in just under 0.5 mile on the right.

Information and Contact

Leashed dogs are allowed. For more information, contact Mount Hood National Forest, Clackamas River Ranger District (595 NW Industrial Way, Estacada, OR 97023, 503/630-6861, www.fs.fed.us and choose "Oregon" and "Mount Hood" from the drop-down menus). For maps, use Green Trails 492 Fish Creek Mountain. When driving, use the USDA Forest Service Mount Hood National Forest map.

16 BAGBY HOT SPRINGS

Mount Hood National Forest

Level: Easy

Hiking Time: 2 hours

Total Distance: 3.5 miles round-trip

Elevation Change: Negligible

Summary: Bagby Hot Springs is a Pacific Northwest landmark – explore a historic bathhouse and hot springs, then enjoy the immense trees of the surrounding forest.

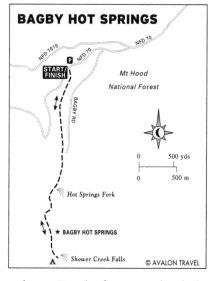

For many Pacific Northwest residents, a visit to one of the local area hot springs is an annual must-do. Bagby Hot Springs is an iconic destination; hot mineral water piped into wooden tubs of varying sizes, in the shade of a forest canopy, offers an experience sure to delight anyone who enjoys outdoor relaxation. The short hike through magnificent old-growth forest and alongside several clear, cold creeks is one almost anyone can enjoy.

This trail, a hiking superhighway, is wide, graveled, and well graded. The path crosses a bridge built of massive timbers and winds its way slightly uphill towards the hot springs. The mature forest boasts Douglas-fir, western hemlock, and cedars in abundance. For the first mile or so, the path heads upriver along Nohorn Creek, which is visible through the trees and from several small viewpoints. About halfway to the second bridge over Hot Springs Fork, a small segmented waterfall drops gracefully into a splash pool. The water looks enticing—and on a hot summer day it's inviting. As you walk on the wide path, take a look around: This is a Pacific Northwest forest in all its big-tree glory—huge Douglas-fir, vine maples to fill in the middle height, and abundant shrubs and wildflowers. Tiny twinflower blooms seem to cover the forest floor along with huckleberry, thimbleberry, rhododendron, and devil's club. Cross the creek on the second footbridge and note some user paths down to the edge of the water. On a really hot valley day the water is a welcome respite—and after a day's hike, the cool water is a balm for hot feet and flagging energy.

soaking tubs at the hot springs

After the bridge the trail gently ascends towards the hot springs. You know you are getting close when the wooden buildings become visible through the trees on the left and a wooden fence appears, discouraging shortcutting. Walk up to the entrance on the left marked by a sign and information display at 1.5 miles. Turn left to walk past some picnic tables and an immense stump and log. If you are going to enjoy a soak, head towards the bathhouses. Changing rooms are located prior to the tubs, but please note that not all bathers wear swimsuits. After your visit, get back to the trail and continue another 0.25 mile through the forest to Shower Creek Falls. This lovely waterfall drops over the rocks to a small pool and grotto. The falls live up to their namesake on hot summer days when a quick "shower" is welcome.

Options

For a day of relaxation, skip the hike extension and just meander to the hot springs and enjoy the waters. On the way back to the trailhead, detour down to the creekside for some more water play; it will be a hit with the kids. It is 3.0 miles round-trip to the hot springs.

Directions

Drive east from Portland on I-84 and take exit 6 to head south on I-205. Drive 8.5 miles to exit 12A/Estacada. Follow the signs about 18 miles to Estacada on

THE
COAST RANGE

© BARBARA I. BOND

BEST HIKES

Hiking Oregon's Coast Range covers a wide

variety of terrain. Here you find families with small children, tourists with a few moments to spend exploring, and valley hikers looking for new territory. The Coastal Uplands extend from the rugged headlands to lower-elevation mountains and offer ready access for recreation. Much of the coast is a temperate rainforest resplendent with the rich green of mosses, lichen, and ferns. Huge Sitka spruce thrive here, taking advantage of the heavy rainfall and mild climate. Moving inland, the middle range, shaped by ancient lava flows and altered by wildfire and the passage of time, offers mid-elevation hikes amongst second-growth Douglas-fir forest and a distinct aura west of the Cascades. Wildlife roam the ridges and valleys of the range. Roosevelt elk run in herds along the Wilson and Nehalem Rivers. Black-tailed deer quietly wander through the forests, as do a wide range of birds, some specifically adapted to nest on the branches of the big trees. Nurse logs litter the forest floor from north to south. In some spots you may see a distinct row of small trees growing – they likely got their start as seedlings along the straight contour of a rotting log. Summer fog keeps many areas cool while inland temperatures soar. When it's hot in the Willamette Valley, you can be sure that hikers will head west to the coast.

The riches of the Coast Range not only allow for a diverse array of wildlife, flora, and fauna, but also create a wide range of activities for outdoor adventurers. Residents of Portland's West Side flock to the Coast Range due to its close proximity and the wide range of easy-access trails ranging from peak-bagging butt-kickers to leisurely river walks. Wildflowers such as violets, vanilla leaf, and western trillium love these damp forests.

Mushrooms grow wonderfully, as do the nonphotosynthetic oddballs like pine drops and candystick. Along State Highway 6, the Wilson River Trail can be climbed by energetic hikers from end to end, although most will want to spend some time revisiting sections of this historic wagon route and envisioning the forest as it was over a century ago. If you are seeking inspiration, tackle the steep trails of Kings Mountain and take in the dramatic views from high above the trees.

Early Oregon explorers visited the Coast Range via the Columbia River. A visit to Ecola State Park is a chance for modern-day explorers to revisit these historic sites along trails and retrace the journeys of old. Further south along the rocky coast are some of the most dramatic scenes in the state, where lava flows created rugged cliffs and dramatic headlands. The public lands of the coast give hikers broad access to these special places. Hiking along the coastal prairie and sweeping headland of Cascade Head is always rewarding. Cape Lookout State Park has a dense forest of Sitka spruce and western hemlock, accentuating the allure of the stunning ocean views.

A drive south along Highway 101 passes a lot of inviting coastal territory. The Siuslaw National Forest encompasses lands from the Pacific Ocean eastward across the crest of the Coast Range to the Willamette Valley. Marys Peak is the high point and offers year-round access for hiking or snowshoeing. The Sitka spruce of this low-elevation forest give way to the dominant Douglas-fir and western hemlock forest that are crisscrossed with recreation trails. A hike in Oregon's Coast Range is sure to satisfy those yearning for easy-to-moderate hiking in scenic splendor.

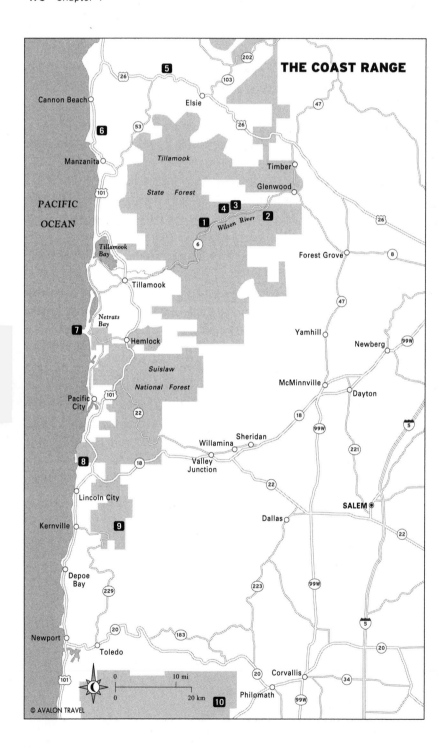

TRAIL NAME	LEVEL	DISTANCE	TIME	ELEVATION	FEATURES	PAGE
1 Wilson River Trail	Moderate	10.8 mi rt	5 hr	950 ft		178
2 University Falls Loop	Easy/Moderate	8.0 mi rt	4 hr	800 ft		181
3 Elk Mountain–Elk Creek Loop	Strenuous	8.4 mi rt	4.5 hr	2,300 ft		184
4 Kings Mountain	Strenuous	5.0 mi rt	3 hr	2,700 ft		187
5 Saddle Mountain	Moderate	5.0 mi rt	2.5–3.0 hr	1,633 ft		190
6 Neahkahnie Mountain	Moderate	8.6 mi rt	4 hr	1,539 ft		193
7 Cape Lookout	Easy	4.8 mi rt	2 hr	525 ft		195
8 Cascade Head	Easy/Moderate	5.0 mi rt	2.5 hr	1,200 ft		197
9 Drift Creek Falls	Easy	3.7 mi rt	2 hr	590 ft		200
10 Marys Peak	Moderate	7.4 mi rt	3.5–4 hr	1,550 ft		203

1 WILSON RIVER TRAIL
Tillamook State Forest

Level: Moderate

Total Distance: 10.8 miles round-trip

Hiking Time: 5 hours

Elevation Change: 950 feet

Summary: Follow this low-elevation trail through the rich Douglas-fir and western redcedar of the Tillamook State Forest.

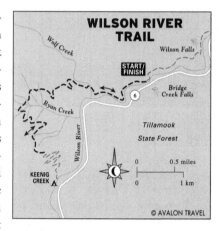

The Wilson River Trail snakes nearly 21 miles from east to west through prime forest of the former Tillamook Burn. This recovering forest was replanted by hand from the 1950s through the 1970s in one of the largest reforestation efforts undertaken in Oregon history. Today's forest contains remaining stands of old growth interspersed with younger stands of planted Douglas-fir. Stands of red alder thrive here; these opportunistic trees fill in disturbed areas and grow throughout the Tillamook State Forest. The Wilson River Trail meanders in and out of creek drainages and past waterfalls, and offers hikers short or long hike choices. Along the trail you may see deer or elk. Frogs and newts are often around in springtime and a variety of birds—Steller's jay, chickadees, woodpeckers, and winter wrens—call this forest home.

The Footbridge Day Use area along State Route 6 is a wonderful starting point for your Wilson River exploration. The Bridge Creek Falls are right across the road and slightly west. To reach the trail, walk west along the road a short distance and then cross the dramatic footbridge high above the river. A short connector trail drops to cross the dry riverbed and head left into the forest to the signed Wilson River Trail junction. Turn left to hike west on the trail alongside lots of sword ferns, giant cedar stumps, and a variety of flowers. Fringe cups are always pretty in springtime, thimbleberry and Oregon grape create a dense thicket, and maidenhair ferns add to the many shades of green. You'll climb gently a few hundred feet, traverse a steep slope, and then wind down 150 feet to cross beautiful Wolf Creek. There are two wooden footbridges at the creek crossing and the area is a great spot for enjoying the forest. There is even a wooden bench that invites one to linger.

a canopy of vine maples across the trail

Once across the creek, the trail climbs and begins a few miles of stream crossings and contours around the Ryan Creek drainage. The trail cuts a swath through the dense growth; in some spots vine maples have grown over the trail, making a natural tunnel. Twisted-stalk, wood sorrel, and anemone thrive along the trail. There are lots of small waterfalls along the streams and dense foliage on the streambanks. Monkey flowers and huge bracken ferns really grow thick near the flowing water. Between 4 and 5 miles there are some burned snags—a solemn reminder of the fires from long ago. When the trail flattens to meet Cedar Butte Road, turn around retrace your steps to the trailhead. Alternatively, if you have a car shuttle you can continue 1.5 miles down to the Keenig Creek trailhead for a 12-mile hike.

Options

For a short add-on, or just a short hike, take the Wilson River Trail east from the footbridge connector junction. Hike 1.5 miles with less than 200 feet of elevation gain to reach the pretty Wilson Falls. The water gently cascades over a rocky ledge as it makes its way down to the Wilson River. The falls are surrounded with thick vine maples, pretty yellow monkey flowers, and several kinds of ferns. Enjoy the falls and then return to the Footbridge Day Use area for a 3.6-mile round-trip.

Visit the Tillamook Forest Center for short hikes, interpretive displays and films, and a chance to view the forest from a replica fire lookout tower. The Forest Center is a stunning complex surrounded by the beautiful forest and a collection of accessible footpaths. The center trails are maintained and wide enough to accommodate a wheelchair. You can even hike west on the Wilson River Trail from here to view the Wilson Falls in 1.7 miles.

Directions

Drive west from Portland on U.S. 26 to exit 53/State Route 6. Turn left (left exit) and drive west 31 miles to the day use parking area at milepost 20.

You can use the Tillamook County public transit system to reach the Tillamook Forest Center from either Tillamook or Portland on State Route 5. For up-to-date information, see www.tillamookbus.com or call 503/815-8283.

Information and Contact

Leashed dogs are allowed. For more information, contact Oregon Department of Forestry, Tillamook District Office (5005 E. 3rd St., Tillamook, OR 97141, 503/824-2545 or 503/359-7402). The Tillamook Forest Center (Wilson River Hwy., State Route 6 at milepost 22, 503/815-6800, www.tillamookforestcenter. com) is always a good source of information, maps, and educational materials. The center is home to nature trails, including a wheelchair-accessible trail; it also has a lookout tower, restrooms, and a theater.

2 UNIVERSITY FALLS LOOP
Tillamook State Forest

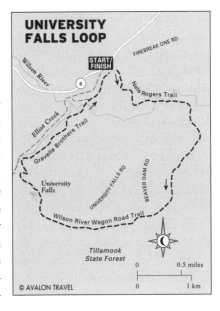

UNIVERSITY FALLS LOOP

Level: Easy/Moderate

Total Distance: 8.0 miles round-trip

Hiking Time: 4 hours

Elevation Change: 800 feet

Summary: Travel through the former Tillamook Burn, visit a beautiful waterfall, and enjoy spring wildflowers while hiking a historic route along the summit of the Coast Range.

The Tillamook State Forest is home to rich second-growth forest largely recovered from a series of wildfires that burned 240,000 acres of timber. Oregon embarked on a huge reforestation project resulting in the growth we enjoy today. University Falls was surrounded by charred snags in 1945; today that same spot has dense tree cover and lush understory. Woodpeckers, chickadees, and the golden-crowned kinglet thrive in this new canopy. The area is also known for elk and deer, and you may also see squirrels or chipmunks from the trail. Begin your journey through time at the trailhead for historic Rogers Camp, where Oregon launched reforestation efforts in 1949.

The University Falls Loop actually consists of three separate historic trails. Start hiking up the gravel Firebreak One Road to the signed trailhead for the Nels Rogers Trail. Turn right onto the trail, which leads through salal, red currant, huge sword ferns, and salmonberry as it makes its circuitous way southeast to cross the Devil's Lake Fork of the Wilson River. The climate here encourages growth and you'll find lots of step moss on the forest floor along with pretty yellow violets, cedar trees, and some big old stumps. Around 0.8 mile you'll cross a small footbridge, and then the trail begins the descent to the Wilson River crossing on a single log footbridge. From the river, bear left on the trail. You'll cross a boardwalk/footbridge and enter an area with a lot of evidence of the burn—lots of old stumps and burned snags. This is a wet section of forest, you'll cross a second boardwalk and then a couple of turn-pikes (sections of trail that are built up to deter erosion, often over a culvert) before an immense stump just before the Wilson River Wagon Road Trail junction at 2 miles.

The next 2.6 miles along the Wilson River Wagon Road Trail traces a wide arc along part of the historic road that opened in the late 1890s. The trail ascends gently under some power lines, then continues through smaller trees as the terrain flattens out atop the shallow ridge. You'll continue past a stand of alders, and then around 3.2 miles begin descending to a nice wooden footbridge. Continue just under 0.5 mile to the junction with the Gravelle Brothers Trail.

hikers enjoy the falls

You are now moments from the University Falls and a well-deserved break. Head northward up the Gravelle Brothers Trail and turn left at the signed side trail to the falls. The falls are a popular destination and are particularly beautiful in the wintertime, when there may be a light dusting of snow on the alder nearby. After enjoying the falls, return to the main trail and turn left to continue north, then northwest, nearly 3 miles to the trailhead. The trail follows Elliott Creek, first ascending slightly and then dropping down to cross the river on another bridge. Pass the Storey Burn Trail junction on the left, and continue to the trail's end at Beaver Dam Road. Turn left and head uphill on the road to reach the ODOT shed. Turn right for the trailhead in 0.2 mile. I'm always surprised that such a scenic hike ends so unceremoniously along the OHV trail and behind ugly cement barriers. Still, it's a small price to pay for a wonderful hike along a historic route.

Options

To enjoy University Falls without hiking the whole loop, you may drive to the University Falls Trailhead. From the turn-off onto Beaver Dam Road, continue 0.7 mile to University Falls Road, passing the Deyoe Creek Trailhead. Keep going uphill a total of 2.6 miles to reach a junction signed Horse Camp. Drive another half mile to the University Falls Trailhead. From here follow the signs 0.4 mile to the falls.

Directions

Drive west on U.S. 26 from Portland. After about 21 miles, turn left on State Route 6/Wilson River Highway. Drive west over the summit and just beyond milepost 33 and turn left on Beaver Dam Road, which is signed for Rogers Camp. Make a quick left and proceed 0.1 mile to the trailhead. This is a shared trailhead with equestrians and OHV users—park on the right.

Information and Contact

Leashed dogs are allowed. For more information, contact Oregon Department of Forestry, Forest Grove District Office (801 Gales Creek Rd., Forest Grove, OR 97115, 503/357-2191, www.oregon.gov/ODF). The Tillamook Forest Center (Wilson River Hwy., SR-6 at milepost 22, 503/815-6800, www.tillamookforestcenter. com) is always a good source of information, maps, and educational materials. The center is home to nature trails, including a wheelchair-accessible trail; it also has a lookout tower, restrooms, and a theater.

❸ ELK MOUNTAIN-ELK CREEK LOOP
Tillamook State Forest

Level: Strenuous

Hiking Time: 4.5 hours

Total Distance: 8.4 miles round-trip

Elevation Change: 2,300 feet

Summary: This challenging hike to the Elk Mountain summit rewards adventurers with forest views and wildflowers galore.

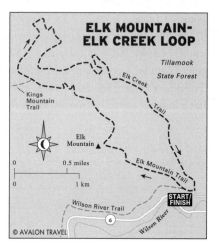

The Tillamook State Forest is sometimes still called the Tillamook Burn. This refers to the series of wildfires from 1933 to 1951 that burned millions of acres of trees and changed the landscape forever. In the time since, Oregonians embarked on a successful and huge replanting process that rehabilitated the land. As you explore the Tillamook State Forest, look around for the silvery snags and charred trunks—they're a reminder of both the fragility and resilience of the forest. This state forest is home to lots of recreation trails. The Elk Mountain–Elk Creek Loop is a popular hike for those looking for a rewarding summit and extended hike along the beautiful Elk Creek. You may even see some of the namesake elk in early morning or evening on the trail—just remember to look down at your path occasionally! Watch for flickers, other woodpeckers, and thrushes in the area around the river and up on the mountain.

The Elk Mountain Trail heads up from the Wilson River Trail about 0.2 mile from the start at the campground. For the next 1.5 miles you will be climbing steeply through the forest of Douglas-fir with an occasional flat spot to catch your breath. Along the bottom of the ridge is a nice viewpoint that allows you to rest briefly and enjoy the views west into the valley. As you return to the ascent, take time to note the abundant flowers along the trail. Yellow violets, serviceberry, purple penstemon, and tiny mitrewort all add to the beauty of the forest. The ridge provides some good views as you get higher—check out the vistas of the state forest and look for the contrasting snags that are a reminder of the fires long ago.

You soon reach the false summit. There are great views here, but push on to finish at the true summit, passing Indian paintbrush, bear grass, and a pretty meadow

foggy-day views from Elk Mountain ridge

along the way. There is a wooden sign on a tree and a summit register. If the day is clear, you may see all the way to the Pacific Ocean, and nearby Kings Mountain just to the west. After enjoying the views, continue northwest on the trail.

The trail descends along a very narrow scramble trail for a short distance. You may have to use your hands for balance as you make your way along the back side of the summit. Continue on the sometimes loose and rocky trail to the old roadbed along a ridgetop that connects to the Kings Mountain and Elk Creek Trails. Once you're on this high ridge, enjoy the views of the amazingly dense second-growth forest, marred only by the clear-cutting along some ridges. In 3.6 miles or so, you will reach the signed junction to Kings Mountain on the left. Continue ahead along the Elk Mountain Trail 0.8 mile to meet the Elk Creek Trail. The trail will duck back into the trees although there are still some nice views occasionally out to the right. Ignore the old road that comes in on your left, this leads up to the ridgetop. You will reach a signed junction with the Elk Creek Trail at mile 4.4 or so; turn right and begin descending the along the old road.

The trail/old road is well-graded and nice and wide as it winds down along some switchbacks and passes a small cliff. There are lots of old stumps scattered around. Some sections of the trail occasionally wash out, and you might have to pick your way across some rocks and around some slide alder. There are lots of red alder through here—they like to fill in disturbed forests. Along the descent, there are some tiny waterfalls. The water gently cascades over the rocks and lots of flowers add to the beauty. You may see wood sorrel, many ferns, bleeding heart, and the intimidating devil's club. Vanilla leaf also loves the shady areas. About 0.5 mile from the trail's end, Elk Creek comes in from the east to meet the West

Fork Elk Creek. The rest of the trail is mostly flat as it heads away from the creek canyon back to the trailhead.

Options

If you just don't feel like climbing—you don't have to! The Wilson River Trail terminates its 20.6 miles at the Elk Creek Campground. Instead of hiking up the Elk Mountain Trail, continue west along the Wilson River Trail to enjoy the pretty Douglas-fir and alder forest with lots of views of the river itself. If you go all the way to the Kings Mountain Trail junction and return, your total distance is 6 miles.

Directions

From Portland, drive west on U.S. 26 and turn left on State Route 6. Drive to milepost 28 and turn north onto Elk Creek Road, which leads to the Elk Creek Campground and trailhead. The trailhead is past the campground and is signed. The trail start is behind the information sign.

Information and Contact

Leashed dogs are allowed. For more information, contact Oregon Department of Forestry, Forest Grove District Office (801 Gales Creek Rd., Forest Grove, OR 97116, 503/357-2191, www.oregon.gov/ODF). The Tillamook Forest Center (Wilson River Hwy., SR-6 at milepost 22, 503/815-6800, www.tillamookforestcenter. com) is always a good source of information, maps, and educational materials. The center is also home to nature trails, including a wheelchair-accessible trail; it also has a lookout tower, restrooms, and a theater.

4 KINGS MOUNTAIN

Tillamook State Forest

BEST ◖

Level: Strenuous

Total Distance: 5.0 miles round-trip

Hiking Time: 3 hours

Elevation Change: 2,700 feet

Summary: The steep Kings Mountain Trail leads to a summit with views all the way to the Pacific Ocean. Along the way you'll see lots of big trees, dense ferns, and wildflowers.

The Tillamook State Forest occupies a special niche in Oregon's Coast Range. Considered a temperate rainforest, the trails here are full of rich growth: sword ferns three feet high, moss hanging from trees, and a recovering forest that illustrates the resiliency of nature. The area is known for herds of elk and you may see some deer (I've seen cougar tracks, but actual sightings are rare). The winter wren, woodpeckers, and chickadees are common in this forest. Kings Mountain isn't the tallest peak in the Coast Range, but it has one of the steepest access trails. It's a rite of passage for many Pacific Northwest hikers; once each spring aspiring mountain climbers test their early season fitness on this popular, if strenuous, trail.

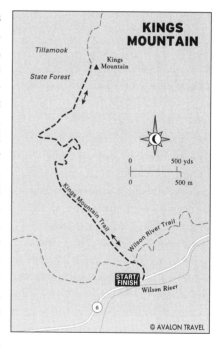

The Kings Mountain Trail is one of my favorite Coast Range hikes. Sure, the climb is steep at times, but the forest is wonderfully diverse, displaying its richness of growth from the start of the hike. Look around the forest of maple, alder, and Douglas-fir for bleeding hearts, thimbleberry, monkey flowers, and fairy slipper as you climb up the first 0.5 mile or so. The trail then flattens for a breather, winding above the creek and through an area of huge stumps, nurse logs, and ferns as far as the eye can see. Soon you'll pass an elevation marker on a tree reading 1,500 feet. Celebrate that if you must and then keep on climbing!

The trail switchbacks up for a bit, then widens to climb up a very steep section

© BARBARA I. BOND

the last push to the summit

before contouring across a tree-covered slope. Around 1.6 miles, there is a 2,000-foot marker on a tree on the left. The trail continues up to pass a nice viewpoint around 2,700 feet. Turn left onto the ridge. There is some pretty flowering red currant, salmonberry, Indian paintbrush, and salal along the trail. Then you reach an even steeper short section, which leads to the false summit; this area features a picnic table. I took my children and two friends on this hike one spring and it is here that they insisted on a treat.

From here it's less than 0.2 mile to the top and the views that await. The final ascent up the summit ridge has views of the sharp west ridge of the mountain, endless forest, and lots of sun-loving wildflowers. Patches of phlox grow amongst the rocky soil on the ridge, as do glacier lilies right after the snow melts. The summit has a little sign on a tree and a summit register. Go ahead and sign it—you've earned it. Relax, enjoy the sights, and return the way you came when you are ready. Enjoy the descent. I find that on this hike you can enjoy the rich forest more on the downhill leg when you're not working so hard. There is a nice spot to hang out right about 0.7 mile from the trailhead where it's flatter. There are a lot of huge trees here that were used in logging days. Most have turned into nurse trees—look for moss and young trees sprouting from them, sometimes in tidy rows. The trail makes a left turn just about 0.5 mile from the parking area for the final descent.

Options

If you want to enjoy this beautiful forest but don't enjoy climbing, then the Wilson River Trail might be what you are looking for. This low-elevation trail has a pretty 3-mile section from the Kings Mountain Trail to its end at the Elk Creek Campground to the east. A hike along this trail gives you fine views of the river, some nice footbridge crossings, and a chance to enjoy the dense stands of red alder that grow happily along here. From the trailhead, just walk up 0.1 mile and turn right at the signed junction for the Wilson River Trail. Trek as far as you'd like or go to the end for a picnic.

Directions

From Portland, drive west on U.S. 26. Turn left on State Route 6 (also known as the Wilson River Highway) and proceed 13 miles to the trailhead on the right near milepost 25. No services are available at the trailhead.

Information and Contact

Leashed dogs are allowed. For more information, contact Oregon Department of Forestry, Forest Grove District Office (801 Gales Creek Rd., Forest Grove, OR 97116, 503/357-2191, www.oregon.gov/ODF). The Tillamook Forest Center (Wilson River Hwy., SR-6 at milepost 22, 503/815-6800, www.tillamookforestcenter.com) is always a good source of information, maps, and educational materials. The center is home to nature trails, including a wheelchair-accessible trail; it also has a lookout tower, restrooms, and a theater.

5 SADDLE MOUNTAIN

BEST

Saddle Mountain State Natural Area

Level: Moderate

Total Distance: 5.0 miles round-trip

Hiking Time: 2.5-3.0 hours

Elevation Change: 1,633 feet

Summary: Enjoy this hike through dense coastal forest as it leads to open summit views to the Pacific Ocean, Columbia River Estuary, Mount Hood, and Mount St. Helens.

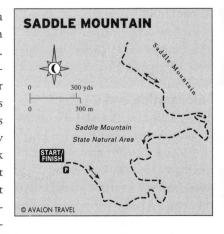

Over 14 million years ago, Columbia River basalts flowed like water from Eastern Oregon to the Pacific Ocean. Hikers familiar with the stately columnar basalt in the Columbia River Gorge are familiar with the sometimes crumbly, dark brown rock. As the flows reached the coast, they cooled quickly and changed into the distinctive rock that makes up Saddle Mountain. Just glance northward from the parking lot and you can see the treeless slopes rising up behind the dense thicket of conifers. The hike to the summit of Saddle Mountain is steep and short—the views are the reward.

From the parking area, head eastward along the well-maintained trail. The trail condition is remarkable considering that the winter of 2007–2008 brought extreme storms to the area resulting in dozens of washouts, downed trees, and rock slides. Enjoy the gradual slope of the first 0.5 mile or so because it gets steep fast. Note the huge cedar stump on the right as you begin your hike—this area was heavily logged at one time.

The Coast Range is typically cool, and even on warmer summer days the forested trail is comfortable. Coyote may be seen early on the trail; look for squirrels or elk in the forest and Steller's jay or gray jays near the start of the hike. Winding through the dense trees, note the carpet of wood sorrel, ferns, and thimbleberry, which in combination seem magical in their rich greens and varied foliage. The trail crosses a footbridge and switchbacks up to pass the first of several viewpoints. The big Sitka spruce and western red cedar provide plenty of shade. You'll want to keep away from the thick devil's club that seems to thrive here. Around 1 mile you will pass through a section of trail that was heavily damaged; it has been rebuilt with a unique new half-log footbridge and wooden retaining walls. As you continue the now-steep climb, you will cross a rocky point covered with the pretty yellow of stonecrop and then pass another viewpoint.

a hiker crossing the saddle after the summit

Occasionally, a mile marker is visible in the thick foliage. The trail leaves the open rock for a quick duck into the forest. You emerge as the scenery opens up to cross another nicely built footbridge with abundant wildflowers lining the trail. Watch for purple aster, larkspur, and foxglove. At around 1.75 miles, there is a dramatic viewpoint. After a short distance you will leave the protection of the forest, drop down to cross the saddle, and then look up—the upper mountain's bare slopes dramatically rise ahead. Yes, those specks are other hikers making their arduous way up the steep, rocky, slippery trail. Take advantage of the hand cable and steps when they are available and carefully climb the remaining 0.5 mile to the rounded summit. Enjoy the tremendous views of the ocean and estuary, Columbia River, Coast Range, and Cascade peaks. Return the way you came.

Options

For a shorter option with amazing coast scenery visit Ecola State Park and hike a section of the Lewis and Clark National Historic Trail. The 2.5-mile Clatsop Loop Trail begins at Indian Creek and heads north to the Oregon Coast Trail's walk-in Hiker's Camp. Turn back south there, adjacent to the Tillamook Head Lighthouse, for incredible scenery high above the Pacific Ocean. This is an interpretive trail, so be sure and carry the brochure to take advantage of this coastal wonder.

Directions

From Portland, drive east on U.S. 26 for about 64 miles. Turn right at the signed entrance for Saddle Mountain State Natural Area and drive north 7 miles. The trailhead is at the end of a paved but rough road.

Ecola State Park is on the Oregon Coast. To reach it, continue west on U.S. 26 from Saddle Mountain and turn south on U.S. 101. Take the first Cannon Beach exit and follow the signs west to the park entrance. Once in the park, follow the signs to the Indian Beach parking area.

Information and Contact

Dogs are allowed on leash only. There are no fees at Saddle Mountain. For more information, visit the website for Saddle Mountain State Natural Area at www.oregonstateparks.org, which includes seasonal camping information. For a map, use USGS Saddle Mountain.

For Ecola State Park (www.oregonstateparks.org), a day-use fee of $3 is required, or you may purchase an annual pass. For a map of the interpretive features of the Clatsop Loop Trail, visit the website to download a nice brochure.

6 NEAHKAHNIE MOUNTAIN   BEST **(**

Oswald West State Park

Level: Moderate   **Total Distance:** 8.6 miles round-trip

Hiking Time: 4 hours   **Elevation Change:** 1,539 feet

Summary: A hike to the top of mythic Neahkahnie Mountain includes history and treasure along the way.

Neahkahnie Mountain has a rich history, which includes Spaniards, hidden treasure, and Native American mythic figures. No matter—it's a rugged and beautiful headland with summit views that go on for miles. This fine adventure begins in Oswald West State Park, winding through old-growth trees and across Necarney Creek on the way to the open western slopes and eventual summit ridge. Hiking on the coast is always fun and unpredictable—if it's hot in Portland head west for almost guaranteed cooler temperatures.

Walk through the campground and follow the signs for beach access. If you have time, take a detour to Short Sands Beach, which is popular with surfers. Back on the trail, keep left and head to

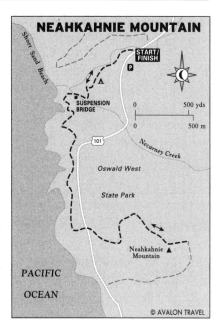

the suspension bridge that crosses Necarney Creek. Now that the first 0.5 mile is out of the way, the fun begins. Turn left at the sign and marvel at the dense forest and huge trees. Sitka spruce inhabit this cool, damp eco-region and they grow big along with the Douglas-fir, western hemlock, and western red cedar. The trail is crisscrossed with thick roots and you even walk through a short "tree tunnel" as you go. At mile 1.6, after wandering southward through a meadow, the trail crosses U.S. 101.

You now begin ascending a series of switchbacks through an open west-facing slope covered with wildflowers. Enjoy the views if there isn't the typical summer fog, and then enter the forest once again. You'll mostly be in the trees now as the trail continues to climb. There is a lot of blowdown—many trees were felled during the huge windstorms that battered Northwest Oregon in winter 2007–2008.

The forest opens up a little around 3 miles, passing lots of snags and continuing upward on more switchbacks. Approaching from the west you will suddenly emerge from the shade of the forest onto the rocky upper mountain just below the small summit. Continue ahead up to the rocky summit. Wildflowers bloom on patches of dirt amongst the rock and there is a summit register in a container. From this lofty vantage point you are about 1,600 feet above the ocean below. On a clear day you can see Smuggler Cove just northwest and down to the Nehalem Valley southward. On a foggy day you may be above the thick clouds and still be able to enjoy views of the rest of the Coast Range. Return the way you came.

coastal cliffs and ocean

Options

You can opt for a shorter and mostly uphill hike by starting where the trail crosses U.S. 101. To find the trailhead, drive south on U.S. 101 from the Oswald West parking area for about 1 mile to a turnoff on the right. The trail comes up on the right from the campground and continues on the north side of the highway. This short hike is 5 miles and still gains nearly 1,300 feet of elevation.

Directions

From Portland, drive west on U.S. 26 for 74 miles to U.S. 101. Merge onto U.S. 101 south towards Cannon Beach. Drive another 12.5 miles to the Oswald West State Park; the parking area is on the right.

Information and Contact

A State Park parking pass must be purchased to park; one-time use passes are $3, and annual passes ($25–40) are available. For park information call 503/368-3575 or visit www.oregonstateparks.org. Check current conditions before you head to the park. For a map, use USGS Nehalem. There is an information sign on the right as you head down the trail.

7 CAPE LOOKOUT   BEST ◖

Cape Lookout State Park

Level: Easy

Total Distance: 4.8 miles round-trip

Hiking Time: 2 hours

Elevation Change: 525 feet

Summary: Wander past gigantic Sitka spruce trees to enjoy excellent whale-watching from a lofty outpost at the tip of a dramatic headland.

Just south of Netarts Bay lies a narrow promontory 1.5 miles long and with 400-foot cliffs. This is the scenic headland of Cape Lookout—protected by a state park and popular with hikers and whale-watchers. The park offers a couple of short hikes through the big trees of the temperate Coast Range forest, bountiful spring trillium blooms, or down to the sandy beach south of

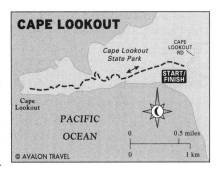

the cape. The Cape Trail is the most well-known route and winds amongst the trees to emerge onto the south side of the Cape en route to the small viewing area high above the Pacific.

The trail begins behind the information sign, walk north to the "Y" and turn left onto the Cape Trail. Pass the signed junction for the South Trail and hike along the wide, level trail through the dappled sunlight of the coastal forest. The trail is lined with ferns and every surface seems to be covered with thick green moss. You quickly pass an old wooden post that was part of the original trail signage. There are views south of the ocean and in the distance you can make out the distinct shape of Haystack Rock. Lots of trillium and violet blooms brighten the trail. On the right, take a moment to read the plaque memorializing the 1943 B-17 plane crash. Continue ahead and soon you'll cross a boardwalk—the first of several that get hikers up off the soggy and muddy forest floor and protect the delicate environment.

As the trail begins descending towards the viewpoint, you wind through the forest and along the north side of the headland for a short distance. Here you catch views through the trees of Netarts Spit and Bay several hundred feet below and northward. There is a trail marker at 1.5 miles just before more boardwalks keep you out of the mud—at least for now. In springtime, be prepared for thick mud that can suck the shoes right off your feet. Also, as my daughter discovered, the mud can result in footing that's akin to walking on ice. Once you get out of the forest you're safe from most of the mud, though. The trail curves southward back towards the south side of the Cape and with good views once more. Western hemlock and red alder round out the coastal forest and contrast with the huge gnarled trunks of the Sitka spruce.

The last 0.5 mile of trail meanders towards the viewpoint along some steep cliffs with amazing views. The trail is open to the south as it approaches the viewpoint with its protective fence and wooden bench. In the spring, you can see plenty of migrating gray whales in the ocean 400 feet or so below. (While binoculars are not necessary, they do bring the huge mammals up close and can be fun for the kids). Also look for common murre, cormorants, and grebes commonly found here. Return the way you came.

Options

To explore the beach, take the South Trail 1.8 miles down to the shore. From the trailhead, walk west on the Cape Trail and then turn left at the signed junction after about 45 yards. Enjoy the beach and remember you have to hike uphill to return to the trailhead.

Directions

From Portland, drive west on U.S. 26 for 21 miles and turn left onto State Route 6 towards Tillamook. After about 51 miles, you will reach the coast and U.S. 101; turn left to head south. Drive south for 0.1 mile then turn right onto Netarts Highway West for 5 miles. At 5 miles, the road turns south into Whiskey Creek Road before merging left into Netarts Bay Road at 1.2 miles. In 4 more miles you will come to Cape Lookout State Park. Follow the signs for the trailhead parking area, nearly 3 miles further, at the south end of the park.

Information and Contact

There is a day-use fee of $3; proof of payment must be displayed. You may also purchase an annual state park pass for $25. If you are camping, then your camping permit is your day-use permit. Dogs are allowed only on a 6-foot or shorter leash. For more information, contact Cape Lookout State Park (13000 Whiskey Creek Rd. W., Tillamook, OR 97141, 503/842-4981, www.oregonstateparks.org). There are no services at the trailhead.

8 CASCADE HEAD

BEST

Cascade Head Preserve

Level: Easy/Moderate

Total Distance: 5.0 miles round-trip

Hiking Time: 2.5 hours

Elevation Change: 1,200 feet

Summary: The basalt promontory of Cascade Head offers unique views of the Salmon River Estuary and Pacific Ocean. In spring, look for dark pink hairy checkermallow blooming.

Cascade Head is a study in contrasts. The preserve is an oasis of older Sitka spruce and western hemlock forest, coastal grasslands, and rare flowers. Formerly managed by a dedicated group of citizens, The Nature Conservancy took over the preserve in the mid-1960s. Today research continues as The Nature Conservancy and its partners work towards full restoration and preservation of its ecological balance.

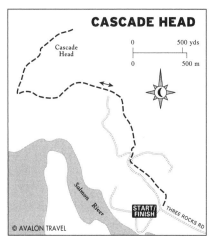

Begin the hike by walking east behind the trail sign at the end of the parking lot. The trail travels a short distance along the road before turning north just past the intersection with North Savage Road, then passes through private lands for the first 0.4 mile. Boardwalks protect the fragile, wet ground. Skunk cabbage grows in profusion, and you might smell these plants before you see the bright yellow flowers in the low area on the right. There already are lots of violets, trillium, and flowering red currant along the trail. The forest has a thick canopy and lots of moss. Walking along the trail, cross the footbridge and continue past towering Sitka spruce amongst the alder. Cross Savage Road and walk a short distance to the former trailhead, 0.5 mile from the start. (Note that there is no parking on Savage Road.) You also get a nice perspective on the Cape from here, clearly showing the open grasslands of the headland.

Begin again on the trail, which is to the left of the old sign. The trail starts climbing up some steps, passing a grove of big trees as it flattens out. Walk across another boardwalk with more skunk cabbage and some tiny wildflowers, then cross a footbridge. Descend nine stairs, cross the creek on a bridge, and note the

high on Cascade Head, hiker looks south to Salmon River Estuary

big wooden water tank on the left. You may see some mule deer along here, they like to wander though the thick understory. I startled several on one visit. A few more stream crossings bring you to The Nature Conservancy's information kiosk with a map and brief history of the preserve.

From here it is 0.6 mile to the lower viewpoint, the westernmost spot that is open to visitors. You will leave the forest and emerge onto the open prairie. Cross the meadow, and then for a short distance drop into a ravine filled with alder. Continue west to the viewpoint at about 800 feet of elevation. If you've done enough climbing, this is a good stopping point for lunch, photos, or just enjoying the scenery. Red-tailed hawks lazily ride the thermals in summer and the view south across the Salmon River is spectacular. On a clear day you can see Salishan Spit and beyond.

If you are heading to the upper viewpoint and beyond, then turn right and begin the 0.5-mile climb, which rises another 900 feet in elevation. The trail is steep in sections and gets very near the cliffs—there are a few ominous warning signs posted. The upper viewpoint has a small marker and can be windy. If the wind is too bothersome, continue east to the forest and duck into the trees for shelter. Avoid the upper meadows; they are under rehabilitation and are closed to visitors. When you've soaked in all the views you can manage, retrace your steps to the trailhead.

Options

A shorter seasonal hike is possible from the upper trailhead. The trail will take you southward through the forest about 1 mile to the upper viewpoint. From here you can continue to the lower viewpoint or enjoy the fine views.

Directions

From Portland, drive south on I-5 for about 42 miles to exit 260A for OR-99. Following the signs, drive west 4 miles to OR-22. Stay left, continuing onto OR-22 for 26 miles, and then merging onto OR-18/22 for another 27 miles to U.S. 101. Turn right to head north on U.S. 101. Just north of the Salmon River, turn west on Three Rocks Road. At 2 miles, take the left fork and park in Knight Park.

To reach the trailhead for the upper trail, which is open from July 16–December 31, continue north on U.S. 101 for 2.4 miles past the Salmon River. Turn left on Forest Road 1861 and drive west 3.5 miles to a small parking lot with a sign.

Information and Contact

There are no fees. Dogs are not allowed. For more information, contact The Nature Conservancy Oregon Coast Office (750 Commercial St., Ste. 212, Astoria, OR 97103, 503/325-3896, www.nature.org and search for "Oregon Cascade Head"). The Nature Conservancy properties are managed for conservation purposes. Please follow the visitor guidelines available at the information signs in the preserve or on The Conservancy's website. The upper trailhead and trail are managed by the Siuslaw National Forest, Hebo Ranger District (3125 Hwy. 22, Hebo, OR 97122, 503/392-5100, www.fs.fed.us/r6/siuslaw).

9 DRIFT CREEK FALLS

Siuslaw National Forest

Level: Easy

Total Distance: 3.7 miles round-trip

Hiking Time: 2 hours

Elevation Change: 590 feet

Summary: The star attractions of this short hike include beautiful the 75-foot Drift Creek Falls and the 240-foot suspension bridge high above Drift Creek.

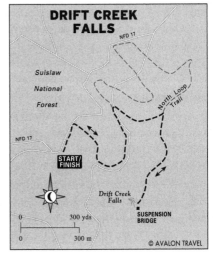

The Siuslaw National Forest is home to dense forest of Douglas-fir with hemlock, adler, and cedar filling in under the canopy. The Drift Creek Trail is nestled in the Coast Range deep in the Siuslaw National Forest. This short and very popular trail draws big crowds on summer weekends due to its proximity to the Oregon Coast and the curiosity about the well-known suspension bridge. Crafted from huge timbers and nearly 500 feet of cable, it's a dramatic highlight to a pretty hike. The wide, well-graded trail descends from the trailhead in less than 1.5 miles and along the way crosses a couple of footbridges and passes trees in the recovering forest.

The trail enters the forest and wastes no time in beginning to take switchbacks down past thick wood sorrel, sword ferns, and violets. The tree trunks are covered with stringy moss and the color green saturates everything in view. The forest consists of smaller trees and huge stumps with nurse logs scattered about. You'll pass a wooden bench about 0.5 mile in, cross a footbridge, and then contour around a ravine. You'll notice a junction for the North Loop Trail; continue straight ahead for the direct route to the falls.

As the trail heads downhill to another creek crossing, check out the thick thimbleberry bushes, salal, salmonberry, red alder, and maples. The sunlight filters through the canopy and the trail keeps cool even on a sunny day. Pass the other end of the North Loop Trail and cross the footbridge. After the bridge, the trail climbs a short distance through some larger trees and passes another small bench and a gigantic old stump. You begin seeing the bridge through the trees then you're there. The suspension towers are impressive, though not as impressive as the immense stump just to the left of the bridge. Cross the bridge and take a moment to enjoy the feeling of hanging 100 feet above the creek below. The falls are off to the right. On the other side of the bridge you can continue the hike another 0.3 mile to the creek's edge. However, most folks will be done here. I think the view back across the creek from this side is the most dramatic, with the bridge deck extending from the forest floor across the chasm. Enjoy the views.

Drift Creek Falls

When you're ready to return to the trailhead, just retrace your steps about 0.5 mile to the signed North Loop Trail. Turn right and uphill onto the 1-mile trail. You'll cross a stream on a footbridge, switchback up a few times, and pass a lot of blowdown. You may even hear some industrious woodpeckers working on the trunk of a nearby tree. The trail ends with a descent back to the main trail. Turn right to reach the trailhead in 0.7 mile.

Options

If you just want to see the falls and bridge, then skip the North Loop. The out-and-back along the Drift Creek Trail is 3 miles round-trip and gains 390 feet in elevation.

As you drive south on OR-99W you will pass the Tualatin River National Wildlife Refuge between King City and Sherwood. The refuge is open year-round and has a small trail system for bird-watching and hiking. There is also a beautiful visitors center with interpretive displays and spotting scopes. You may also reach the refuge via the no. 12 TriMet bus. Only a handful of other National Wildlife Refuges around the country can be reached using public transportation.

Directions

From Portland, drive south on I-5 for 7.8 miles to exit 294/OR-99W towards Newberg/Tigard. After 22 miles, take State Route 18 towards the Oregon Coast.

Drive 48 miles on State Route 18. Turn left on Bear Creek County Road and drive for 3.5 miles; continue on Forest Road 17 straight ahead for 7 miles to the trailhead on the left.

If you are at the Oregon Coast, drive south from Lincoln City for about 5 miles on U.S. 101. Turn left and go east on Drift Creek Road for 1.6 miles, then right on South Drift Creek Road for 0.25 mile. Turn left on Forest Road 17 and follow it for 10 miles to the trailhead on the right.

Information and Contact

A Northwest Forest Pass ($3) is required. Leashed dogs are allowed. For more information, contact the Siuslaw National Forest, Hebo Ranger District (3125 Hwy. 22, Hebo, OR 97122, 503/392-5100, www.fs.fed.us/r6/siuslaw). The trailhead will accommodate at least 20 vehicles and has a vault toilet. A self-issue forest pass box is on the trailhead information sign along with trail information and facts about the bridge. A refuge map is available on the website for the Tualatin River National Wildlife Refuge (19255 SW Pacific Hwy., Sherwood, OR 97140, 503/625-5944, www.fws.gov/tualatinriver).

 MARYS PEAK
Siuslaw National Forest

Level: Moderate

Hiking Time: 3.5-4 hours

Total Distance: 7.4 miles round-trip

Elevation Change: 1,550 feet

Summary: One of western Oregon's most well-known peaks, Marys Peak offers hikers old-growth trees, abundant wildflowers, and panoramic views of the Coast Range, Willamette Valley, and Cascade Range.

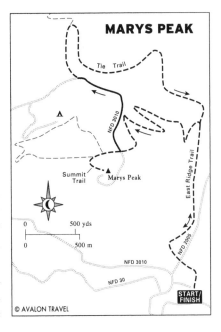

Corvallis-area residents have a recreation treasure in nearby Marys Peak. The heavily forested slopes contain miles of hiking trails, multiple trailheads and day-use areas, and a campground with trail access to an old-growth noble-fir grove. The trails get a lot of use year-round and summer is no exception. Explore the multiple layers of the rich forest by ascending the East Ridge Trail and linking to the Summit Trail for a fun survey of the forest diversity. Once on the rounded summit, you will enjoy views of the Pacific Ocean and snowcaps of nearby Cascade volcanoes.

The East Ridge Trail begins with a short section of trail that leads to a road crossing. Once you cross the road, the trail enters rich forest of fir, hemlock, and Douglas-fir. Vine maple fills in the understory and adds a vibrant light green to the surroundings. The forest floor is covered with salal, Oregon grape, huckleberries, ferns, and a multitude of flowers. It's recommended that you brush up on your wildflower identification skills or bring along a field guide in peak season. A mile quickly passes as you reach the Tie Trail junction; keep left to stay on the East Ridge Trail. Continue climbing as the trail switches back and enjoy the last views eastward. As you climb, the forest surroundings change, featuring more blowdown and a dense canopy that lets in little light.

Nearly 2.5 miles in, you will reach a signpost and trail junction with the Summit Trail. Turn left on the Summit Trail and immediately climb up the five wooden steps. You now will ascend across a steep slope past a row of trees with trunks curved nearly across the trail. Heavy blankets of wet winter snow permanently alter the shape of these old trees. You'll blink at the change when you suddenly emerge to cross a green grassy meadow with wildflowers including tiger lilies, penstemon, and lupine. Some scattered big fir trees adorn the meadow. The trail deposits you onto the summit road; across the way is the trail you'll return on. Turn left and ascend the road about 0.25 mile to reach the summit. Ignore the radio equipment on the summit and just enjoy the great views.

along the trail on Marys Peak

© BARBARA I. BOND

After your break, walk off the north side of the summit on a short trail that leads back into the fir and hemlock forest and reaches the junction with the Meadowedge Trail in 0.25 mile. Continue on through the trees west to emerge on the road; look across the road to see the trail you came up on. Turn left on the road and descend quickly to the observation area parking lot. Cross the lot and pick up the North Ridge Trail on the right of the lot's end and adjacent to the road. The trail descends northward towards the junction with the Tie Trail. Again the forest floor is dotted with wildflowers—starry-eyed Solomon's seal and queen's cup are just a couple. Take a look at the twin snag on the left. Turn right onto the Tie Trail and continue to wind southward back to the East Ridge Trail. The Tie Trail immediately has a different feel—the trail becomes more narrow and rocky; it undulates through a damper forest with red cedar and tall menacing devil's club trailside. The trail contours around several ravines as it makes its way back to the junction with the East Ridge Trail. Retrace your steps 1.2 miles to the lot from the junction.

Options

The Meadowedge Trail 1325 loops through an incredible old-growth noble-fir grove just below the summit of Marys Peak. The 1.6-mile loop begins at the campground just before milepost 9 along Marys Peak Road. From the campground, hike a very short distance on a spur that leads to the loop trail.

Directions

From Portland, drive south on I-5 for about 74 miles to exit 223 for State Route 34. Follow State Route 34 west, through Philomath, to milepost 49.7 and a sign for Marys Peak. Turn right onto Marys Peak Road and proceed to the turnoff for Connor's Camp at about mile 5.5. Turn right for the parking lot. The trailhead is on the north side of the lot near the road you came in on.

Information and Contact

A Northwest Forest Pass ($5) is required to park. For more information, contact the Siuslaw National Forest (541/750-7000, www.fs.fed.us/r6/siuslaw). The Sierra Club Marys Peak Group (www.oregon.sierraclub.org) is very active and may have scheduled outings, current conditions, or other useful trail information.

SOUTHWEST WASHINGTON

© BARBARA I. BOND

BEST HIKES

This region contains a contrasting collection of

hikes amidst a wide range of terrain. There are freshwater wetlands in the wildlife refuges close to the Columbia River. These lowlands present a sharp contrast to the rugged alpine terrain of Mount Adams, or the hundreds of lakes in the Indian Heaven Wilderness. As with Oregon, the Cascades are the major geologic feature of the state and dominate the landscape and pursuit of outdoor adventure. Fragile alpine meadows burst with wildflowers in mid-summer. Glacier lilies, Indian paintbrush, and lupine create a rich palette of color. All types of hikers will find a unique and fitting experience along Southwest Washington trails.

Close to the Portland area are the historic trails of Cottonwood Beach, on the shore of the Columbia River. Adjacent to a wildlife refuge, this area provides city dwellers with a quick and easy way to enjoy a bit of natural splendor. Bird-watchers will want to bring along their binoculars and check out the nearby waterfowl habitat. Moving away from the Columbia River, the terrain shifts to the rich coniferous forests we often associate with the Pacific Northwest. Nestled between the two major peaks of the Gifford Pinchot National Forest are two small wilderness areas that offer hikers very different outdoor experiences. The Indian Heaven Wilderness is dotted with over 100 lakes and is interspersed with mid-elevation peaks. The Trapper Creek Wilderness offers hikers and backpackers fewer and more rustic trails among immense old-growth trees coupled with a feeling of deep solitude. Both wildernesses feature rich displays of wildflowers throughout the summer.

Mount St. Helens, Washington's most famous volcano, draws visitors from around the world each year. Locals get to enjoy its unusual features as often as they want! Nearby, the hulking Mount Adams attracts wildflower lovers, berry pickers, and hikers drawn to the drama of glaciers, treeless ridges, and dwarf subalpine forest. Native Americans have a rich cultural history in Southwest Washington. Some of the huckleberry fields surrounding Mount Adams are the tribal berry-picking grounds for the Yakama Nation. Today a long-standing treaty guarantees that those traditions of gathering, along with hunting and fishing, are preserved. Hikes near these areas have plenty of huckleberries for anyone venturing onto the trails.

The highest terrain attracts both the seasoned explorer and the neophyte — each looking for their own unique experience. The higher elevation trails of Mounts Adams and St. Helens wind through dense fir and hemlock forest, past the rushing water of snow-fed creeks. Here hikers pass through the rugged landscape sculpted by lava flows and glaciation. Although summer is the most popular time of year, many lower-elevation trails can be reached year-round by using snowshoes in winter. For many Portlanders, there is a misperception that Washington trails are far afield and hard to get to. Yet many of these trails are well mapped and have good access. Introduce some variation and wonder into your hiking routine by exploring Southwest Washington trails.

SOUTHWEST WASHINGTON

Mt St. Helens
National Volcanic
Monument **12**

11

13

Cougar

Woodland
Park   Yale

Yale
Lake

Lake
Merwin

Amboy

RAILROAD AVE

LUCIA FALLS RD

2

NE 182ND AVE

3

W 1200 RD

WASHINGTON

500

140

Camas **1**

Washougal

Troutdale

Gresham

212

224   **211**

Sandy

26

Zigzag

Brightwood

OREGON

Mt Hood ▲

© AVALON TRAVEL

Gifford Pinchot
National Forest

Swift Creek
Reservoir

CURLY CREEK RD

NFD 90

MEADOW CREEK RD

5

6

4

Trapper Creek
Wilderness

WIND RIVER RD

Stabler

Gifford Pinchot

National Forest

Carson

Columbia River

Cascade
Locks

Skamania   Bonneville

Dodson

84

14

Dee

Parkdale

35

Mount Adams
Wilderness

14

Gifford Pinchot

National Forest

NFD 120

NFD 30

9

8

7

Indian Heaven
Wilderness

10

NFD 65

NFD 66

WOODS CREEK RD

FR 83

NFD 25

NFD 81 RD

503

503

504

0   5 mi
0   10 km

TRAIL NAME	LEVEL	DISTANCE	TIME	ELEVATION	FEATURES	PAGE
1 Lacamas Park *9-20-14*	Easy	3.0 mi rt	2 hr	200 ft		212
2 Moulton Falls *2-2-14, 1-4-14*	Easy	5.0 mi rt	2.5 hr	100 ft		215
3 Silver Star Mountain *4-13-14*	Moderate	7.6 mi rt	4 hr	2,100 ft		218
4 Soda Peaks Lake *5-9-15*	Easy/Moderate	4.4 mi rt	2.5 hr	1,300 ft		221
5 Observation Peak *9-27-14*	Easy/Moderate	5.5 mi rt	2.5 hr	600 ft		224
6 Falls Creek Falls *5-16-15*	Easy/Moderate	6.3 mi rt	3 hr	700 ft		227
7 Indian Race Track	Moderate	7.6 mi rt	4 hr	1,598 ft		230
8 Indian Heaven Lakes Loop	Moderate	9.7 mi rt	5 hr	1,300 ft		233
9 Lemei Rock	Moderate	7.6 mi rt	4.5 hr	1,900 ft		236
10 Little Huckleberry Mountain *5-23-15*	Moderate	5.0 mi rt	2.5 hr	1,850 ft		239
11 Butte Camp-Loowit Trail	Moderate	9.0 mi rt	4.5 hr	1,650 ft		242
12 Ape Canyon	Butt-kicker	11.0 mi rt	5.5 hr	3,000 ft		245
13 Upper Ape Cave	Moderate	2.8 mi rt	3 hr	375 ft		249
14 Stagman Ridge	Strenuous	11.4 mi rt	5.5-6.0 hr	2,300 ft		251

9-20-14

1 LACAMAS PARK
Lacamas Lake

Level: Easy

Hiking Time: 2 hours

Total Distance: 3.0 miles round-trip

Elevation Change: 200 feet

Summary: This hike can be done year round with special attention in spring due to the fields of camas lily blooms.

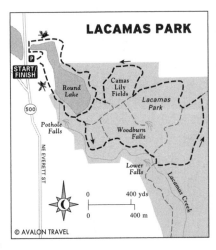

Lacamas Park is a wonderful winter and spring outing for city dwellers with Northwest cabin fever. Whether rain or shine you can hike along gently rolling trails to view waterfalls and wildflowers amongst the conifer and oak forest. This hike generally traces a path along the outer trail system in a counterclockwise loop. Begin hiking from the parking area and head for an information kiosk on the northwest corner of Round Lake. Round Lake, a smaller section of Lacamas Lake, anchors the northwest corner of the park and provides anglers the opportunity to catch brown and rainbow trout which are stocked annually.

After learning about the geology of the lake(s) begin hiking south along the lake on a wide trail. You may be sharing this trail with mountain bikes so be aware. At the southern tip of the lake the trail crosses a dam which drains the lake into Lower Lacamas Creek. Cross the dam, viewing the huge gears which operate the hand-cranked mechanism, continuing on the trail. You'll quickly reach a junction, bear right and keep on what is now a smaller trail that stays close to the creek and leads to stunning views of Pothole Falls. (Note: Don't take a side trail that leads to the high school; if you do just backtrack.)

This trail winds past large Douglas-fir, sword ferns, a variety of mosses, and wildflowers. Vine maple, Oregon grape, and other understory trees and shrubs make the forest dense even in winter. Everything here is coated with thick green moss. The first large waterfall along the trail is Pothole Falls. In winter, due to the influx of rainwater, the falls are very dramatic. After viewing the falls continue along the winding trail which largely parallels Lacamas Creek southward.

Enjoy the rich forest as you approach the junction with a bridge just below Lower Falls. Don't cross the bridge unless you want to add an out-and-back extension to two parking areas and some boggy areas loaded with skunk cabbage and cottonwoods.

After the bridge and Lower Falls views continue on the path which begins curving east away from the creek. You will eventually move from the smaller trail to a wide hiking-superhighway which leads to a junction ahead. There, turn left towards the camas lily fields. As you trudge up a short hill note the huge downed trees on the left side of the trail. Imagine the sound when they hit the ground!

On the right will be sign and fence (hikers only) for the Camas Lily Loop.

descending through forest

In early spring the rocky, exposed outcrops will be covered with what look almost like green onion stalks. In mid-April the lush green is transformed by the bloom of hundreds of camas lilies. The camas was an important food source for Native Americans and early explorers. Enjoy the fields of flowers before continuing along the path. At a junction, keep right to descend away from the flowers back into the forest. You will soon reach a trail junction near Round Lake. Turn right if you want to circumnavigate the lake along its eastern shore. Turn left to return to you car by again following the wide trail, crossing the dam and outlet to Lacamas Creek.

Options

You can take a much shorter interpretive hike around Round Lake. Pick up a Round Lake Loop Interpretive Trail Guide at the park information kiosk. Follow the directions for a pleasant and informative 1.2 mile hike around the lake with numbered guideposts marking points of interest.

Directions

From Portland drive east on I-84 for 4.9 miles to the I-205 north exit. Take I-205 north across the bridge and exit onto SR-14 east to Camas. Take exit 12 and wind through Camas. Turn left on Garfield Street, then follow the signs for SR-500W

(SR-500 is also NE Everett Road). Drive north a short distance to the park. The parking lot is on the right and is clearly marked.

Information and Contact

There are no fees. Dogs on leash are allowed. Park hours are 7 A.M.–dusk. Restrooms, picnic tables, interpretive signs and guides are available. Lacamas Park is managed by Clark County. The city of Camas does have a webpage for the park at www.ci.camas.wa.us/parks/lacamas.htm. For a trail map visit the Vancouver Parks & Recreation website at www.ci.vancouver.wa.us/parks-recreation.

2 MOULTON FALLS
East Fork Lewis River

2-2-14
1-4-14

Level: Easy

Total Distance: 5.0 miles round-trip

Hiking Time: 2.5 hours

Elevation Change: 100 feet

Summary: Hike along the East Fork Lewis River through restored greenway, past fir and alders, and enjoy the drama of Moulton Falls. Bonus – crossing the river on a stunning arch bridge.

The East Fork Lewis River Trail is a wonderful low elevation hike with pretty waterfalls and a short accessible section leading to a picnic table and pond. The trail is a wonderful mid-winter hike and is the northern trail-head for the 9-mile Bells Mountain Trail. From the Hantwick Road trail-head the trail starts out as a wheelchair-accessible trail. The paved section ends

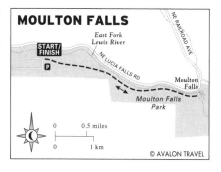

in less than a half mile but the wide, flat trail continues along the river past lots of small falls and pretty streams. The thick forest, rushing waters of the river and wildlife watching are just some of the highlights hikers enjoy on the way to the lovely Moulton Falls.

Leave the parking lot at Hantwick Road and hike east on the path which quickly takes you across a small footbridge and enters the forest. It's hard to miss the huge Douglas-fir trees and thick salmonberry along the trail. Songbirds fill the quiet and wildflowers dot the forest floor along the trail. The pavement ends in about 0.5 miles at the west end of a pond.

As you continue east along the path you'll cross several small footbridges. There are many small streams that come down off Bells Mountain into the river and some with flowers and small falls. The trail winds closer to the river for nearly a mile; you can catch a glimpse of the water occasionally and the sounds of rushing water filters though the trees. The Bells Mountain Trail junction is at 2.1 miles on the right. Stop a moment and take a look at the dedication at the trailhead. The Bells Mountain Trail climbs steeply a short distance then works its way south along the broad north/northeast flanks of the mountain.

The river trail continues, across another footbridge and past a series of wa-terfalls visible through the trees. The main section of Moulton Falls Park is less

an arch bridge across the East Fork Lewis River

than a half mile away. You enter the park before crossing the river on the amazing arch bridge. After crossing the bridge, bear left and follow the trail through the park to view the waterfalls from the north banks. There are a number of places to explore and enjoy the falls as they drop over the volcanic rock worn smooth by the flow. To view more waterfalls cross Lucia Falls Road on the left side of Big Tree Creek. This short path will take you past some picnic tables and waterfall viewing spots at the north end. The trail then crosses the road to bring you back through the forest to the main path leading back to the arch bridge. Return the way you came.

Options

For a shorter hike with more time to explore begin at Moulton Falls Park. Hike down to the water's edge from the parking lot to enjoy the waterfalls. The short trail along Big Tree Creek also offers a chance to see more waterfalls and enjoy more the park.

Directions

From Portland, drive east on I-84 for 4.9 miles and exit onto I-205 North. Drive across the bridge on I-205 North to WA-503. Turn left to go north on SR-503 12.5 miles to NE Rock Creek Road. Drive a half mile and continue on NE 152nd Avenue then NE Lucia Falls Road for a total of 8.3 miles. Pass Lucia Falls Park and turn right on Hantwick Road. In a half mile you will see the trailhead parking area on the left side of the road. The trail is north of the lot.

Information and Contact

There are no fees. Restrooms are available at the Hantwick Road parking lot and Moulton Falls Park. The park also has picnic tables, fishing, swimming, and interpretive information. Park hours are 7 A.M.–dusk. For a map and more information visit the Clark County website page for the park at www.co.clark.wa.us/parks-trails/moultonfalls.html. You can download a trail map for the park and also for the Bells Mountain Trail here.

4-13-14   5.6 miles

3 SILVER STAR MOUNTAIN   BEST ◖

Gifford Pinchot National Forest

Level: Moderate   **Total Distance:** 7.6 miles round-trip

Hiking Time: 4 hours   **Elevation Change:** 2,100 feet

Summary: Get your heart rate up and enjoy great views from this former lookout site atop Silver Star Mountain.

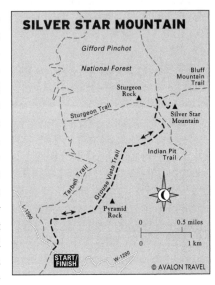

Silver Star Mountain occupies a neglected corner of the Gifford Pinchot National Forest adjacent to and surrounded by the Yacolt Burn State Forest. In 1902 the Yacolt fires roared through the forest and changed the landscape irrevocably. The soils were altered, some tree replanting took place, and native flora and fauna fought to establish a foothold. The recovered lands are good for hikers—open, rocky ridges with unobstructed views and a hardy collection of wildflowers amongst smaller trees. The 15 million-year old rock of the mountain complex is rich in minerals and at one time had a number of active mines.

Hike up the Grouse Vista Trail which begins steeply climbing from the start. This trail is rocky and wide, winding northerly towards the Pyramid Rock ridge. You'll quickly pass the trail junction with the Tarbell Trail on the left; keep right for Silver Star Mountain. The second-growth forest is thick in places, barely letting the understory survive. Still, a number of flowers thrive here, you can watch for the rich green leaves of false lily of the valley and beargrass. Stands of alder have filled in areas, and some vine maples add to the layers of trees.

South of Pyramid Rock you emerge from the trees onto the hillside below the rocky ridge. The views from here will keep you motivated as you contour around on the flatter trail past inviting knobs and spurs. Continue along the open slope, passing Pyramid Rock and at 2.1 miles ignoring the closed road that joins from the south. In another half mile you pass another junction on the right—this trail leads to the Silver Star Indian Pits. It's worth the detour now or later, to check out this cultural landmark. It isn't clear whether this was a vision quest site or food cache for Native Americans. Sites like this are scattered around the Columbia River Gorge area. You'll reach the site of the pits about 0.8 mile from the junction.

The last half mile or so winds in and out of the trees before the final bit of trail on the open upper ridge to the Silver Star summit. There is a good view of the columnar basalt of Sturgeon Rock out to the west and you'll see fir and hemlock trees amongst the green. Note that there is a second summit just south of the main one, look past it for a nice look at Mount Hood. The summit has wonderful views and some remaining foundation from the fire

on the trail to Silver Star Mountain, hikers stop at Pyramid Rock

© BARBARA I. BOND

lookout it once housed. You get a good look at the Bluff Mountain Trail as it winds south around Little Baldy. This is a great place for a long break or just tag-and-go. If you want a quiet lunch spot, retrace your steps to the Indian Pit Trail junction and make that your destination. Retrace your steps back to the car.

Options

If you prefer a loop hike and a little extra mileage you can return using the Sturgeon Rock Trail 1.3 miles to the Tarbell Trail which continues southward 2.8 miles to the "Y" you passed on the way up. The loop total distance is 7.8 miles.

Directions

From Portland, drive east on I-84 for 4.9 miles and exit onto I-205 North. Drive across the bridge on I-205 North and turn right on State Route 14 (east). Take SR-14 east about 10 miles to Washougal, then turn north on SR-140 for nearly 10.5 miles. Turn left on Skye Road and drive 3.7 miles to Skamania Mines Road. Turn right and head north on Skamania Mines road to the junction with Road W-1200. Bear left onto Road W-1200 and follow it 5.6 miles to the Grouse Creek Vista trailhead. This road may have large potholes and some very rough patches.

Passenger cars will do fine as long as you take your time. Nearly the last 7 miles of road are unpaved.

Information and Contact

There are no services at the trailhead except an interpretive sign. For more information, contact the Gifford Pinchot National Forest, Mount St. Helens National Volcanic Monument Headquarters (42218 N.E. Yale Bridge Rd., Amboy, WA 98601, 360/449-7800). The Washington State Department of Natural Resources has a nice map of the area at www.dnr.wa.gov.aspx. For a pretty good map with all the trail options, visit the Gifford Pinchot National Forest trail pages for Silver Star at www.fs.fed.us.gpnf/recreation.

4 SODA PEAKS LAKE
Trapper Creek Wilderness

5-9-15
Saw a bunch of
Elk

Level: Easy/Moderate

Total Distance: 4.4 miles round-trip

Hiking Time: 2.5 hours

Elevation Change: 1,300 feet

Summary: Hike the southwest corner of the Trapper Creek Wilderness to a pretty lake in a beautiful wooded setting.

Soda Peaks Lake sits in a glacial cirque surrounded by dense trees and an imposing rocky ridge. This scenic spot in the southwest corner of the Trapper Creek Wilderness is a great destination for either a short dayhike or a quick backpack and fishing trip. According to the fisherman I saw down there, brook and rainbow trout were biting. The hike to Soda Peaks Lake is short but don't let that fool you. On the way out you must regain the elevation you lose as you make your way down to the lakeshore.

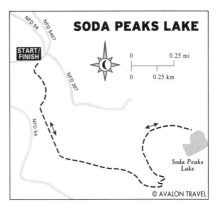

The Soda Peaks Lake Trail leaves the road alongside an old clearcut full of young trees and enters the deep forest of old-growth. In the open areas lupine and beargrass grows amidst the huge weathered stumps. Once inside the cool dark of the forest the color palette shifts to earth tones—duff on the forest floor, massive tree trunks, and the distinctive stalks of reddish coralroot. Lots of downed trees litter the trail as you begin climbing up to the ridgetop where you can catch a glimpse of the lake below. The trail gets steep, crosses a rock slide around 1 mile with some vine maple, salmonberry, and the ubiquitous huckleberry. You'll reach the wilderness boundary around 1.2 miles after topping out in a short flat with a Mount Adams view. The trail now drops slightly then makes a sharp left in the saddle to begin the descent to the lakeshore. The trail switchbacks down steeply but don't let that distract you from the sudden abundance of ferns.

You will end up at the north/northeast corner of the lake in a clearing/campsite on the lakeshore. This is your spot—there's a log to sit on and the beautiful lake is less than a stone throw away. The trees are dense along the lakeshore—most of the trees come right down to the water. Oddly there are huckleberry bushes all

© BARBARA I. BOND

Soda Peaks Lake

around the lakeshore, enjoy these tasty treats in late summer or early fall. Osprey nest at the top of some of the tall snags along the lakeshore—listen for their distinctive call. Return the way you came.

Options

If you can arrange a car shuttle this is a nice one-way hike of about 5.5 miles. After your lake visit continue on the trail east 3.15 miles to the endpoint near Government Mineral Springs. You will descend rather sharply from high above Trapper Creek and end nearly 2,800 feet below your high point for the day. After you pass the wilderness boundary and ignore a trail junction to the Trapper Creek Trail 192—finish the 0.65 mile to end at the trailhead at the end of the FR-3065 loop. This is the trailhead beyond the gated road FR-3065 and north of the campground. As you walk to your car take a look at the impressively large old-growth trees along the roadway.

Directions

From Portland, drive east on I-84 to Cascade Locks exit 44. Cross the bridge after paying the toll ($1 each trip, ticket book available for $.75 each trip) and turn right on SR-14. At the sign to Carson, turn left onto the Wind River Road. Drive north on the Wind River Road 8.6 miles. Turn left on Hemlock Road then make a quick right on Little Soda Springs Rd/Szydlo Rd for 3.6 miles. Turn left on FR-54 and drive 9.1 miles to the trailhead which is at a three-way road junction. There is secondary Forest Service Road 307 on the right at the trailhead; the start of the trail is on the south side of the spur. There is parking space available for several vehicles.

To do the shuttle hike, leave a car at Government Mineral Springs. Drive north from the Carson Fish Hatchery on Wind River Road. Keep left on FR 3065 and drive almost to the end. Follow the signs to the trailhead lot.

Information and Contact

There are no fees. For more information, contact the Gifford Pinchot National Forest, Mt. Adams Ranger District (2455 Hwy. 141, Trout Lake, WA 98650, 509/395-3400, www.fs.fed.us/gpnf/recreation/current-conditions/). For maps use Green Trails No. 396 and 397 or USDA Forest Service Mount Adams, Indian Heaven, and Trapper Creek Wilderness map (2005). For the roads use the USDA Forest Service Gifford Pinchot National Forest map.

9-27-14

5 OBSERVATION PEAK　　　　　　　　BEST ◖

Trapper Creek Wilderness

Level: Easy/Moderate　　　　　　**Total Distance:** 5.5 miles round-trip

Hiking Time: 2.5 hours　　　　　　**Elevation Change:** 600 feet

Summary: Hike to the site of a former fire lookout atop Observation Peak in the Trapper Creek Wilderness.

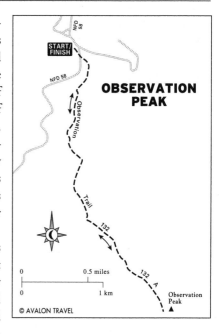

The Trapper Creek Wilderness provides protection for the anadromous fish of the Wind River Watershed and offers hikers a chance to see some huge old-growth trees while enjoying lots of solitude. Occupying a small corner of the Gifford Pinchot National Forest, and dwarfed by its nearest neighbors— the wilderness is a destination worthy of a visit. Elk and black bear make this their home and the fall huckleberries are a delicious snack as you make your way to the bare summit.

The Observation Trail 132 begins winding through the deep forest just north of the Wilderness boundary, only entering right around 1 mile. The trail of thick duff is easy on the feet and the forest floor is covered with shade-loving flowers like vanilla leaf. Watch for beargrass as you climb and you may also see some wild strawberry and roses. Just after the wilderness boundary you may see a small way-trail on your left leading to a rocky viewpoint. Walk over the short distance and check out the nice views including the bulky Mount Adams on the horizon. Back on the trail you descend and pass a couple of trail junctions and signed Berry Camp at one of the nice-looking campsites. Just ignore both the Big Hollow Trail then the Trapper Creek Trail junctions. Violets, lupine, and, if you're right after the snowmelt, avalanche lilies seem to thrive along here.

The trail traverses a steepish slope then reaches the Observation Peak Trail 132A—a short spur to the summit. Turn right at this signed junction at 2.25 miles and climb the final few hundred feet up the north ridge of the peak. The

on the rounded summit of Observation Peak

trail winds along the southern slope of the summit before petering out. The views from up here are great—Mount St Helens is visible northward through the trees, Mount Adams dominates east, and Mount Rainier is visible northeast. You can even see Mount Hood far to the south. The deep drainages and dense forest fill in the near view. Asters, tiger lily, cat's ear lilies are interspersed amongst the summit rock. We saw a lot of elk scat too—but no elk! Retrace your steps to return to the trailhead. Take a small detour just as you begin your descent north along the summit ridge. Bear right on a short way-trail to Observation Peak's north summit.

Options

If you want to see some huge trees, experience naturally-carbonated mineral water, and skip the hike, you can visit the site of the restored Government Mineral Springs Guard Station. Although you aren't quite in the wilderness there are immense old-growth trees along a gated gravel road just north of the mineral springs. The Government Mineral Springs once boasted a hotel—destroyed by fire long ago. All that remains is a pump for the healing waters, which you can sample (although I will say it's an acquired taste!). Enjoy the quiet of the primitive campground which only has six sites and is ringed by Douglas-fir and hemlock trees. Just continue north from the Carson Fish Hatchery on Wind River Road, bearing left on FR 3065 nearly to its end. Follow the signs to the springs and/or campground.

Directions

From Portland, drive east on I-84 to Cascade Locks exit 44. Cross the bridge after paying the toll ($1 each trip, ticket book available for $0.75 each trip) and turn right on SR-14. Turn left onto the Wind River Road, following the sign to Carson. Drive north on the Wind River Road 16.5 miles. Turn left on Dry Creek Road/FR-64 and follow the winding (some potholes) gravel road 6.1 miles. Continue on FR-58 2 more miles to the trailhead. Parking is available for a few cars. The trailhead is on the east side of the road.

LEFT *LEFT AT 1.8*

Information and Contact

There are no trailhead parking fees. If you camp, pay at the self-issue permit station as you enter the campground. For information, contact the Gifford Pinchot National Forest, Mt. Adams Ranger District (2455 Hwy. 141, Trout Lake, WA 98650, 509/395-3400, www.fs.fed.us/gpnf/recreation/current-conditions/). For maps use USGS Bare Mountain or Green Trails No. 396 or USDA Forest Service Mount Adams, Indian Heaven, and Trapper Creek Wilderness map (2005). For driving use the USDA Forest Service Gifford Pinchot National Forest map.

5-16-15
Awesome! Saw Elk

6 FALLS CREEK FALLS BEST 🄲

Gifford Pinchot National Forest

Level: Easy/Moderate

Total Distance: 6.3 miles round-trip

Hiking Time: 3 hours

Elevation Change: 700 feet

Summary: Hike across a suspension bridge en route to a tremendous view of a tiered waterfall.

Washington's Wind River Valley is home to wildlife, mixed-age forests, and enough hiking to keep anyone busy. This area north of Carson sees few visitors yet is close enough to visit year-round for outdoor activities. The short hike to view Lower Falls Creek Falls is a classic and is sure to please almost anyone. The beautiful three-tiered falls drop over a rocky precipice over and over again resulting in a scenic wonder.

The hike begins on the Lower Falls Creek Trail 152A. Start south of Falls Creek and meander easterly to pass the trail junction for the return loop then cross a short footbridge within the first half mile. The flowers are abundant amongst the vine maples, salal, and Oregon grape—look for wild roses, false solomon's seal, anemone, bead lily, and the everpresent bunchberry. There are a lot of smaller trees typically found in second-growth forests yet watch for some bigger cedars and Douglas-fir as you reach a dry creekbed crossing around 0.8 mile. The trail is gently ascending as it winds through the trees above the creek.

Pass a signed junction with the Falls Creek Trail 152 at 1.2 miles and continue east then south while approaching the falls. The creek crossing at a second bridge brings you even closer and you get to check out the rushing water of Falls Creek from the bridge deck. Now, 0.4 mile to the base of the falls, the trail flattens out as it contours along a steep slope. Look to the right and you will begin catching glimpses of the falls through the trees southeast. The trail now goes below a section of rock wall then climbs up to the viewpoint. The three-sections of the falls all have their own brilliant character and you can hear the thunder of the water crashing below into the creek. Take your time and hang out a bit—it's a great spot for photos and a break.

stunning Falls Creek Falls

Once you've had your fill of waterfall retrace your steps to the signed trail junction around a half mile back. Turn right onto a short connector leading to the Upper Falls Creek Trail 152. Now the trail climbs steeply north before turning right and heading east then southeast to some nice viewpoints and spots along the creek. There are some saprophytes in the forest along here—they don't have any chlorophyll and live off the tree roots. Striped coral root is especially abundant. The trail flattens out in a few more minutes and at around 2.5 miles watch for a side trail on the right. There are a number of these that just head south/southwest to the edge of the cliffs to view the falls below. For a nice flat spot near the creek continue along a half mile or so and pick your pleasure. After enjoying the pretty creek retrace your steps to pass the trail junction back down to the lower falls trail. Continue west on the trail through the trees while descending back down to the creekside. The trail is dry for about a mile as it heads back to the cool of the creek and there are some bigger trees near the water. Around mile 5.8 the trail jogs left and crosses a bridge then turns nearly 180 degrees to return to the junction with the short segment to the trailhead. Turn right and you're there.

Options
If you want a shorter hike just do an out-and-back to the lower falls viewpoint. This will be about 3.2 miles roundtrip.

Directions

From Portland, drive east on I-84 and take the Cascade Locks exit 44. Cross the bridge after paying the toll ($1 each trip, ticket book available for $0.75 each trip) and turn right on SR-14. At the sign for Carson, turn left onto the Wind River Road north, passing the Carson National Fish Hatchery. Turn right on Highway 30 and continue 0.75 mile. Turn right on FR-3062 for 2 miles and turn right on Forest Service Road 057 to the trailhead.

Information and Contact

There are no fees. For more information, contact the Gifford Pinchot National Forest, Mt. Adams Ranger District (2455 Hwy. 141, Trout Lake, WA 98650, 509/395-3400, www.fs.fed.us/gpnf/recreation/current-conditions/). For maps use Green Trails No. 396 and 397 or USDA Forest Service Mount Adams, Indian Heaven, and Trapper Creek Wilderness map (2005). For the roads use the USDA Forest Service Gifford Pinchot National Forest map.

7 INDIAN RACE TRACK
Indian Heaven Wilderness

Level: Moderate

Hiking Time: 4 hours

Total Distance: 7.6 miles round-trip

Elevation Change: 1,598 feet

Summary: Nestled between Mounts St. Helens and Adams is Washington's Indian Heaven Wilderness. Visit the Indian Race Track for the wildflowers then climb Red Mountain to experience the whole wilderness from up high.

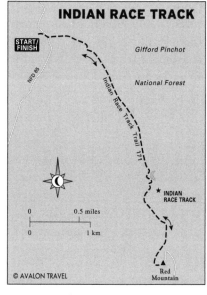

The Yakama Nation has a rich history in and around the Indian Heaven Wilderness. The 20,000 acre wilderness contains volcanic remnants, rugged peaks, more than 100 lakes and ponds, and is home to huckleberry bushes galore. The hike to the Indian Race Track wanders through thick second-growth forest to reach the race track meadows. Enjoy this visit rich in cultural and natural history.

Start hiking on the level Indian Race Track Trail 171 in the mossy forest. Lots of fun stuff grows here and you'll see bear grass, lupine, lots of huckleberries (go ahead, taste them), and too many wildflowers to name. One odd looking flower that thrives here is sickletop lousewort—look for the pinkish flowers atop slender stalks. You'll reach a quick trail junction with a self-issue permit station. Keep left after getting a permit. The trail on the right is a connector trail leading back to the road (ignore it). Cross the creek on a single log footbridge. You will begin climbing near the wilderness boundary at 0.75 mile. The next mile or so climbs 700 feet on the sometimes narrow and rocky trail. In the areas with thick duff on the forest floor look for the yellowish pinesap with its delicate fringed petals.

Pass a pond just before reaching the open meadow of the race track around 2.5 miles. In the late 1800s, Native Americans would gather here to race horses and socialize. Cross the signed PCT connector trail, jog right a very short distance then left again to continue on Trail 171 southward to its end partway up Red Mountain. If you go straight ahead you will reach a signed dead-end!

the Indian Race Track meadow

The forest is suddenly very thick again, a surprising contrast after the open meadow. Climb rather steeply up the north ridge of Red Mountain. There is a clearing with views part of the way up on the left side off the trail. Continue to the south trailhead for Indian Race Track, which also is the wilderness boundary. Take the dirt road another 0.4 mile up to the Red Mountain Lookout. When I visited there was some restoration work going on at the lookout. There are a few outbuildings in addition to the lookout itself. There are good views all around; particularly nice is the view north into the Indian Heaven Wilderness. Red Mountain obviously got its name from the dark red volcanic rock that covers the upper mountain. Retrace your steps to the car when you've exhausted the views.

Options

You can do a shorter hike by driving to the south trailhead for Indian Race Track. From FR-65 turn right at Four Corners onto FR-60. Drive east to FR-6048 and turn left. Head north on this rough road 3.2 miles to the trailhead. You may need either 4WD or high clearance vehicle to travel on this road. In early summer either check the website for current road conditions or call ahead to be sure the road is open.

Directions

From Portland, drive east on I-84 to Cascade Locks exit 44. Cross the bridge after paying the toll ($1 each trip, ticket book available for $0.75 each trip) and turn right on SR-14. At the sign to Carson, turn left onto the Wind River Road.

About 6 miles north is the junction with FR-65, which is signed for Panther Creek Campground. Turn right and then left, following FR-65 northward, passing the Four Corners/ FR-60 intersection. Continue nearly 5 miles to the trailhead. The Falls Creek Horse Camp is on the left. Slightly north is the trailhead, on the right. There is room along the road to park. There is also an unmarked connector trail across from the camp entrance. This leads to the trail junction mentioned above.

Information and Contact

There are no fees. The Falls Creek Horse Camp has vault toilets, parking, and camping and picnic tables. For more information, contact the Gifford Pinchot National Forest, Mt. Adams Ranger District (2455 Hwy. 141, Trout Lake, WA 98650, 509/395-3400, www.fs.fed.us/gpnf/recreation/trails/index.shtml). For maps use USGS Gifford Peak or Green Trails No. 365S or USDA Forest Service Mount Adams, Indian Heaven, and Trapper Creek Wilderness map (2005). For driving carry the USDA Forest Service Gifford Pinchot National Forest map.

8 INDIAN HEAVEN LAKES LOOP

Indian Heaven Wilderness

Level: Moderate

Hiking Time: 5 hours

Total Distance: 9.7 miles round-trip

Elevation Change: 1,300 feet

Summary: Indian Heaven is known for it's hundreds of lakes, ponds, and tarns. This delightful hike takes you past at least a dozen. Be ready for amazing scenery.

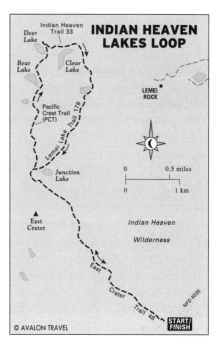

The East Crater Trail 48 leaves the road and climbs gently through the beautiful eastside forest of fir, western white pine, and hemlock. The trail is nice and wide and luckily lined with lots of huckleberry bushes. You might spy some twisted stalk and beargrass too. It's really damp here and there is a lot of fungus to prove it—watch for a variety of mushrooms in the pine duff. I saw some shelf fungus and at least four or five other mushrooms I couldn't identify. As you make your way up to Junction Lake you will cross a couple of footbridges and boardwalks—and meadow after meadow filled with flowers. There are also lots of tiny ponds and streams. The flowers are a nice contrast to the green and you may see shooting stars, lupine, Indian paintbrush, and, if you time it right, avalanche lilies. At 2 miles you pass the east ridge of East Crater then a short distance later reach the PCT and Junction Lake. Note there are some old PCT signs on the trees near the lake—most of these have been replaced over the years. Take a moment to visit the lake—it's beautiful and has hemlock, fir trees, and flowers in its meadows. It's even pretty on a rainy day with fog drifting along the water and the different shades of green accentuated by the soft light.

From here head north on the PCT through more dense forest. The trees are loaded with lichen, such as witch's hair. You'll cross a creek and pass a washout.

a footbridge leads through the meadows and dense trees

Ignore the Elk Lake Trail, which is in 1 mile. You'll pass a couple of other "animal" lakes then turn right just past Deer Lake onto the Indian Heaven Trail 33. If you are doing this hike mid-summer you might think this area is called "mosquito heaven." The many lakes and ponds provide plenty of breeding ground for these pesky insects. Nevertheless, it helps to hike on cooler summer days or wait until fall when nighttime temperatures begin to fall.

This next 0.8 mile may be my favorite of the hike—you'll be climbing along the north shore of Clear Lake and below a boulder field of gigantic rock. The lake is nestled amongst huge trees and has the ever-present huckleberry along its shore. Continue up to the junction with the Lemei Lake Trail 179 and turn right to head south back to Junction Lake. This is the wet part of the hike, particularly after a rain. There are numerous boggy sections of trail, creek crossings, and muddy slogs. To distract you from all this are thick green meadows bursting with flowers and dense heathers. Return the way you came once you reach Junction Lake.

Options

For the obvious shorter hike skip the additional 4.5-mile lake loop and make Junction Lake your destination. The little lake has plenty of shoreline to explore and the meadows are inviting. Bring a picnic and stay all day. Hike as above but at the PCT hike north just a bit then turn right onto Lemei Lake Trail 179 along the north shore.

Directions

From Portland, drive east on I-84 for 60 miles to exit 64 and follow the signs for White Salmon. After crossing the bridge turn left on SR-14 for 2.5 miles to Alt-141. Turn right and continue north to Trout Lake. From Trout Lake it's another 15 miles to the trailhead. At the "Y" keep left on SR-141 as it turns west then turns into FR-24. Eight miles from Trout Lake is the junction with FR-60 (at Peterson Prairie). Turn left and drive south to FR-6035, signed for the Forlorn Lakes Campground. Drive up the road about 3 miles, past the campground to the trailhead.

Information and Contact

There are no fees. For more information, contact the Gifford Pinchot National Forest, Mt. Adams Ranger District (2455 Highway 141, Trout Lake, WA 98650, 509/395-3400, www.fs.fed.us/gpnf/recreation/trails/index.shtml). For maps use USGS Gifford Peak & Lone Butte, Green Trails No. 365S, or USDA Forest Service Mount Adams, Indian Heaven, Trapper Creek Wilderness map (2005). For driving carry the USDA Forest Service Gifford Pinchot National Forest map.

9 LEMEI ROCK

Indian Heaven Wilderness

Level: Moderate   **Total Distance:** 7.6 miles round-trip

Hiking Time: 4.5 hours   **Elevation Change:** 1,900 feet

Summary: Hike past a stunning lake overlook with views of Mount Adams. Turn around after a break at the base of jagged and crumbly Lemei Rock.

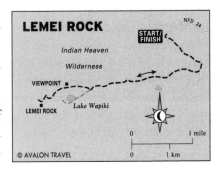

Indian Heaven is home to several volcanic remnants that tower dramatically above the rest of the wilderness. Lemei Rock is one of these ragged peaks—a collection of multicolored basalt literally crumbling from the ravages of harsh winter weather and time. The view of the east side is amazing and is a good spot to enjoy a break. The hike through the thick second-growth forest of fir, pine, and hemlock features berry picking and abundant wildflowers—add in a dose of solitude and you get a near-perfect destination.

Begin hiking from Little Goose Horse Camp on the Filoon Trail 102. This short and nearly flat trail meets the Lemei Trail 34 in just 1 mile and eliminates some climbing. The forest starts out thick and dark, quickly changing though as you pass the wilderness boundary. The forest is thick with growth—vanilla leaf covers the forest floor in places, the distinctive and beautiful bear grass flower occasionally appears amidst the thick grassy stalks, and ferns add both color and texture. At the signed trail junction, which is out in the open, turn right onto Lemei Trail 34. You may also see some mountain ash here and there—look for the red berries in fall. There are a few big Douglas-fir trees along the trail—you might see one with lots of holes in its thick bark. I watched a pair of woodpeckers industriously searching for bugs on a tree trunk, flinging scraps of bark down as they hammered along.

The trail climbs steadily the next 2 miles to the junction with the Lake Wapiki Trail 34A. You will cross a dry creek bed, ascend up a couple of switchbacks, then continue climbing. The undergrowth thins out and some queen's cup and spiraea bloom in the duff. There is a lot more bear grass along here and some huckleberry bushes with a smaller variety of berry. Approaching the junction with the Lake Wapiki trail you'll pass a huge boulder then meet the signed junction. Turn right

Lemei Rock

and head up the steepish trail through the trees. Things start changing—the trees thin and you might catch a glimpse of Mount Adams. Soon there are more views northward towards Mount Rainier. You'll cross a small footbridge just before some switchbacks and now Mount Adams really comes into view. The trail continues climbing. Check out the side trail to a Lake Wapiki viewpoint—it's really a dramatic view and the views of Mount Adams on the left aren't bad either. After enjoying the views continue on the trail across an open slope then travel a short distance in the trees to the base of Lemei Rock. This is a good spot to hang around and explore, taking care to stay on rocky surfaces as not to damage the delicate alpine meadow. There is some delicate white mountain heather, lots of lupine and paintbrush, phlox and bright cinquefoil. Lemei has a smattering of alpine trees managing to survive the harsh conditions—look for some fir and mountain hemlock. When you are done enjoying the scenery, return the way you came.

Options

Hike up to Lake Wapiki for a day relaxing along the shore. The lake is ringed with trees and lots of pink mountain heather. From the Lake Wapiki Trail 34A junction it's only a half mile to the east shore. Continue along the lakeside trail westward past some ponds to some pretty spots along the south side. Explore all you want—the cliffy north side showcases the region's volcanic past. When you're through it's 3.5 miles back to the trailhead.

Directions

From Portland, drive east on I-84 for 60 miles to exit 64 and follow the signs for White Salmon. After crossing the bridge turn left on SR-14 for 2.5 miles to Alt-141. Turn right and continue north to Trout Lake. From Trout Lake it's another 15 miles to the trailhead. At the "Y" keep left on WA-141 as it turns west then turns into FR-24. Continue on FR-24 to the Little Goose Horse Camp turnoff on the left side of the road about two miles past the junction with FR-6020. Drive up the short road to the trailhead at the end. There is a sign and information board for the Filloon Trail 102, including wilderness information.

Information and Contact

There are no fees. For more information, contact Gifford Pinchot National Forest, Mt. Adams Ranger District (2455 Highway 141, Trout Lake, WA 98650, 509/395-3400, www.fs.fed.us/gpnf/recreation/trails/index.shtml). For maps see Green Trails No. 365S or USDA Forest Service Mount Adams, Indian Heaven, Trapper Creek Wilderness (2005). For driving carry the USDA Forest Service Gifford Pinchot National Forest map.

10 LITTLE HUCKLEBERRY MOUNTAIN
Gifford Pinchot National Forest

5-23-15

Level: Moderate

Hiking Time: 2.5 hours

Total Distance: 5.0 miles round-trip

Elevation Change: 1,850 feet

Summary: Hike up this steep, deep-forest trail to a rocky summit and views of the Big Lava Bed Geologic Area. For all your hard work you get to eat your fill of huckleberries as you climb.

Little Huckleberry Mountain is a comma-shaped mountain with a long north/northeast trending summit ridge. The mountain forms the east boundary of the Big Lava Beds, which dominate to the west. Little Huckleberry is a fine summit if you are into peak bagging—but the real lure is the dense huckleberry bushes that make up the forest understory. The trail is unrelenting for the first mile but you can distract yourself from the pain by stopping often for a snack of these tiny delights.

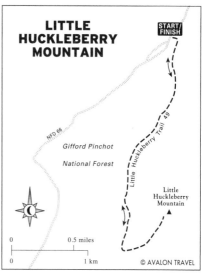

The Little Huckleberry Trail 49 wastes no time in heading uphill. Right from the start this trail is going one way—up. The first mile takes you through a dense thicket of trees with an equally dense collection of huckleberries covering the forest floor as far as one can see. Some vine maples fill out the forest and you may occasionally see some wintergreen, lots of pine drops and vanilla leaf, twin flower, or bear grass. Catch your breath around 1.3 miles, when the trail flattens and dips a moment, before resuming its uphill march south. After the break, the climbing begins again around 1.6 miles. As we hiked through the thick trees in this area one summer evening, we startled a few elk—which in turn startled us. A little further up you might notice an old sign on the right announcing Spring Camp. There may be a spring here but play it safe and carry your own water.

After passing an unofficial milepost "2" on a tree, the trail makes a sharp left and begins a traverse across a steep slope a short distance before the final summit push. Ascend the last 0.2 mile of the south summit ridge through rocky patches

© BARBARA I. BOND

enjoying sunset on the summit

alternating with huckleberries, tiger lily, columbine, lupine, and paintbrush. Some bear grass completes the greenery along with mixed forest including the beautiful sculpted boughs of fir trees. A final turn left and you're there. The summit views west are across the Big Lava Beds. You can also follow the summit ridge of Little Huckleberry northeast where it drops off sharply. You are virtually surrounded by dense deep-green forest, punctuated by steep ridges and deep valleys. Retrace your steps to the trailhead.

Options

You can head to the Indian Heaven Wilderness for a hike by continuing north on FR-66 to FR-60. Turn left and drive west to the trailhead for the Pacific Crest Trail at Crest Camp. From the trailhead hike north along the PCT 3 miles to the junction with the shortcut trail 171A. Turn left for the 0.6 mile to the Indian Race Track. Retrace your steps for a 7.2-mile hike that climbs gently but steadily from the trailhead.

Directions

From Portland, drive east on I-84 to Cascade Locks exit 44. Cross the bridge after paying the toll ($1 each trip, ticket book available for $0.75 each trip) and turn right on SR-14. Drive east, passing the Wind River Road exit to Carson, and continue 9 miles to Cook. Turn left and head north up Cook-Underwood Road (also called County Highway 86). Drive north 7 miles through Willard

– Take a left on Willon. Rd

where the road changes to FR-66. Continue north on FR-66 about 13 miles to the trailhead. Park on the right, adjacent to the trailhead sign.

Information and Contact

There are no fees and no services at the trailhead. For more information, contact the Gifford Pinchot National Forest, Mt. Adams Ranger District (2455 Hwy. 141, Trout Lake, WA 98650, 509/395-3400, www.fs.fed.us/gpnf/recreation/trails/index .shtml). For maps use USGS Little Huckleberry Mountain or Green Trails No. 398. For the Indian Heaven Wilderness use Green Trails no. 365S. For driving carry the USDA Forest Service Gifford Pinchot National Forest map, although the Green Trails map will cover the roads north from Willard.

11 BUTTE CAMP-LOOWIT TRAIL

BEST C

Mount St. Helens National Volcanic Monument

Level: Moderate

Total Distance: 9.0 miles round-trip

Hiking Time: 4.5 hours

Elevation Change: 1,650 feet

Summary: Explore the dramatic and varied Mount St. Helens landscape including old lava flows, massive fir trees, and the austerity of the mountain's timberline.

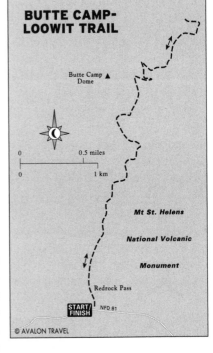

What is it about Mount St. Helens that attracts Northwestern outdoor folks? It must be a combination of the stark beauty of the diminished giant along with the allure of the dangerous. Of course, Mount St. Helens has been mostly quiet since the eruption that changed the landscape in 1980. In the fall of 2004 the mountain awoke and began a three-year period of dome building inside the massive crater. It's quiet again now and is a fantastic place to see the devastating effects of volcanism in a real-life working laboratory.

The Toutle Trail 238 heads north from Red Rock Pass, passes by a few big trees and climbs gently through a jumbled bed of black lava nearly 2000 years old. Bear grass grows in huge clumps and break up the dark expanse as you hike toward some fir and hemlock trees in the distance. Mount St. Helens looms up over the dark green trees—its southwest flanks looking dusty and barren in contrast. This is the joy of hiking near the big mountain—you never get tired of the view—I know I don't. Pass an old trail sign and junction around 1.2 miles and continue northward 0.5 miles more to the Butte Camp Trail 238A. You begin climbing in earnest at 1.5 miles and it really doesn't let up until you reach 4800 feet and the Loowit Trail.

There is still a lot to enjoy as you climb through the old-growth. Nearing 3 miles you begin passing through pretty meadows dotted with an array of flowers.

lava beds on the trail to Butte Camp

Hellebore thrives here and if you look down at the trail you may see some elk or deer hoof prints. Butte Camp has a lower campsite situated amidst beautiful meadows and there is a little stream running just to the west. There is also a side trail on the right that leads to a rocky outcrop with good views of the surroundings. As you continue north and upward you'll pass the twin domes on the left then begin a traverse across a steep slope covered with old fir trees with bent trunks. The years of heavy snow cause this odd characteristic—some tree trunks are so curved it's amazing they survive. The end of the climbing is near as you cross a rock slide then another beautiful meadow with lots of lupine. A couple of switchbacks and you emerge from the trees as the trail meets up with the Loowit Trail at 4800 feet and 4.5 miles. For some nice places to explore or just hang around and enjoy turn left onto the Loowit. The trail undulates a bit through lots of meadows loaded with penstemon, phlox, wild strawberry, Indian paintbrush and lupine. Pink mountain heather and some scattered subalpine fir and whitebark pines complete this open wonderland. You may see some oddly-shaped forms high on a ridge about 0.25 miles west of the trail junction. This is just part of the collection of equipment used to monitor the mountain. Return the way you came.

Options

Hiking the Loowit Trail 216 part of the way around Mount St. Helens is a wonderful way to really get a feel for our famous volcano. If you arrange a car shuttle to the Climber's Bivouac (you pass the side road to Climber's Bivouac halfway to the Redrock Pass Trailhead) you can turn right on the Loowit Trail 216 and hike 2.5 miles to the junction with the Ptarmigan Trail 216A. Check out the climber's trail heading north on Monitor Ridge before turning south to reach the trail's end at Climber's Bivouac. The round-trip distance for this one-way hike is 9.1 miles. A Northwest Forest Pass ($5) is needed to park at Climber's Bivouac.

Directions

From Portland, drive north on I-5 to the Woodland exit for SR-503. Drive east on SR-503, through Cougar and continue on FR-90. At 7 miles past Cougar, keep left on FR-83. Drive north 2.9 mile on FR-83 and bear left onto FR-81. The trailhead at Redrock Pass is another 1.7 miles on the north side of the road.

As of winter 2009, FR-81 was washed out west of Climber's Bivouac and was impassible. Park at a wide spot before the road narrows and walk west along FR-81 for 0.5 mile to the trailhead.

Information and Contact

There are no fees. A Northwest Forest Pass ($5) is required. For more information, contact the Mount St. Helens National Volcanic Monument (42218 NE Yale Bridge Rd., Amboy, WA 98601, 360/449-7800, www.fs.fed.us/gpnf/mshnvm). For maps use USGS Mount St. Helens or Green Trails 364 and 364S. See also the USDA Forest Service Mount St. Helens National Volcanic Monument map (1997).

12 APE CANYON

Mount St. Helens National Volcanic Monument

Level: Butt-kicker   **Total Distance:** 11.0 miles round-trip

Hiking Time: 5.5 hours   **Elevation Change:** 3,000 feet

Summary: This exploration of Mount St. Helens brings you up close to the Muddy River Lahar, a distinctive canyon and expansive pumice plain – it's a geologic time capsule.

Mount St. Helens' recent volcanic history is a familiar story. It's one thing to read about it, it's entirely another to hike alongside unique geologic features that illustrate the violence and renewal of volcanism. This hike leads northward along the east side of the Muddy River Lahar. This wide channel was formed when mix of water, rock, and mud flowed down the volcano's flanks toward the valley below. It's a dramatic sight. After meandering through thick forest of mixed conifers, which include huge old growth noble fir, you suddenly emerge on the edge of Ape Canyon—a

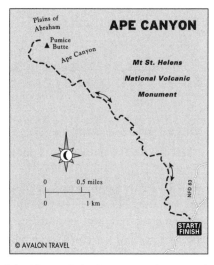

dramatic crevice in the earth southeast of the Plains of Abraham. Here the scoured pumice plain reveals a nearly featureless surface unlike any encountered.

The trail leaves the road and begins gently climbing right away. Here the forest has thick canopy which keeps it shady and relatively cool. Wildflowers line the trail and break the monotony of the forest floor. Huckleberries are abundant in many locations—be sure and sample some of these delightful treats when you find them ripe. During the first 2 miles the dominant feature visible to the west is the barren lahar. Here a river of mud took away trees, topsoil, and anything else in its path. The trail soon turns away from the lahar to begin a circuitous path through the forest for several miles. It's amazing to hike amongst these giant trees as the trail traverses some steep slopes and switchbacks to the ridge.

Once on the ridge, and after contouring past a washout where the trail gets quite narrow (careful here), the trees thin and it's suddenly a subalpine forest with stunted pines and hemlock, lupine, paintbrush, and pink mountain heather.

© BARBARA I. BOND

rock cairns mark the trail along the Plains of Abraham

Pass the westbound Loowit Trail junction which leads into the trees and continue west, then north along the trail. As the trail follows along you will suddenly see the ground open up on your right as the canyon spreads out before your eyes. As the trail winds along the edge of the canyon, look for the occasional marmot here, towards the pumice plain. The trail surface has now become light gray with pumice and dotted with larger volcanic rock of darker basalt composition.

The trail will now wind down to cross two dry creek beds, one with a washout. Climb out on the other side and now work upwards another 0.5 mile to reach the edge of the Plains of Abraham, a huge, nearly featureless pumice plain. The trail is marked with large rock cairns as it makes its way eastward then cuts back north. Hike a little further to a viewpoint just past Pumice Butte; it's a good spot to enjoy this unusual destination and take in the views of the mountain's rugged east side. On clear days as you gaze west it's hard not to be mesmerized by Mount St. Helens upper mountain rising above the plains. Return the way you came.

Options

You can still enjoy the drama of the lahar from the Lahar Viewpoint. The viewpoint is 0.3 mile west of the Ape Canyon Trailhead. There are interpretive signs at the parking area. A Northwest Forest Pass is required.

Directions

From Portland drive north on I-5 to the Woodland exit for SR-503. Drive east on SR-503, through Cougar and continue on FR-90. Seven miles past Cougar turn left on FR-83. Drive north then east on FR-83 to the Ape Canyon Trailhead on the left 8.3 miles past the junction with FR-81.

Information and Contact

A Northwest Forest Pass is required ($5). For more information, contact the Mount St. Helens National Volcanic Monument (42218 NE Yale Bridge Rd., Amboy, WA 98601, 360/449-7800, www.fs.fed.us/gpnf/mshnvm). For maps use USGS Mount St. Helens or Green Trails 364 and 364S. See also the USDA Forest Service Mount St. Helens National Volcanic Monument map (1997).

13 UPPER APE CAVE

Mount St. Helens National Volcanic Monument

Level: Moderate

Hiking Time: 3 hours

Total Distance: 2.8 miles round-trip

Elevation Change: 375 feet

Summary: Hiking Upper Ape Cave is a fun exploration of one of the longest lava tubes in North America.

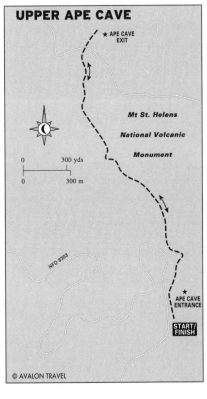

UPPER APE CAVE

★ APE CAVE EXIT

Mt St. Helens

National Volcanic

Monument

0   300 yds

0   300 m

NFD 8303

★ APE CAVE ENTRANCE

START/ FINISH

© AVALON TRAVEL

Many people remember the catastrophic eruption of Mount St. Helens in 1980. What you may not know is that there was a eruptive period nearly 2,000 years ago that covered the southern mountain and its surroundings with thick lava flows. The Ape Cave lava tube formed during this activity and remains the third longest lava tube in North America. There is nothing like the thrill of walking along the cool, dark cave to explore its mysteries. I took my children through the upper cave when they were 6 and 7 years old; kids love the excitement of hiking with headlamps and lanterns. Plus, the little scramble up the 8-foot lava fall makes it all the more fun for kids and adults alike.

Walk past the Ape's Headquarters and pick up the trail north to the cave entrance. Spend a few minutes reading the interpretive signs at the kiosk on the left, then walk around to the cave entrance and stairway. You might want to light your lantern now. Descend the stairs into a large, lit chamber. At the bottom of the stairs walk forward and around to your right heading away from the obvious path to the lower cave. You now will find yourself engulfed in utter darkness— no ambient light enters the cave except occasionally through breaks in the tube ceiling such as the skylight. For now, use your lantern and make your way along the uneven "trail" northward. Scramble up and over boulder piles formed when

© BARBARA I. BOND

entrance stairway to Ape Cave

parts of the ceiling collapsed during the tubes cooling period. Don't worry—the lava tube is stable now.

It's hard to keep track of your distance inside the cave as the usual navigation cues are all distorted down here. Just keep moving forward with your lantern held high! About a third of the way up you will have to keep scrambling over the boulder piles on your way to the lava fall. This is the only real obstacle in the cave and it's about 1.2 miles up. Send someone up first with one lantern and have them set it down nearby. Then they can help anyone who needs a hand. Give kids a boost and have them scramble up and over. After that continue upward over more breakdown.

You'll see a bright column of light entering from the skylight, continue up an-other 0.3 mile to the exit. The light from the exit seems extra bright after the total darkness. Head out by climbing the ladder into the daylight. Turn left and walk around a dozen yards to catch the trail back to the Ape's Headquarters. Along the way enjoy the fir trees, some vanilla leaf and thimbleberry, and vine maple. In the darker forest you may catch a glimpse of pine drops with their unique form and odd colors. As you descend the gentle grade there are a few places with inter-esting lava flows and patterns—take a minute to explore these flows. It's a great way to see how adaptable plants are; in some places stunted trees have rooted in cracks in the lava. You'll pass the Ape Cave main entrance 0.1 mile before the 1.3-mile trail ends.

Options

If you don't like exploring the netherworld of caves, take a hike on the Trail of Two Forests. This is a lava cast forest with a short 0.3-mile loop trail and interpretive information. It's a wonderful example of the power of a volcano.

Directions

Take I-5 north to the Woodland exit for SR-503. Drive east on SR-503, through Cougar and continue on FR-90. Seven miles past Cougar turn left on FR-83 (signed to Ape Cave) and drive 1.6 miles. Turn left on FR-8083 to the Ape Cave parking lot. At 0.7 mile before Ape Cave you will pass the parking area for Trail of Two Forests. (The road is gated here in the winter.)

For a fun snowshoe trip head up the road to the Ape Cave entrance. It's always open and is a good addition to the short snowshoe. Remember to bring extra lights when you are planning on entering the cave.

Information and Contact

A Northwest Forest Pass ($5) is required to park. For more information, contact the Mount St. Helens NVM (42218 NE Yale Bridge Rd., Amboy, WA 98601, 360/449-7800, www.fs.fed.us/gpnf/mshnvm). Caves are fragile environments; please don't touch the walls of the cave. The cave is always 42°F inside, so wear long pants and a hat. It can be very damp and drippy when the snow is melting or in winter so a raincoat helps. Gloves and hiking boots that cover your ankles are good protection from the sharp lava. Lantern rentals, interpretive guides, and tour information is available at the Ape's Headquarters near the trailhead. Caving safety includes always having extra light sources—carry three sources of light for your outing. A lantern illuminates a large area making it easier to negotiate the uneven ground.

14 STAGMAN RIDGE

BEST

Mount Adams Wilderness

Level: Strenuous

Total Distance: 11.4 miles round-trip

Hiking Time: 5.5–6.0 hours

Elevation Change: 2,300 feet

Summary: Get up close views of the southwest flanks of magnificent Mount Adams on this lesser-known hike.

Mount Adams is Washington's second highest peak and is the second largest stratovolcano in the United States. This hike, to the 6,000-foot level, won't get you on top of the 12,276 monster. It will get you high enough to enjoy tremendous mountain close-ups and allow you to drink in all the wildflower displays you can handle.

Walk past a couple of big Douglas-fir as the trail begins a gentle ascent through the forest. The first 0.5-mile of trail is wide enough to be a road and winds through second-growth forest with a dense understory of vine maple and thimbleberry bushes. Thimbleberry is edible and is similar to raspberry

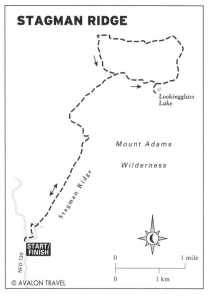

although a little less flavorful. The trail turns left and becomes narrower, passes a clear-cut with small trees, then re-enters the forest. Note the old wood Wilderness Boundary sign on the right. The next 1.5 miles takes you to the top of the ridge. Along the way stop and sample some huckleberries from one of the bushes that line the trail and seem to extend as far as you can see. Lots of wildflowers share the forest floor, including queen's cup, and you may catch some salal and vanilla leaf when the huckleberries thin out.

You'll continue ascending to 5,100 feet, then the trail jogs northwest then northeast around Grassy Hill, dropping down about 200 feet before resuming the climb amid bear grass, lupine, cat's ear lilies, false Solomon seal, and penstemon. At 3.4 miles you will reach a signed junction. A sign on the left reads PCNST (right arrow) and Road 120 (left arrow). On the right is a trail with a sign on a tree that says "Graveyard Camp" (I never did figure out what this meant)! Turn

© BARBARA I. BOND

Horseshoe Meadow and Mount Adams

right here to make your way to Lookingglass Lake on a pleasant loop. You can do this loop in either direction but I choose to go counterclockwise. There are multiple creek crossings and the water level is usually lower in the morning.

The trail winds easterly, dipping down several times to cross dry creek beds. The next few creek crossings have no bridges but the water is usually low. Around 4.1 miles you reach a creek with a log ford upstream—that will change from season to season so just use caution and turn back if the water seems too high or fast. After the upstream crossing get back onto the trail, ascend the east side of the drainage, and cross an old washout with dozens of small trees. Re-enter the forest and in a short distance is the junction with the side trail south to Lookingglass Lake. Visit the pretty lake—it's got clear green water and a couple of nice campsites for backpackers.

Return to the trail which is now officially Lookingglass Trail 9A. The trail climbs through stunning wildflower displays and crosses a couple more creeks along the 0.9 mile to the Round the Mountain Trail 9. Turn left to head westerly on this 6,000-foot trail that contours along with great mountain views back to the northeast. Enjoy the profusion of alpine flowers along the trail including purple asters, lupine, and several kinds of penstemon. Reach Horseshoe Meadows just before the junction with the PCT in just over 1 mile. After drinking in the views from the meadow, continue past the trail junction with the northbound PCT and continue ahead 0.4 mile to the signed junction with Trail 12—the Stagman Ridge Trail. Turn left and follow the trail south 4 miles to the trailhead.

Options

To do a shorter version of this hike and avoid the creek crossings, keep left at the 3.4-mile trail junction. Continue along the Stagman Ridge Trail 12 to the junction with the Pacific Crest Trail (PCT) at 4 miles. At the PCT junction turn right for the 0.4-mile hike to Horseshoe Meadow. This meadow has flowers and stunning mountain views. Return the way you came for about a 9-mile hike.

Directions

From Portland, drive 60 miles east on I-84. Take exit 64, turn left and cross the bridge to White Salmon and SR-14. Turn left onto SR-14 and drive 1.5 miles to SR-141 Alt. Turn right and follow this north (it turns into SR-141 in 2.2 miles, bear left) for 19 miles to Trout Lake. At the "Y" keep right on FR-23, driving north for 9.1 miles to the junction with FR 8031. Follow FR 8031 for just under 0.5 mile then turn right onto FR 070 at a sign for Stagman Ridge. Drive 3.2 miles, turn right on FR 120 and continue 0.8 mile to the trailhead in a clearcut. There is plenty of parking, some old picnic tables, and a trailhead information sign with wilderness permits. Please fill out a permit before heading onto the trail.

Information and Contact

Leashed dogs allowed. For more information, contact the Gifford Pinchot National Forest, Mt. Adams Ranger District (2455 Hwy. 141, Trout Lake, WA 98650, 509/395-3400, www.fs.fed.us/gpnf/recreation/trails/index.shtml). There is an information sign out front with current weather conditions, vault toilets at the end of the parking lot, and a small lot at the south end of the building to leave extra vehicles when you carpool from the ranger station.

For maps use either Green Trails No. 367S Mount Adams, WA or USDA Forest Service Mount Adams, Indian Heaven, and Trapper Creek Wilderness map (2005). For navigating the roads use the USDA Forest Service Gifford Pinchot National Forest map. If you want a pre-hike breakfast or post-hike slice of huckleberry pie, visit KJ's Bear Creek Café (2376 Hwy. 141, 509/395-2525) in Trout Lake at the "Y".

RESOURCES

NATIONAL PARK SERVICE

Mount St. Helens
National Volcanic Monument
Monument Headquarters
42218 NE Yale Bridge Rd.
Amboy, WA 98601
360/449-7800
www.fs.fed.us/gpnf/mshnvm

U.S. FISH AND WILDLIFE SERVICE

Steigerwald Lake
National Wildlife Refuge
Ridgefield National
Wildlife Refuge Complex
P.O. Box 457
Ridgefield, WA 98642
360/887-4106
www.fws.gov/ridgefieldrefuges/
    steigerwaldlake

Tualatin River
National Wildlife Refuge
16507 SW Roy Rogers Rd.
Sherwood, OR 97140
503/590-6702
www.fws.gov/tualatinriver

Willamette Valley
National Wildlife Refuge Complex
26208 Finley Refuge Rd.
Corvallis, OR 97333-9533
541/757-7236
www.fws.gov/willamettevalley

PORTLAND PARK PASSES

Many Portland-area trailheads require passes or permits, while some locations have self-issue permit stations at the trailhead. If you're a serious hiker, you may want to purchase the most flexible option – the Washington and Oregon Recreation Pass. Whatever your choice, be sure to plan ahead and purchase any neccessary passes at local outdoor stores or through Nature of the Northwest (www.naturenw.org).

Annual Northwest Forest Pass: $30

Interagency Annual Pass (Forest Service, National Park, BLM, U.S. Fish and Wildlife): $80

Oregon State Park Pass: $3 daily pass, $25 one-year pass, $40 two-year pass

Single Day Northwest Forest Pass: $5

Washington and Oregon Recreation Pass: $100; this is the same as the Interagency Pass, but includes Oregon State Parks and some other sites that charge recreation fees.

U.S. FOREST SERVICE

The Columbia River Gorge
National Scenic Area
902 Wasco Ave., Ste. 200
Hood River, OR 97031
503/308-1700
www.fs.fed.us/r6/columbia/forest

Barlow Ranger District
780 NE Court St.
Dufur, OR 97021
541/467-2291

**Clackamas River Ranger District, Esta-
cada Ranger Station**
595 NW Industrial Way
Estacada, OR 97023
503/630-6861

Gifford Pinchot National Forest
Mount Adams Ranger District
2455 Hwy. 141
Trout Lake, WA 98650
509/395-3400
www.fs.fed.us/r6/gpnf

Hood River Ranger District
6780 Hwy. 35
Parkdale, OR 97041
541/352-6002

Mount Hood National Forest
16400 Champion Way
Sandy, OR 97055
503/667-1700
www.fs.fed.us/r6/mthood

Siuslaw National Forest
Hebo Ranger District
31525 Hwy. 22
P.O. Box 235
Hebo, OR 97122
503/392-5100
www.fs.fed.us/f6/siuslaw

Zigzag Ranger District
70220 E. Hwy. 26
Zigzag, OR 97049
503/622-3191

STATE MANAGEMENT AGENCIES

Cape Lookout State Park
13000 Whiskey Creek Rd. W.
Tillamook, OR 97141
503/842-4981

Ecola State Park
Nehalem Bay Management Unit
P.O. Box 366
Nehalem, OR 97131
503/368-5943

**John B. Yeon State
Scenic Corridor**
I-84, Exit 35
Cascade Locks, OR 97014
800/551-6949

**Oregon Department of Fish
and Wildlife**
Sauvie Island Wildlife Area
18330 NW Sauvie Island Rd.
Portland, OR 97231
503/621-3488
www.dfw.state.or.us/resources

Oregon Department of Forestry
Tillamook Forest Center
45500 Wilson River Hwy.
Tillamook, OR 97141
866/930-4646
www.tillamookforestcenter.org

Oregon Parks and Recreation
725 Summer St. NE, Suite C
Salem, OR 97301
www.oregonstateparks.org

**Oregon State University
College Forests**
McDonald Forest/
OSU College Forests
College of Forestry
8692 Peavy Arboretum Rd.
Corvallis, OR 97330-9328
541/737-4452
www.cof.orst.edu/cf/recreation

Oswald West State Park
U.S. Hwy. 101
Cannon Beach, OR 97110
800/551-6949

**Saddle Mountain State
Natural Area**
U.S. Hwy. 26
Necanicum Junction, OR 97138
800/551-6949

Silver Falls State Park
20024 Silver Falls Hwy. SE
Sublimity, OR 97385
503/873-8681, ext. 23

Starvation Creek State Park
I-84, Exit 54 (eastbound)
Hood River, OR 97031
800/551-6949

Tillamook State Forest
Forest Grove District Office
801 Gales Creek Rd.
Forest Grove, OR 97116
503/357-2191
www.oregon.gov/ODF/TSF/tsf.shtml

Tryon Creek State Natural Area
11321 SW Terwilliger Blvd.
Portland, OR 97219
503/636-9886

**Washington Department
of Natural Resources**
P.O. Box 47000
1111 Washington St. SE
Olympia, WA 98504-7000
360/902-1000
www.dnr.wa.gov

LOCAL MANAGEMENT AGENCIES

Portland Parks and Recreation
1120 SW Fifth Ave., #1302
Portland, OR 97204
503/823-7529
www.portlandonline.com/parks

**Vancouver-Clark Washington Parks and
Recreation**
P.O. Box 1995
Vancouver, WA 98668-1995
360/397-2000
www.co.clark.wa.us

MAP SOURCES

USDA Forest Service

National Forest Store

P.O. Box 8268

Missoula, MT 59807

406/329-3024

www.nationalforeststore.com

The U.S. Forest Service publishes the widely distributed national forest maps. Ordering information is available online ($1 service charge per order), or check the local national forest website.

Nature of the Northwest

800 NE Oregon St., Ste. 177

Portland, OR 97232

503/872-2750

www.naturenw.org

Perhaps the best source of maps in the Portland area, Nature of the Northwest has the complete Oregon and Washington collection of USGS 7.5 minute maps, USDA Forest Service maps, and many other maps and mapping software. They also have recreation permits, including the Northwest Forest Pass ($5).

Green Trails Maps

P.O. Box 77734

Seattle, WA 98177

www.greentrailsmaps.com

Green Trails publishes topographic maps for Oregon and Washington.

TRANSPORTATION

**Oregon Department
of Transportation**

www.tripcheck.com

Check this website for road conditions and road construction reports within Oregon.

**Tillamook County
Transportation District**

P.O. Box 118

Tillamook, OR 97141-0188

503/842-8283

www.tillamookbus.com

The Wave provides intercity bus service between Portland and Tillamook ($10 one-way, $15 round-trip). Call them or visit their website for detailed route information.

TriMet

503/238-7433

www.trimet.org

TriMet is the public transportation provider for the Portland metro area. Call for trip-planning assistance or visit the website for detailed bus, rail, and streetcar route information.

**Washington Department
of Transportation**

www.wsdot.wa.gov/traffic/

Check this website for road conditions and road construction reports within Washington.

OUTDOORS ORGANIZATIONS

The Chemeketans

P.O. Box 864

Salem, OR 97308

www.chemeketans.org

The Chemeketans is a nonprofit membership organization based in Salem, Oregon. They organize day hikes, ski trips, and other outdoor activities, as well as overnight trips to a mountain cabin.

Friends of the Columbia Gorge

522 SW Fifth Ave., Ste. 720

Portland, OR 97204

503/241-3762

www.gorgefriends.org

This organization is committed to protecting and preserving the Columbia River Gorge National Scenic Area.

Klickitat Trail Conservancy

P.O. Box 512

Lyle, WA 98635

www.klickitat-trail.org

This nonprofit organization is committed to preserving and promoting the Klickitat Rail-to-Trail.

Mazamas

527 SE 43rd Ave.

Portland, OR 97215

503/227-2345

www.mazamas.org

Oregon's premier mountaineering organization was founded on the summit of Mount Hood more than 100 years ago. Their website has loads of resources for hikers.

The Nature Conservancy

Oregon Field Office

821 SE 14th Ave.

Portland, OR 97214

www.nature.org

The Nature Conservancy has many Oregon preserves, including Camassia Natural Area, Little Rock Island Preserve, and Sandy River Gorge Preserve. For more information, check the specific websites for these preserves.

Trails Club of Oregon

P.O. Box 1243

Portland, OR 97207-1243

503/233-2740

www.trailsclub.org

The Trails Club is made up of enthusiastic supporters of outdoor recreation; the club hosts year-round hiking and a variety of events.

Washington Trails Association

2019 Third Ave., Ste. 100

Seattle, WA 98121

206/625-1367

www.wta.org

The WTA provides a wide range of Washington state resources for hikers.

SUGGESTED READING

Cox, Steven M., and Kris Fulsaas, eds. *Mountaineering: The Freedom of the Hills.* 7th ed. Seattle: The Mountaineers Books, 2003.

Jensen, Edward C., and Charles R. Ross. *Trees to Know in Oregon.* Rev. ed. Corvallis: Oregon State University Extension Service and Oregon Department of Forestry, 1999.

Letham, Lawrence. *GPS Made Easy: Using Global Positioning Systems in the Outdoors.* 4th ed. Seattle: The Mountaineers Books, 2003.

Mathews, Daniel. *Cascade-Olympic Natural History: A Trailside Reference.* 2nd ed. Portland: Raven Editions, 1999.

McArthur, Lewis A., and Lewis L. McArthur. *Oregon Geographic Names.* 7th ed. Portland: Oregon Historical Society Press, 2003.

Orr, Elizabeth L., and William N. Orr. *Geology of Oregon.* 5th ed. Dubuque: Kendall/Hunt Publishing Company, 2000.

Pojar, Jim, and Andy MacKinnon, eds. *Plants of the Pacific Northwest Coast: Washington, Oregon, British Columbia, and Alaska.* Redmond, WA: Lone Pine Publishing, 1994.

Randall, Glenn. *The Outward Bound Map and Compass Handbook.* Rev. ed. New York: The Lyons Press, 1998.

Thorson, T.D., and others, eds. *Ecoregions of Oregon.* Reston, VA: U.S. Geological Survey, 2003.

INTERNET RESOURCES
Cool Trails
www.cooltrails.com
This website provides backcountry trail reports written by hikers for Oregon, Washington, and rest of the Pacific Northwest.

GORP
http://gorp.away.com
GORP offers a wealth of information on hiking, gear, campgrounds, and National Parks. Click on Activity Guides, then Oregon, for a list of hikes and trail descriptions.

Leave No Trace
www.lnt.org
Visit this informative website to learn how to lower your impact on the natural areas you visit.

Northwest Hiker
www.nwhiker.com
This website offers interactive hiking guides for Oregon, Washington, Idaho, and Montana.

Oregon Adventures
www.oregonhiking.com
Oregon author William L. Sullivan's website breaks down a list of activities (including hiking) by region within the state.

Portland Hikers Field Guide
www.portlandhikersfieldguide.org
Portland hikes broken down by skill level, type, environment, views, waterfalls—the list is endless!

trailsNW.com
www.trailsnw.com
Over 150 trails are described with interactive comments and blogs from readers and hikers alike.

Index

Acknowledgments

This book could not have been completed without the help of many people. My partner, Cathy, was unwavering in her support, as were my children, Taliah and Evan. Thanks to each for making suggestions for hikes, for accompanying me on hikes, and for providing inspiration. You're my favorite trail partners.

Thanks to The Mazamas. I used their extensive library for my initial research and their quiet meeting room regularly as my "office." I also talked with many members about their favorite hikes and was the beneficiary of their incredible generosity.

Many people came along on hikes, some for one or two, others for a few. Thanks to you all for keeping me company under sometimes less-than-ideal conditions. Due to Portland's extraordinary 2008 winter and spring, I dragged trail companions through rain, mud, and lots of cold, wet snow. My sister, Leslie, came along for more than a dozen hikes. She hiked in light snow in the Eastern Gorge, wind and rain in the Coast Range, and dense fog in the Cascades. Finally, she even consented to read most of the hike descriptions. Thanks, Les!

Finally, thanks so much to all the rangers, volunteers, and staff at the various land management agencies in Oregon and Washington. I appreciate your kind response to my queries. The Klickitat Trail Conservancy was kind enough to take us on a tour of their trail, and provide lots of history along the way. I also had wonderful assistance from the Cape Horn Conservancy. Judith Zineski expanded my wildflower identification skills exponentially. Thanks, Judith.

It's been my pleasure to work with the professional team at Avalon Travel Publishing. Their patience helped make an otherwise stressful process less so.

www.moon.com

DESTINATIONS | ACTIVITIES | BLOGS | MAPS | BOOKS

MOON.COM is all new, and ready to help plan your next trip! Filled with fresh trip ideas and strategies, author interviews, informative blogs, a detailed map library, and descriptions of all the Moon guidebooks, Moon.com is all you need to get out and explore the world—or even places in your own backyard. As always, when you travel with Moon, expect an experience that is uncommon and truly unique.

 OUTDOORS

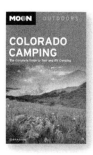

"Well written, thoroughly researched, and packed full of useful information and advice, these guides really do get you into the outdoors."

—GORP.COM

ALSO AVAILABLE AS FOGHORN OUTDOORS ACTIVITY GUIDES:

250 Great Hikes in
   California's National Parks
California Golf
California Waterfalls
California Wildlife
Camper's Companion
Easy Biking in Northern
   California
Easy Hiking in Northern
   California

Easy Hiking in Southern
   California
Georgia & Alabama Camping
Maine Hiking
Massachusetts Hiking
New England Biking
New England Cabins
   & Cottages
New England Camping
New England Hiking

New Hampshire Hiking
Southern California
   Cabins & Cottages
Tom Stienstra's Bay Area
   Recreation
Utah Camping
Vermont Hiking
Washington Boating
   & Water Sports

MOON TAKE A HIKE PORTLAND

Avalon Travel
a member of the Perseus Books Group
1700 Fourth Street
Berkeley, CA 94710, USA
www.moon.com

Editor and Series Manager: Sabrina Young
Copy Editor: Maura Brown
Graphics and Production Coordinator:
    Domini Dragoone
Cover Designer: Domini Dragoone
Interior Designer: Darren Alessi
Map Editor: Kevin Anglin
Cartographers: Kat Bennett, Lohnes & Wright
Illustrations: Bob Race

ISBN-10: 1-59880-197-X
ISBN-13: 978-1-59880-197-2
ISSN: 1944-4702

Printing History
1st Edition – May 2009
5 4 3 2 1

Some photos and illustrations are used by permission and are the property of the original copyright owners.

Front cover photo: A hiker carefully navigates the narrow cliffside trail of Tunnel Falls on Eagle Creek trail in the Columbia River Gorge, © Jonathan Kingston / Aurora Photos
Title page photo: Lemei Rock, © Barabara I. Bond
Table of Contents photos: © Barbara I. Bond
Back cover photo: © Peter Cade / Getty Images

Printed in the United States of America
by RR Donnelley

Keeping Current

We are committed to making this book the most accurate and enjoyable hiking guide to Portland. You can rest assured that every trail in this book has been carefully reviewed in an effort to keep this book as up-to-date as possible. However, by the time you read this book, some of the fees listed herein may have changed and trails may have closed unexpectedly.

If you have a favorite gem you'd like to see included in the next edition, or see anything that needs updating, clarification, or correction, please drop us a line. Send your comments via email to feedback@moon.com, or use the address above.